Latin America

Latin America

Economic development and regional
differentiation

Arthur Morris

BARNES & NOBLE BOOKS

Totowa, New Jersey

First published in the USA 1981 by
BARNES & NOBLE BOOKS
81 Adams Drive
Totowa, New Jersey, 07512

ISBN: 0-389-20194-4 (cloth)
     0-389-20195-2 (paper)

Printed in Great Britain

Contents

Figures

Tables

Preface

Regional development studies at varying geographic scales and with varying standpoints between applied and theoretical are already abundant and a fair number refer either directly or indirectly to parts or the whole of Latin America. Some kind of apology or justification is therefore required for the addition of yet another work on this subject.

This justification is in two parts, because the work rests on two kinds of approach to the subject not yet widely adopted in the English language. In the first place, an attempt is made to bring in a historical analysis, not merely to show the background with which modern planners must contend, but also to demonstrate process, and in particular the long-term continuity of some processes since the colonial period or earlier. This continuity in itself implies a resistance to change which will be difficult to overcome and must be allowed for by those who seek change. Historical approaches have indeed been employed by writers of various academic, intellectual and political complexions, but those who have sought to utilize such approaches for the study of regional development have for the most part written in Spanish for a Latin American readership. The first chapters of this book must therefore be acknowledged as little more than an English-language synthesis of these writings flavoured by a personal concern to relate economic processes more intelligibly to social structures than is commonly the case in 'development studies'.

In the second place, I have tried to catch something of what would appear to be a paradigm change, a change in the way of thinking about regional development. The manuscript was largely completed when I read the latest contributions of John Friedmann and Walter Stöhr on the subject, in works which are interesting not only for their content, but also as demonstrations of a 90 degree, or perhaps even a 180 degree, change in their philosophical stance.

This change has been from an insistence on innovations and change at the centre or top of the hierarchy, followed by downward filtering through a hierarchical regional structure, to encouragement of local 'grassroots' initiatives and development of an *intra*-regional rather than *inter*-regional character.

Regional and national development plans and actual achievements since World War II have been found to fail in their purpose of achieving a better balance of development between poorer and richer, and regional planning has been seen as yet another arm of national planning promoting central, metropolitan development as against that of the regions to which the measures refer.

There is an interesting coincidence of the paradigm change (if we can decorate this philosophical reorientation with such an impressive name) in regional development planning, with parallel changes in national and international attitudes to resources and their use, and to the organization of planning. The prophetic works of Ernst Schumacher have demonstrated that 'small is beautiful', but beyond any aesthetic qualities of size there lie also questions of economic and social necessity, given the rise of socio-economic expectations and their decreasing changes of fulfilment by large-scale technology and large institutions.

Small-scale organization, linked where possible to 'alternative' or 'intermediate' technology, implies a much greater regional conscience on the part of the state and the need for national planning to incorporate regional planning as a fundamental part – not, as at present, as an additional and almost independent function of the state. This is particularly important because national sectoral planning has at the moment much more significance for regional success or failure than regional planning, and the regional effects of sectoral, non-regional measures must be taken into account in any attempt to predict regional evolution.

There are, of course, political movements towards regional separation and independence in Europe which exaggerate and in some cases confuse the socio-economic regional problem. Such separatist and nationalist movements are not common or strong in Latin America at the present time and it might be thought rash to begin planning on a separate basis for a variety of regions which might thereafter call for regional autonomy and a breaking-up of the state. It is therefore necessary to insist that regionalization of the social and economic life of a country does not necessarily imply political balkanization, and that by anticipating regional demands for help and encouragement of local and regional institutions, the central government may provide for long-term stability, since in this way it is demonstrating its good will towards, and acceptance of, a diversified set of regional components. It is indeed logical to suppose that a combination of both centrally organized and regional institutions is the best compromise for harmonious forward development, and this proposition is examined in a spatial context in the book's concluding section.

1 An introduction to development processes

This first section is partially concerned to introduce the developmental experience of Latin America in a geographical and historical framework. But it is also intended to present a personal view of developmental processes, not solely those of a single region or time period but also those at a level more general than that of the individual region, however large. Some of the processes may be studied from examples in Latin America, but for most the information does not permit precise exemplification. This work differs from standard contributions to regional development theory both in seeking a broader framework, embracing social as well as economic values, and in emphasizing strongly the specific historical and spatial context of Latin America. In this region the degree of subjugation to a colonial mother country, the reliance on precious metals in the case of Spanish America and the powerful influence of outside powers into the present century are all special factors which must be taken into account in any assessment of regional planning measures and possible alternatives. In the post-1970 search for an alternative paradigm to the growth pole and related policies for regions, it seems desirable both to categorize growth processes in general and to evaluate the particular circumstances which have made this kind of policy a failure.

An obvious advantage of the use of a broad set of geographical and historical observations is that the attempts at theory may be related to real-world processes and structures. This point is worth making because the majority of economic development writings by economists have been little concerned with applicability in concrete circumstances; while, on the other hand, geographers and other social scientists have concerned themselves with detailed observation of often minor aspects of the overall process and have failed to fulfil their supposed integrative function.

The counterbalancing disadvantage, if it is such, of continuous reference to specific historical and geographical canvas is that a certain eclecticism, the lack of a single, unified, encapsulated theory, becomes inevitable, as will become obvious in later pages. In effect, real-life processes which relate to completely different abstractions or models are seen to overlap and intertwine with one another in space and time in different combinations. The spatial and chronological divisions of the study are only a partial solution to this problem.

Spatial economic development theories

In this section an outline of development theories is provided, emphasizing those with a spatial framework. This is followed by a broader framework of types of growth in space and time within which development may be classified. This should make it evident that different kinds of development are possible within a single country at the same time, as well as over a period of several centuries.

A wide selection of models of economic development exists, and there are therefore various ways in which they may be categorized: according to the type of factors emphasized (capital, resources, labour, entrepreneurship); according to their empirical or theoretical bias and basis, contrasting historical models with mathematical–economic ones; or according to whether they are descriptive or analytic models. For the purpose of identifying spatial growth processes in development, the discussion here is first in terms of *endogenous* versus *exogenous* development models. No precise definition of development is attempted, as an objective definition is scarcely possible, and the definitions used seem to have varied periodically to suit the models presented. But there seems to be a fairly general current agreement that development involves elements of social welfare (access to social services, hospitals, education, police protection and so on) and 'quality-of-life' elements, such as fresh air, water, landscape, countryside, which have no readily determinable monetary value, alongside the more standard components such as income, production and consumption of goods and services, and the existence of infrastructure such as transport, power installations and the like.

Whether explicitly recognized or not, theories of development have an important spatial component. Not just in the naive sense that they occur at some place or region, but because the mechanisms of development are in most cases mechanisms of *transmission* or *non-transmission* of growth or innovation or their obverse, or because (in the case of autochthonous, non-transmitted growth) the process of forward movement is seen as based on local resources, the propensities of the populace, existing social structures, such as class divisions or existing economic structures.

Endogenous development

Development as an endogenous process, or at least overlooking the intervention of outside forces, is the theory or model applied by some writers to economic development. Possibly the best known endogenous model in the English-speaking world is that of W. W. Rostow (1960) who, in following the thought of various nineteenth-century German economists, views the process as one which all nations traverse, so that present states of development represent stages along the road towards 'modernity', that is towards the status of the most advanced countries, a status of 'high mass consumption' by the population which is final and apparently fixed. We need not stay to consider here the criticized concepts of fixed initial and final states of development and the lack of any real mechanism for moving the country from one stage to another; what is important to the present discussion is that each nation is seen as having the same kind of evolution and that therefore the influence of exogenous factors cannot be important. The model is one of independent evolution along parallel lines, without any chance of short-circuiting through outside influence or of outside factors from different sources leading to a different history of change in each case. Rostow's instrument of development is a growing savings ratio, an instrument which is itself undifferentiated and therefore leads to similar results for all nations.

Another economist taking development as an endogenous growth process is Colin Clark. In *The Conditions of Economic Progress* (Clark 1957) the inference is that economic development is a simple process of advance in employment structure (used as an index of economic activity in general) from a predominance of agricultural employment, to manufacturing-industry dominance and then to the dominance of services, the tertiary sector. Such a view is based on the real and quite general observation of a broad correlation between levels of wealth, the complexity of the economy and the proportion of labour engaged in primary, secondary and tertiary sectors. The factors thought to be operative in moving from the dominance of one sector to another were the changes in the comparative costs of products and in the income elasticity of demand. As nations or regions become more prosperous, they demand more manufactured goods, though their consumption of food and other raw materials is limited; and as development advances still more, the greatest demand is for more and more specialized services of all kinds, helping the growth of this sector. A view similar to that of Clark is held by Kuznets (1959) who uses different terms – agriculture, mining and services – but sees the same progression. Hoover and Fisher (in Holland 1976, ch. 6) endorse a broadly similar view of development.

Clark (1967) gives a slightly different view in his later work on population and land use, where population growth is seen as a positive influence for development, bringing economies of scale and more intensive agricultural land use with higher technology; and (at least in the case of Europe) a strong association is found between population densities or market potential and industrial growth. This, however, remains an endogenous view of development, as in his previous work. It may be compared with a number of other statements concerning development as a result of resource poverty rather than resource wealth. Writers who support a resource-poverty basis for development adopt an essentially endogenous view of development (Boserup 1965: Wilkinson 1973; North and Thomas 1973), since scarcity of natural resources within an area is seen as stimulating effort by the natives of that area, independent of outside influences; while resource strength is the essence of the export-based kind of explanation, exogenous because it relies on exports to outside areas.

One geographer's view of the process follows in part the concept of endogenous growth (Hodder 1968). In this work, although there is no direct indication of whether this is an endogenous or exogenous process, Hodder indicates (p. 166) that in the early stages of development a rising population density (internal or endogenous factor) is most important, promoting changes towards mechanization and the intensification of land use in agriculture; later on industrial feedback is thought to be a major feedback to agricultural development, and this may be internal or external.

Another very different but also essentially endogenous view is that of Carol (1964). Rather than take narrow indices of economic prosperity, Carol categorized five stages of technology:
1 adaptation to natural environment, a primitive stage;

2 domestication of nature, plants and animals included;
3 diversification of activity based on higher productivity – the rise of urban places and urban functions allowing a surplus to be used in support of the townspeople;
4 mechanization and higher productivity with more specialization;
5 automation.

Such a wide-ranging scheme begs the question of what is understood by economic development, but it may be noted that Carol's stages of increasing complexity of life will, of themselves, produce increases in the kind of indices most economists would regard as indicative of development. The scheme is essentially an endogenous one, though it allows for technological transfers and short-circuits of the stages, because the agents of change are technological advances in man's mastery of his environment occurring in a single society. The scheme is expounded further as a geographical–economic model by Kay (1975).

Exogenous development

More acceptable today than endogenous growth theories are those which rely on the intervention of outside forces, whether in the form of the demand or supply of goods and services from the exterior, outside sources of technical innovation or outside control and coercion. We may start with the argument of the neoclassical economists (Borts and Stein 1962; Williamson 1965) who extended the ideas of national economic growth to regional growth. Growth of regional income Y_i in region i is seen as a result of growth of the labour force L_i and capital K_i in the same region. But these two factors of production have an optimum balance or ratio, so that any excess of either one will lead to adjustments through factor movement. A labour-rich (overpopulated) region with poor capital endowments will attract the inwards movement of capital because higher returns on capital investment are available using the pool of cheap labour, while labour itself will tend to move out, seeking regions of higher wage level, that is, those regions with a labour shortage. Optimal growth depends on the free movement of these factors between i and all regions j to bring in the scarce factor and evict the abundant one.

The theory depends on many restrictive assumptions, notably the idea of constant returns to scale – that is, the lack of any difference in the efficiency of production between large and small units, which always acts to help increase differences between industrial regions at different levels of development. It also assumes complete, or at least equal, levels of information about all possibilities for economic enterprise in each region; the absence of non-economic factors such as community feeling, which might make an obstacle to movement for any of the community's members; and historical-cultural associations of particular groups with particular areas. It even assumes the absence of technological advance of any one region over the others. No geographical barriers or obstacles to factor movements are posited, so that the economy is in effect space-less, although it concerns regions. Given all these assumptions, the theory predicts equal payments to factors and, allowing for changes in the character of the mobile factors before and after their movement, a convergence between regions in their total incomes. Some variants of the neoclassical theory relax various of these assumptions to approach more closely real-world conditions, but the introductions do not change the basic form of the theory. It is an exogenous growth theory in the sense that regional income growth relies on inter-regional factor movements which help both donor and receiver regions. Evidence supporting the ideas of convergence has been scanty and hard to interpret, but if we accept that the poor countries are following the rich or developed ones, then a pattern of increasing divergence, followed by a levelling out and finally convergence, may be taken as the result of neoclassical forces operating over a period of time, as postulated by Williamson (1965). But it is equally possible to make different interpretations of Williamson's kind of evidence and to conclude, from Latin American evidence, that convergence is not taking place at all (Gilbert 1976).

Counter to such ideas are those which identify the geographical barriers to movement through incorporating transport costs, emphasizing the economies to be achieved through urban–industrial agglomeration, and place the advance of technology through innovation as the central force in development. Gunnar Myrdal (1957) in his picture (not a tightly expressed model or theory) of economic development through cumulative and circular causation processes, predicted a growing divergence of income levels between nations because of inherent advantages in the advanced industrial economies, together with the very limited real mobility of labour and capital and substantial obstacles to movement through geography or through institutional, essentially political factors, associated with the nature of modern capitalism. Various kinds of advantage in production technology and control mechanisms over production and trade throughout the world, which are retained by the richer countries, have acted in snowball fashion to allow wealth to accrue to the wealthy, poverty to the poor. Hirschman (1958), also considering national rather than regional development, took a less pessimistic view, identifying the economic but not the political obstacles to convergence and the agglomeration economies favouring the more advanced lands. In place of Myrdal's 'backwash' effects, he emphasized factors leading to 'spread' or, as he termed it, 'trickle-down' processes through which modern technology was diffused to all parts by the gradual elimination of barriers to mobility of information and capital. 'Trickle-down' effects would lead to the interregional convergence of income levels. For both these writers there is a reliance on outside factors, and their opposite conclusions relate only to the forces of the different factors of convergence and divergence.

Many writers have extended the Hirschman viewpoint into studies of the regional aspects of development, to the point where we can identify a whole school using 'modernization diffusion' as the principle of regional development and where the success and rate of development depend on the proper functioning of the vehicles for transmission of developmental impulses (Berry 1972; Boudeville 1966; Friedmann 1966, 1971; Gould 1969; Johnson 1970; Pred 1975; Riddell 1970). Recognizing the role of the city in economic development, and noting that in many countries the urban structure is one of a single great city or metropolis plus a large number of very small settlements with a lack of intermediate-sized settlements, they propose aid to development through improvement of the hierarchy structure in order to create more nodes for transmission of development. Berry, Gould and Riddell, among others, without involving themselves closely in the study of development, drew attention to the pattern of modernization spread from centres of innovation and were able to map its contagious and hierarchical aspects, focusing especially on the latter, which were taken as the most important. At a regional, 'mesoscale' level, this spread is dependent on the main urban centre within the region (Brown and Lentnek 1972); at a macroscale, it moves from the largest city centres, through smaller cities, to country towns and rural areas.

Approaching more directly the theme of regional development, which was seen as a concrete problem by the 1960s in most countries, Boudeville (1966) and others took François Perroux's idea of a growth pole, a lead sector in an economy which, through its dynamism and its extensive linkages, pulls the rest of the regional economy along with it, and applied this as a spatial model. The growth pole then became a geographical place, an urban centre which acts as stimulator of growth in its vicinity. Combining this idea with that of the central place or urban hierarchy, growth poles were seen as those places which fill in the gaps in this hierarchy, as well as being centres for growth industries. The growth-pole paradigm became the dominant one in the young science of regional planning in the 1960s and early 1970s, appealing in its simplicity, in its obviousness, and in its ties to urban planning and industrial planning, already the subject of considerable academic and practical efforts at planning by this time.

There were many variants on the growth-pole theme. Johnson (1970) applied the argument about filling gaps in the hierarchy of the poor countries with only a tangential reference to growth poles; he found that in India particularly there was a need for small centres of, say, 20,000 inhabitants immediately above the village level. His method to stimulate development focused entirely on the provision of this urban structure, and the lack of a smooth hierarchy following the rank-size rule is interpreted as being a major cause of poverty and underdevelopment. On the other hand, Friedmann (1966), writing on Venezuela, and most of the writers in the volume edited by Kukliński (1972) advocated a growth-pole kind of development primarily out of concern for the advance of technology and the redirection of metropolitan growth, not with any direct reference to the urban hierarchy. Others found it hard to relinquish the advantages of the great city through growth-pole advocacy and instead argued for a single 'counter-magnet' to the principal city, of comparable size and importance (Geisse and Corraggio 1972). A variant of this theme was the use of development corridors, retaining metropolitan advantages along a single line of development, but still spreading these advantages because the line has more extension than the single point, and perhaps achieving an integration through specialized production of different goods at different points along the line (Pottier 1963).

There is insufficient evidence from historical studies to weigh the relative merits of the neoclassical and modernization-diffusionist school of thought on regional development, and it is possible that one's view should depend on the time-scale and period chosen. For the modern period, Chapter 6 will show some evidence relative to this argument. It may be noted, however, that apart from this debate there is another one between, effectively, followers of Hirschman and of Myrdal. Following the latter's view, especially as regards the importance of political factors, to their logical end, a school of dependency writers has emerged, first in Latin America itself and then, since the late 1960s, in the English-language literature. Some writers, such as Prebisch (1971) and Furtado (1970), simply emphasize the structural problems which prevent convergence of international or inter-regional income levels. This structuralist branch is surpassed by the true dependency school, which insists on the institutional problems underlying the structural ones and takes the whole economy as a subsidiary and dependent process under the control of a small number of leading nations who decide between them the development of all others, the 'dependent' lands (Frank 1969; Cardoso and Faletto 1979). O'Brien (1974) and Lall (1975) have summaries showing the various shades of opinion within this school. For the most part, as it stresses the political character of the development problem, dependency theory does not apply with great force to the region, though some writers have attempted an application – as, for example, Slater's (1975) study of Peru or Rofman's (1974) of Latin America, based on Argentina.

Another kind of exogenous model of development can be shown to have only very limited applicability to specific regions and time periods. This is the economic base model. Douglass North (1955) applied the base concept to the development of the Pacific Northwest of the United States. As applied at this level, the idea is that a leading export commodity from a newly opened region will induce growth within the region by earning an income for it that may be reinvested in the export sector (or in a variety of derivative industries which depend on the export industry) through linkages of labour supply, service provision, processing or otherwise using the product. This is an exogenous theory inasmuch as it relies on an export market for the product.

Over the first half of the present century North viewed the Northwest as maintained by a succession of bases, from lumber in the 1880s to grain farming, power production and aeroplane manufacture. This model might be considered important in the Latin American context because reliance on one or more export commodities has been, and is still today, a fact in most countries of the region. Resource wealth which backs these exports might be seen as the key to development.

But such a model stands in contrast not only to current views of the United Nations, which look with ill favour on policies of dependence on a single major commodity export, but also to another theory advanced by the same author (in North and Thomas 1973) concerning, admittedly, European development in medieval times rather than the more modern American experience. In this theory, also subscribed to in part by Wilkinson (1973), the development of industry and of the services of the modern state is an essentially endogenous process, relying not on resource abundance but resource scarcity. Scarcity is seen as having induced a search for substitutes, and the process of industrialization, with its improvements in transport and services, is one of substitution of manufactured products for previously abundant but now scarce natural products. In agriculture intensification is an adjustment to increased demographic pressure rather than autonomous 'progress' towards higher technology. In industry the use of manufactured products such as textiles is a reaction to the increased scarcity of natural furs or hides which once provided the optimal solution. Boserup's conception of agricultural development in Datoo, (1978) has much in common with this line of argument.

Boserup's (1965) concept of agricultural development is that population growth forces groups to increase the intensity of land use by increasing frequency of use, in a five-stage sequence from forest fallow (shifting cultivation), through bush fallow and short fallow, to annual and multiple cropping. Advances in technology, usually exogenous, do not determine the shifts from one stage to another more intensive one, because technology in advance of what is commonly used has usually been found to be available long before it has been permanently adopted. The main stimulus to change comes from increasing population density, which forces changes in farming systems and thus in technology.

The very possibility of completely different interpretations of the role of resources in relation to development is undoubtedly a warning to us of the limited possibilities of a grand general theory based on this kind of factor. In the specific context of Latin America, indeed, Browning (1975) showed that the export base has an effect which is strongly dependent on the social and institutional context of production. Tobacco in Cuba in the eighteenth century or coffee in nineteenth-century Colombia were useful export bases for development because they were not connected to a plantation economy. But almost universally sugar cane, though a major export base, could have little developmental effect because of its plantation associations. No incentive to private initiatives in any branch of the economy could be given under slavery.

Applied models

Some theories of economic development of the exogenous kind, as well as some concepts which have never been formally set out as theories, have been applied in trying to remedy the poor countries' plight. One well-known set of public policies has been that associated particularly with the United Nations Commission for Latin America (ECLA). The content of its analysis and consequent policy has changed over time, but the central ideas remain the same. Raul Prebisch, the Argentine economist who became head of ECLA, saw a structural inequality in the 1950s between nations, based on their 'terms of trade'. Primary products received, according to his arguments, progressively lower prices relative to manufactured goods, so that the primary producer countries tended to be the under-developed countries and manufacturing countries tended to advance.

This analysis recognized the power of outside influences in its stress on the factor of trade. The solution was logically to change the trading relations by encouraging domestic industry in Latin American countries, behind the protection of tariff barriers. In the 1970s this policy was modified in view of the evident inability of Latin American countries to achieve thresholds beyond which industry would be self-maintaining and competitive; their tiny and dispersed internal markets could not bring into being new industries demanding large market size; only the consumer industries which were already in existence did that. Instead a policy designed to promote the macroregional industrialization of groups of countries was now endorsed, in order to create a large initial market, and tariff barriers were lowered wherever possible to achieve this. The lowering of internal tariffs had no direct effect on external trade and aid, but these were de-emphasized as agents of development, aid in particular being questioned as a vehicle for promoting long-term development.

Despite the partial rejection of aid as the formula for development and an increased reliance on internal groupings, the basis of the ECLA approach remains the need for modernization, transference from agriculture to industry by adoption of techniques from the outside world and modernization of agriculture itself by means of mechanization. Diffusion of modern technology is still the desideratum in the process for change.

Growth-pole policies, mentioned already in the context of Venezuela and adopted as a means of promoting regional development by several countries in the late 1960s and 1970s, are also applications of development theory which rely on exogenous kinds of factors. Perroux's idea of an *'industrie motrice'*, a motor industry or lead sector which would propel the total economy through its linkages, was applied in France at a regional level in establishing the concept and the fact of growth poles, centres from which economic prosperity would have spread effects out into the surrounding countryside and into linked industries. The policy was well publicized, became part of regional-planning lore in the 1960s and was adopted by Latin American countries such as Bolivia, Argentina, Chile and Colombia (Conroy 1973) in the course of that decade. It suffers as a concept from the same strictures as apply to its intellectual parents, the ideas of Hirschman and Myrdal on spread and polarization effects. Whether or not it is effective depends on a host of other factors, which are highly variable from place to place and from time to time.

Growth processes

Before presenting a specific view of development, it is necessary here to regress to a more basic level of understanding and to categorize growth processes and related processes of differentiation. The reason for doing this, in the present writer's view, is that most of the writing on socio-economic development has been too narrow and tendentious in its search for a single and simple explanation of the processes, and that a view encompassing various different possible processes occurring simultaneously or following one another over a period of time at one place is more correct.

In recent years geographers in particular among social scientists have been subject to a kind of narrowing influence in the study of growth, both in spatial and temporal dimensions and in terms of the content and methodology of study. Diffusion, and in particular diffusion as modelled in quantitative terms by stochastic or deterministic methods, has been the primary focus of interest, and while this has achieved important results in terms of our understanding of the mechanisms and spatial structure – that is, contagious, hierarchical, or mixed forms – of spread processes, it has also had some unfortunate side-effects. Attention has been concentrated on the spread of what might be termed 'simple' innovation, items whose content does not change in any important respect across space or time, whose target population is readily identifiable and fixed over the dimensions of the study and whose spread is not linked to, or limited by, other innovation-spread processes. In practice this has often meant a restriction to consumer goods and their spread, usually reaching the vast majority of a population and moving rapidly so that changes in the course of spread may be ignored.

Even within the category of single-item growth processes, one may identify some which suffer distortions and changes, either in the object being spread or in its use by man. Some examples which spring to mind are the long-term spread of domesticates, which involved a change from wheat to barley in the Middle East and to rye substitutes in northern and western Europe, and to millets and sorghum in Asia and Africa (Isaac 1970). This was a process lasting thousands of years, giving ample time for change in content; but more recent and rapid changes, according to environment, are in the use of corrugated iron for cheap-hut roofing in the industrial West and for house roofing in the Third World shanty towns, where oil drums and cardboard have similarly been pressed into service for emergency housing. An intermediate case of changing use is that of maize, which spread from Central America as a tropical grain crop across all the tropics but in recent decades has been extended into middle latitudes as a feed crop grown for its green-matter content.

Other kinds of growth are not single-item but multiple and offer much greater opportunities for changes in content or use. To take an example cited sometimes in the literature on diffusion (see, for example, Pounds 1969), the spread of urbanization is obviously not equivalent to the spread of any one of its parts, such as manufacturing, services, transport, administration, religious or military functions. Urbanization has, rather, a shifting, variable content across time and space, moulding itself to the requirements of distant political or economic centres or more local contingencies of social structure or local resource mix.

To this simple point it might be objected that functions may be changeable, but urbanization viewed as a geographic structure (the town) will still be capable of being mapped as a single spread, forgetting functional differences; the simple fact of concentrated settlement may be studied. This is admissible but begs the question of what it is we seek to study: the architectonic form of the settlement or the underlying processes which give rise to it and are usually so varied?

Another phenomenon whose spread has been traced across territory and time is 'modernization'. In this it is apparent that we do not have a single, unified or stable phenomenon, although geographers have tried to identify it by various indices, combining a number of factors (Slater 1975; Riddell 1970; Cole and Mather 1972). In this case it seems that modernization was roughly equated with economic development, so that development is simply a spread process moving across territory, a view which has been widely held. For the moment we may simply note, on the unlikely assumption that agreement on what is meant by the term could be reached, that modernization has many components and that it is liable to change; in short, it is a multiple rather than a single innovation.

Other examples of complex multiple growth could be given. It might be useful to consider the Agricultural Revolution or Improvement Movement of the eighteenth and nineteenth centuries in this light. The improvements in Britain, for example, consisted of a number of permutations from a list including enclosures, drainage, fertilizers, tree planting, crop rotation and animal breeding as physical measures, and individual tenure replacing joint tenancy as an institutional change. The mixture of these elements varied from place to place and over time, so that improvement in the mild, wet pasture lands of the south-west might mean farm enclosure and the improvement of cattle farming and stock pedigree, while in the south-east it was more a matter of stock and management improvements in sheep farming, increases in farm size and improved crop rotations involving feed production for the sheep (mostly turnips and improved grasses). Yet again, in the Highlands the movement focused on sheep and forest plantation, as it did in the uplands of northern England. An underlying concept of improvement is certainly diffused about the country, but the form it takes is highly variable according to local resource possibilities.

Still other kinds of growth must be identified as those which involve also differentiation as an integral part of the growth process, and it should also be noted that differentiation may occur without growth. Here we refer not to a set of diversified changes in different directions (as described above in the case of the agricultural improvements of the eighteenth century) but an organized separation into parts distinctive in function and form as the growth process goes on.

Human phenomena achieve a differentiation of their component parts as they grow, each part tending to become more specialized over time as the need for its special function asserts itself. The large modern firm, for example, as it grows to national and international scale, produces functional links between specialized branches and depends for its existence on strong links between these branches and the organizing centre. Car manufacturing firms commonly establish assembly lines in distant regions of low labour cost and component manufacture in others where labour may also be relatively low-cost but skills are relatively high; design, administration and planning are retained in the centre.

The same principle may be applied to socio-political or economic organizations, whether politically formalized as states or empires or of a more informal nature, like the present-day Soviet and United States economic empires. As they grow, such organisms call into being economically specialized zones for the production of raw materials, minerals, farm produce, power and fuels, timber and so on, zones where manufacturing is concentrated, and urban concentrations of tertiary-level activities.

This is a process of epigenesis, to use the biological term coined early in the last century to distinguish the new concept of unified growth plus differentiation of parts from the older concept of growth from an egg or cell which held in it all its specialized parts in embryo. The biological analogy cannot be pressed too far; within the economic or social 'organism' sub-units with various degrees of distinctiveness may separate out to a greater or lesser degree (within a country such as the United Kingdom, for example, Scotland, Northern Ireland and Wales have varying degrees of separate identity). Such intermediate states are not normal in nature, where the integrity of the individual organism is maintained and the production of offspring involves the creation of entirely separate units.

Nevertheless, epigenesis may be seen as important to our understanding of socio-economic development, more central than any individual growth process involving only a simple spread. To aid understanding of the different classes of growth envisaged here, a classification scheme is shown in Table 1.

The three major categories are called levels, the implication being that there exists some sort of order of priority among them. Level 1

Table 1 *Growth processes*

	Level 1: epigenetic process	Level 2: multiple growth	Level 3: single growth
Features	Central organizations; growth is accompanied by differentiation, and both are complex, involving many elements	Not centrally organized; involves differentiation but not of a systematic kind; many elements in variable mix	Not centrally organized; individual items do not change, i.e. no differentiation; modelled by diffusion
Examples	Large economic enterprises with vertical linkages among processes; political and economic bodies, economic empires	Agricultural revolution; agrarian reform movement; urbanization	Motor car, hybrid corn, television, tractors

processes, and the structures they produce, determine in part the limits for Level 2 processes, and in turn Level 2 dominates or restricts Level 3. Thus the spread of Britain's nineteenth-century empire as an epigenetic process, formal and informal, set approximate limits for the growth of modern agricultural methods and structure. In turn, individual innovations at Level 3, such as the Hereford breed of improved cattle, could only spread within the confines of the complex growth which we call the Agricultural Revolution. These are maximum limits at both levels, so that the actual spread of many items was far less. Neither an agricultural revolution nor the spread of improved cattle was found in the Indian subcontinent. These are challengeable concepts because the question is in part one of priorities as between political, economic and social processes, and there are entrenched academic and intellectual stances on the matter. For this reason the matter will be returned to in later discussion.

Growth processes and development

Having identified and classified some different growth processes, it is now possible to relate socio-economic development to them and also – to the extent that the writer's position is made clear – to relate some existing theories, outlined earlier in this work, to the schemata of growth. In doing so, we will have to enlarge the classification of Table 1 and to include further types.

First of all, from the classification in Table 1 it would appear that all three levels may be involved in development, and indeed phenomena from all levels have been used as indices of development. Indices from Level 3, such as the percentage of households with television, motor cars or amount of railway track per unit of population or area, are common as representations of development; and it has been noted that the 'modernization' theories of development equate the process more or less with the adoption of these innovations.

Other indices commonly used in the measurement of development, such as the percentage employed in manufacturing and agriculture, the level of farm mechanization or the proportion of owner-operator farms, are examples portraying the broader complex diffusions of Level 2. At Level 1 the operation of large institutions and political bodies is to be observed, as envisaged in dependence theory and some of the 'backwash' effects identified by Myrdal, as well as the structuralist arguments of Prebisch.

On the other hand, it is at first sight difficult to reconcile the classification made earlier, into endogenous and exogenous processes, with the growth categories mentioned. But a fresh start may be made in an attempt to use both kinds of concept. If we allow a degree of priority to the Level 1 processes, simply because of their greater scale and the fact that they incorporate within them the various lower-level processes, these processes may be examined first as possible generalizations of socio-economic development.

Without entering into a detailed discussion of the geographical patterns of a Level 1 structure, such as an economic empire, and simplifying it to the Von Thünen-like set of rings of different intensity of production (Figure 1), the growth of the overall structure is indicated by the arrows, each of the zones 1, 2 and 3 expanding their outer limits under pressures such as improved transport and higher demand at the centre.

Within such a scheme, one possibility for development is the course followed by Y in the innermost circle. As nerve-centre to the whole system, and as the system grows from A to B, Y's functions become more complex (more administration, management functions and perhaps some kinds of manufacturing), and many of the

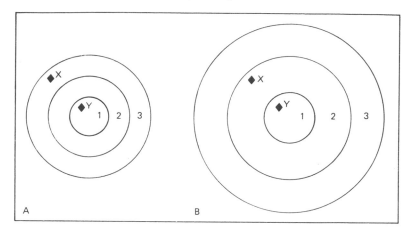

Figure 1   *Development by growth of the system. The growth of an economic system is indicated by the increase in the size of the rings from diagram A to diagram B.*

commonly accepted indices of development see an increase. Another possibility is that of X, which also undergoes development, not through an endogenous force but through the overall expansion of the system. From A to B it moves from the outer circle (which may be supposed, for the sake of simplicity, to be one of ranching) to the intermediate one, of arable farming, and in terms of the common indices (density of roads or railways per square kilometre, percentage urban population, level of use of machines such as tractors), there is an increase in developmental level.

Within this Level 1 process, Level 2 expansions such as urbanization may be followed through in detail, with changes occurring not only in the proportion of urban population in the total but also in the function of towns and their relation to hinterlands and to other towns, as we move from the ranching to the arable and then to the central zone.

Putting the two types of development together – changes from Y through the growth of its system, and changes in X through its changing relative position in the system – a simple model of development is at once suggested. Outer regions and countries will benefit from the expansion of the system and improvements in technology which make it more 'central', either in simple distance or in terms of access to information and communications, input to industry and markets for products. But the central region, if not overtaken by diseconomies of congestion, will always move further ahead – indeed it must do so, if this is a long-term development, in order to be able to provide the stimulus, by way of innovation and organization, for the remainder of the system or organism.

In other words, in adopting this kind of pattern as the only one for development, we are constrained to a dependency-type theory of spatial development, with options open for only a few central countries. And if the same processes may be presumed operative within countries (and the individual nation-state may well be regarded as one of the entities considered at Level 1), then centre–periphery models of the Myrdal–Friedmann type may be said to operate always to maintain interregional differences and disparities, and even to increase them. This would be true in all cases of growth at the centre, and only where the central region or country is undergoing a serious recession or debilitating political or military turmoil would the balance become more even, though in this latter case no region is likely to benefit.

But the scheme of Table 1 is incomplete as a representation of developmental processes and does not properly cover differentiation types. In addition to those processes which may be related to growth, there are others, more correctly termed differentiation, which may occur either with or in the absence of growth. The situation may be re-diagrammed as in Table 2.

In this table two major categories of process are envisaged,

Table 2 *Growth and differentiation*

| *Growth* | | *Differentiation* | |
| | *Epigenetic* | | |
Simple (usually single items)	Complex (usually multiple)	Dependent	Disjunctive
TV, hybrid corn, tractors, railways	Agricultural revolution, urbanization, agrarian reform	Large firms, internal national growth, external urban region, military, educational systems, industrialization	Geographic isolation, social isolation

growth and differentiation. The first encompasses the types discussed earlier, simple and complex growth. The epigenetic process is seen as straddling growth and differentiation, and the examples indicate its multi-faceted nature. Industrial growth, for example, proceeds through the outward spread of factories to different regions, as a straightforward growth process and might be studied as such, but it also involves inter-regional specialization as one city or region acquires a specific industrial complex and induces a counterbalancing specialization in other regions.

Differentiation processes may also occur on their own, so that separate categories for differentiation of disjunctive and dependent types are included. Dependency, in fact, as a process, might be viewed as epigenesis, and it is so viewed by the more optimistic of the dependency writers. Others, like Frank (1964), would place the process as one of simple differentiation with no overall forward movement. Beyond these processes one of disjunctive differentiation is identified.

To compare this evolution with the simple diagrams of Figure 1, disjunctive development (Figure 2) implies a separate centre of economy emerging from the framework of the first one.

The point X in this socio-economic scheme, instead of becoming developed through association with Y, achieves a separate development, with its own structure of zones. In fact, the scheme is more understandable if Y and X start as separate centres with no

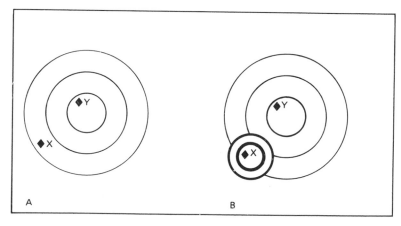

Figure 2 *Disjunctive development model. Instead of growth through movement from an outer to an inner ring, an independent system is created.*

relation between them, for this allows X to emerge without any struggle to emancipate itself from Y.

How does this kind of development relate to what has already been said about the biological analogy or to the various known models of development? First, as has already been noted, the biological or organism analogy (growth occurring with specialization) is one that cannot be pressed too far in socio-economic terms. The process envisaged in Figure 2 is one of separation out of a part within an existing organism, so that it finally becomes a new one; if birth of a new organism is the nearest analogy, it is still not close to what is contemplated in the present process. Indeed, the latter often involves, as in the case of colonial territories achieving independence and separating from their mother country, an increasing change in the style of development (different political structure, social aims and economic mechanisms); the daughter organism does not resemble the parent and increasingly dissociates itself from it.

In relation to existing theories, it would seem closer to the endogenous than to the exogenous type of growth, because an independent and separate path of development may be identified. This may be allowed, except that the simple theories of endogenous development assume that all countries develop in a similar manner, and the idea of disjunctive development is that there is at least the possibility of completely different kinds of development.

If the barrier between X and Y in Figure 3 is of a physical type, a different kind of development was likely in pre-modern times simply because of transport difficulties (across mountains, deserts or water barriers). If cultural factors, such as religious and linguistic differences, operate (usually together with the physical), then the differentiation is almost certainly one of kind as well as of degree. Economic and political institutions may act as limiting barriers and operate either artificially to cut off segments within a single major type or organization (as do tariff barriers between the otherwise similar economies of, for example, some Latin American countries) or to reinforce real differences in development directions (as with the Iron Curtain of Central Europe). Disjunction may thus be regarded as endogenous, but with the proviso that it does not resemble existing endogenous theories.

It is perhaps possible to show why isolation and disjunctive differentiation have been little aired in academic discussion and have failed to enter into any current theory. On the one hand, disjunction runs counter to the idea of dependency, and Frank

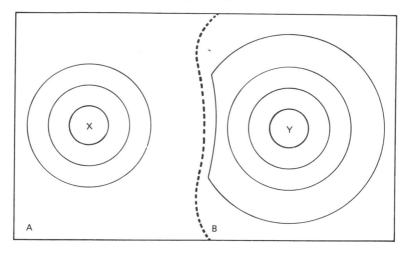

Figure 3 *Independent development. X is separated from Y by a physical, cultural, economic or institutional barrier.*

(1967) and the other dependency writers make much of the concept that all areas of the periphery, in Latin America and elsewhere, are all linked in to the metropolis and that their underdevelopment is due to these links. In fact, it is necessary, for Frank's thesis, to have good linkages, for otherwise the criticism is easily made that at least some regions fail to develop because they have fallen behind in 'modernization' or simply because they have been isolated and out of touch with the centre.

If dependency theory is anxious to prove that there is no real isolation, disjunction and isolation as factors are not really taken up by the other side in the debate. 'Modernization' and 'spread' theories of development have something in common with dependency, for they both rely on outside forces to influence local events; both are exogenous theories. For the 'modernization' theorists, however, isolation and disjunction are seen solely as negative elements, disadvantages to be overcome if development is to occur at all. Disjunction is thus not a mechanism by which growth can generally be achieved, except where a temporary aid to separate development is seen as a possibility, with tariff barriers to protect infant industries.

Synthesis

Pulling these different views together, it is possible to make some general statements about development without confining ourselves to any one line of argument but allowing eclecticism to match the very varied character of the real-life experience. Development may be either endogenous or exogenous in nature, either under the dominant influence of some external political or economic power, or the product of a process of national or regional transformation. In the case of exogenous development, as applied to colonial territories, this will often be of a dependent nature, a controlled and limited development, though the active 'underdevelopment' process of Frank may be challenged as a view of Latin American processes. Exogenous development in a dependency pattern characterizes much of colonial Spanish and Portuguese America, as it does the remainder of the present-day Third World.

The alternative form of exogenous development theory noted, 'modernization' – diffusion, may be regarded as related to dependency, as suggested in the earlier discussion, differing mainly in the force allowed to individual factors. 'Modernization' may occur as a process, but its scope for operation in geographic and social terms is limited by a set of social and political or institutional factors. It may also operate at various levels; simple, complex and epigenetic growth processes are possible, and these may be ordered as earlier indicated so as to allow diffusions only within higher-order frameworks.

A considerable segment of the underdeveloped world was, however, allowed to remain outside the realm of colonial enterprise and is characterized, rather, by isolation and its effects. The vast interior of Africa until the late nineteenth century and the Chinese realm in East Asia, like most of Latin America beyond the coasts and the settled upland districts, had only peripheral contact with Europe. When such territories developed in any sense it was by endogenous processes, though sometimes with an external impulse to start or react to. For large areas, what took place was a process of increasing differentiation through isolation, because primitive and traditional societies did not change to align themselves with the European but remained more or less static. The barriers in the case of the Latin American area were both physical and social. Physical barriers made contact with primitive people in the Amazon Basin difficult and unrewarding because of the few resources that might easily be harnessed to the colonial machine; social barriers were erected between people oriented to different ideals and with a different set of motivations. Frequently the physical and social barriers reinforced one another and have caused longstanding differences in the type of development which are still felt today.

Geographical and social structures

To understand more fully the last point, concerning the social barriers between peoples, it is necessary to explore further the possible ways in which socio-economic structures may be formed. A useful format, which directly indicates possible spatial structures and relates them to kinds of economy and society, is that of Polanyi (1977). Three kinds of exchange systems are identified by him – reciprocity, redistribution, and market exchange – each connected with a specific social organization and a particular kind of economy, though not at all mutually exclusive in time or place. These three socio-economic types may be identified today in the palimpsest of Latin America's human landscape. Their distribution in the region at different points in time may be described, as well as their internal spatial structures, and we may relate them to growth and differentiation.

Reciprocity is the system of economy practised dominantly by primitive peoples, whereby exchange between groups (clans, extended families) of objects and services is controlled by the status of these individuals in the community, and the movements are symmetrical between each pair or at least over the whole set of groups (Polanyi 1977, pp. 37–9). Polanyi cites the Trobriand Islanders studied by Malinowski as a classical example of this structure, which is based not on communal action, however, so much as on a chain reaction of aid *from* one set of neighbours *to* another defined set. In most parts of the world, and certainly in Latin America, a more familiar structure would be communal aid in common tasks among members of the village group, such as the harvesting of each individual farmer's crops by the whole group. This is also an illustration of reciprocity, in that each individual must help with all others' harvests and is himself helped in his own work by all others. The structure is not simply one of exchange, however, but explicitly involves a social set of relations and a political structure. An egalitarian society, in Fried's (1967) terminology, is implied, because no individual or subgroup is established as leader or receiver of a special share in work effort, goods or services. Reliance on the principle of mutual aid requires that each family, each individual, is similarly endowed. Such a society obviously implies no political structure, for none is required in the homogeneous social and economic structure. It is a stable, static socio-economic structure, because no obvious pressures for change are built into it, and this no doubt explains the survival of primitive societies into the twentieth century. Change from this to the next system of relations requires some special force, such as population pressure, combined with favourable resources to set off a self-reinforcing process of expansion and change towards another exchange system. As a spatial expression of this type of exchange system a homogeneous landscape is proposed, without, on the one hand, concentrations of economic activity implied by urban places, which are unnecessary to this self-sufficient society, nor, on the other, the specialized economic structures (landscapes of specialized agricultural production of one or two commodities or specialized industrial extraction zones) which characterize the other kinds of society. Thus the only variations in pattern are those imposed by nature – denser settlement in more fertile soil zones or on coasts or rivers with a richer fish resource.

Redistribution, by contrast, relies on the principle of centralization. In Polanyi's terms (1977, p. 40): 'Redistribution obtains within a group to the extent that in the allocation of goods (including land and natural resources) they are collected in one and distributed by virtue of custom, law or *ad hoc* central decision.' This kind of economic exchange principle is more typical of what Polanyi (1957) terms the 'ancient empires', large territorial units such as the empires of pre-Conquest America and of the Aztec, Maya and Inca, and the classical economies of Egypt, Sumeria, Babylon.

As a general mechanism for movement from reciprocity to redistribution and on to markets, Polanyi suggests that one possibility is war, perhaps allied to, or alternating with, trade. A situation of general stability in reciprocity systems may be imagined, but one which may be destabilized whenever inter-tribal or inter-group rivalries flare up and war results in the defeat of one group. The military leaders established for the purposes of war may have become permanent chiefs over the enlarged domain, and their success in administration may have been a snowballing factor helping them to expand still further and gain still more power, which society legitimized by the elevation of these leaders to the position of god-kings. In other words, the possibility of inequality in worldly possessions, counter to the principles of reciprocity, could only be tolerated by allowing a non-human quality to the recipients. But as the god-kings could only be a small group or family, power was necessarily highly centralized and usually focused in one city.

It is, of course, true that as the group or community grew with increasing power, the large new units made a new exchange system imperative in many cases. Differences in time of harvest or type of product were likely, so that the collection of the various products and their redistribution would be required. It is also likely that the disciplined central organization, whether theocratic, military or civil, which had accompanied the first expansion also allowed the community to organize itself for central collection of tribute or trade and redistribution. But these arguments also allow us to predict a change to a market economy, so that it becomes necessary to fall back on the social principle of organization around a single leader as responsible for the structure.

A spatial centre for collection and redistribution, with transport links to it, is essential with this scheme. Instead of homogeneity, there is a centripetal/centrifugal pattern in urban systems. Urban life is both possible and necessary with this system: possible, because the concept of trade and tribute implies a surplus which is used to maintain the city; necessary, because a centre to receive tribute and administer it, and to provide a home for the king and his entourage, is essential. The transport system will reflect this polarization; most roads lead vertically to the centre, directly or through intermediate small towns, and there are few 'horizontal' linkages among similar-sized towns.

Harvey (1973, p. 209) indicates that a redistributive society will generate an urban structure which is hierarchical in the way that Christaller's (1966) and Lösch's (1954) models of economic landscapes predict. This seems inherently improbable, for these models, even if we discount their normative character, do not include any distinctive social-structure element; they assume an economy which is essentially autonomous and independent of social structure. In support of his assertion, Harvey cites E. A. J. Johnson (1970), but this work is quite explicit (see especially chs. 1, 5, 6 and 7) in stating that no regular hierarchy of towns is found in what Johnson terms the 'developing countries', and that, in fact, a major purpose of economic development planning should be remedying this situation by the establishment of medium-sized towns. In general, it is more likely (and, as will be seen later, the contention is supported by observation) that poor countries will have an urban structure dominated by a single primate city and other centres which are only small, with purely local functions. Although complex social-ranking systems may exist under this form of exchange, this does not necessarily imply a set of ranked urban centres, for the hierarchy of administration may itself be very small and entirely concentrated in one major centre. Harvey's attempt to relate social-rank structure and urban structure seems to be straining the relationship between the two, which is at best loose; indeed, the link between social structure and type of exchange system is itself looser than he implies in following Fried's categorization of egalitarian, ranked and stratified societies and in equating these with Polanyi's exchange systems, reciprocity, redistribution and markets. What seems important to establish is that rigid social ranking systems are likely with this kind of economy, dictated both by positions of privilege or subservience within the society and by an economic division of labour which is related to the social division and to the size and complexity of the socio-economic structure.

The third type of economic system is that of price-making markets, the economy of which we have most experience of in the Western world. In this system each individual acts separately, competing in an open market to supply or to acquire goods and services. Such a system requires market centres of many different sizes to fulfil its functions, and an efficiency principle is adhered to because competition eliminates non-optimal markets, just as it does non-optimal producers.

In spatial terms, and ignoring the variations due to resource patterns and physical barriers, the urban pattern is that described in normative terms by Christaller and Lösch or, in more sophisticated manner, with allowances for information factors, by Robson (1973) and Pred (1977). An elaborate hierarchy of urban centres, with spatial and size relationships carefully adjusted, comes into being and maintains a considerable stability over time. In keeping with the urban structure, a transport system characterized by multiple linkages, both horizontally between similar-sized towns and vertically from them to smaller towns and larger cities, will be typical. Such a spatial structure is, of course, idealized in the diagrams of the writers on the subject of central place theory, but its overall validity as a normative model can scarcely be challenged. This is because in the modern market society the economic principles do have a dominant effect in determining spatial structure, tempered only by physical or institutional factors. In such an economy society effectively endorses the operation, in apparent independence of economic laws, so that the constraints imposed by rank or blood relationships are no longer important.

It may be apposite to ask here what is the relation of some structures or models, developed specifically to portray the growth of urban and transport systems in colonial territories, to the ideas set out in the foregoing paragraphs. We may consider two models, one specifically of transport in a colonial territory (Taaffe, Morrill and Gould 1963, and the other of economic development in general, with an emphasis on the spatial structure (Vance 1970). These models, which are all we have in the way of general spatial models showing the distinctive patterns of developing countries, apart from the centre–periphery type of models, have much in common with each other. They both consider the case of an essentially modern economy entering and taking over a land where either there is a homogeneous previous pattern of human exploitation or none exists at all. The transport model assumes an initial pattern of many small ports along a coast, presumably of primitive fishermen, but an interior vacant or ignorable for the purposes of the model's development. Initial spread is in linear form, followed by a dendritic pattern, with feeder lines taking goods out to the exterior. In the latter stages of the model an integrated network begins to appear, reflecting local development of manufactures or services and the growth of interior urban centres where these activities take place. In effect, the early stages resemble those of a redistribution economy and for good reasons. While the market economy in Europe or North America operates as such among competing regions or countries, permitting the interdigitation of markets and supply hinterlands that gives us networks of transport and graded urban hierarchies, in areas of 'underdevelopment', where there is either no competitor or one that can be ignored, the market exchange system is virtually replaced by a redistributive one. Resources such as metals, farm produce and other raw materials are found and exploited, then taken out via linear transport systems to a port and thence to a home country. A meagre counterbalancing flow operates in the opposite direction, primarily bringing equipment for the extraction operations and salaries and goods for the administrators working in the country. In the absence of a varied market economy in the region, the trade pattern is one of the gathering in from the few isolated resource areas of the goods for export to the home country, in the manner of the centralized redistributive society, and the areal pattern is one of linkages to that home country, the long lines in the colonial area representing the outer parts of a large radial system of links. In parallel with the older redistributive societies, trade is not extended out from small centres within the colonial territory, so that it grows up 'naturally', but is administered by institutions outside the control of the local inhabitants.

Vance calls attention to this fact – that trade grows up commonly as a result not of local linkages but of long-distance contacts – and makes it the basis of differentiation between his model of colonial settlement and that hypothesized for European homelands, where a central-place type of emergence might be supposed to be correct, each small place generating trade hinterlands that gradually grow and compete one with another. In Vance's model the details of conversion from the dendritic penetration-line system of settlement and transport to a central-place type are discussed in detail; once the colonial economy becomes diversified, there is a need for a more network-like transport system and for a hierarchical urban structure to replace the primate one. But in this case, as in the Taaffe–Morrill–Gould model of transport, the discussion is entirely spatial-economic. Social underpinnings are almost ignored, in contrast to Polanyi's model, which would arrive at the same spatial structure if extended from its basic tenets. In some cases it might be supposed that the social structure could be ignored because new territory was being occupied; but even in such cases it is necessary to consider the social factor because the willingness of the colonizing people to engage in colonization of the pattern described is itself a matter of social will.

The topic of Polanyi's different exchange types was introduced to show the possibility of social barriers to development and their replacement by differentiation processes of a disjunctive nature. While some areas might come under the influence of market economies and societies, others remain under the older traditions of redistributive or reciprocal structures; what is more important, there seems to be no 'natural' way for the traditional societies to move towards more modern structures. Instead they remain internally in balance; in the words of Pearson (in Polanyi *et al.* 1957, pp. 307–19), the economy operates within a social integument which itself is stable. Primitive economies produce no necessary surpluses for trade until society demands them, and centrally controlled economies exert no pressures towards a market economy which might replace them.

If this matter has been given a more extensive treatment than might be expected in most discussions of economic development, it is because it is felt by this writer that this kind of social structure is important in the Latin American context, and also that the spatial structures which relate to the various kinds of exchange system present a format for our understanding of colonial and more recent geography. This writer (Morris 1978c) has developed the social-economic/spatial structure model in a study of Latin America in the Spanish language.

In the models assembled by Taaffe, Morrill and Gould and by Vance there is no hint of the social-barrier effect, and transition is direct from one spatial structure to another. What is proposed here is that the three exchange systems be recognized as distinct, and that the transition from one to another be seen as a major shift. What are the normal means of movement from one system to another? We may refer back to the division at the beginning of this chapter into endogenous and exogenous factors; given the stability of traditional systems, change has usually come from outside factors or groups, typically from movements of colonization. Thus the colonial empire constructed by the Spanish and the Portuguese contained within it the germs of transition from reciprocity and redistribution to markets. Internally there were possibilities for movement forwards but they were limited. Polanyi (1977) himself provides some key for forward movement in the growth of the spatial system. As a primitive society expands its territories through acts of aggression on the part of the displaced groups seeking a new home (one is reminded of the early Aztecs), it occupies increasingly larger territories and must needs move away from reciprocity to some system providing different goods from different regions and at different seasons. Society thus alters and, with it, the economy. The rulers take powers associated with their office as the military leaders and retain them afterwards as civilian rulers. Thus they become the kings at the centre of a redistributive system. Change from a redistributive to a marketing system may occasionally emerge out of the need for a money system to replace tribute in goods. Again, this is associated with the increasing size of the social political unit and reflects the difficulties of moving such items as cattle or timber, bulky objects, over great distances. Money or some kind of universal token system is employed instead of objects, and a market system is thereby facilitated. These shifts are unlikely to happen often, however, and, as has just been said, the most common changes are these introduced from the outside.

Summary and some conclusions

In the early part of this chapter a variety of growth processes were outlined, both endogenous and exogenous, that might contribute to economic development in different contexts. Simple and multiple growth processes proper, however, were seen to be limited to one kind of socio-economic structure: as most of the processes we regard as economic development are parts of the modern market economy, they were seen to spread readily only within the confines of existing economies which exhibit most of the features of the modern market economy. The spread of technical advances such as hybrid corn, tractorization, mechanization in general and the adoption of fertilizers, insecticides and new cultivation techniques is easy only within the market context, where there is no resistance to it.

In many poor countries processes of differentiation, not development, have been and continue to be the most likely. Two kinds of differentiation may be identified: dependent differentiation, relating to the dependency relations between colonial exploited area and mother country, and disjunctive differentiation, a product of social and physical barriers between different parts of a territory or between one territory and its neighbour. It is not implied that these differentiation processes represent negative development or the absence of it; they represent development in different directions. It will be a purpose of the final chapter of this book to show how the historically and geographically based differences may best be made use of in order to promote regional development on sound long-term bases.

2 Physical environment and indigenous settlement

Major aspects of the physical framework

Three principal geological-topographical units may be identified in Latin America. To the west are the mountains which front the Pacific; east of them are great valleys and plains of sedimentation; and further east are the shield masses, with their plateau topography.

The western mountain belt is a series of roughly parallel ranges running approximately north–south and of variable but usually considerable height, rising continuously to over 3000 metres in the South American continent. They thus constitute an important barrier to east–west movement and generally form the continental divide between Pacific and Atlantic drainage. Being of recent geological formation, they are generally steep-sided, and the continuing earth movements result in earthquakes and active volcanoes all along the line. Mountain building and erosion have given rise to an irregular topography, with many small separate valleys and interior basins, each with very limited and often fragmented areas of flat valley land. To the north, in Mexico, the ranges that form the mountains are well separated from one another and flank a larger interior basin-plateau between them. Most of Mexico belongs to this interior plateau, at altitudes of 1000–3000 metres. In South America the ranges again separate in Peru and Bolivia to produce broad upland basins, at around 3000 metres in the Peruvian Sierra and well over 3000 metres in the Lake Titicaca Basin and the Bolivian *altiplano*. Mountain-building processes in the western belt have involved the emplacement of mineral veins of commercial importance (copper, tin, iron ores, silver and zinc), in association with the intrusion of great magmatic bodies. Where erosion has subsequently removed much of the overlying sediments, as in Bolivia and southern Peru, these veins have been exploited, in colonial times principally for silver, in modern times for copper (Peru) and tin (Bolivia).

To the west the mountains drain out to deep oceans, and the only coastal plains are narrow erosional terraces or structural plains. Eastwards, however, there are large interior river plains, where sediments have accumulated. On the northern flank the Orinoco plains are shared by Colombia and Venezuela. Southwards the Amazon drains the long eastern slopes of the Andes in Colombia, Ecuador, Peru and Bolivia. A third sedimentary plain is that of the Paraná–Paraguay river system draining out to the south. Metallic minerals are not found, but oil-bearing formations are typical of the broad belt approximately 160 kilometres wide just east of the Andes. Only a few of these oil basins have been exploited to date, and there are probably large reserves, the area from which they may come being about 1.53 times that in the USA.

The shield masses are the Guiana shield, in the Guianas and in Venezuela south of the Orinoco, the Brazilian shield south of the Amazon and the Patagonian plateau in Argentina. In contrast to the mountains of the west and the central plains, the plateaux have table surfaces over large areas, bounded by sharp edges and deep-cutting valleys. This characteristic is heightened by the sandstone or volcanic rocks covering the shield, which tend to produce steep slopes at their margins. These overlying rocks are responsible for spectacular scenery in the Guiana shield country and remarkable waterfalls where big rivers leave the volcanic overlay, as on the edge of the Paraná Plateau at the Guayra Falls on the Paraná and the Iguazú Falls on the Iguazú.

The remarkable topographic contrasts and the landscapes they produce are perhaps more impressive than climatic, soil or vegetation variations but these latter are equally significant to human life. Seventy per cent of the region is climatically tropical, either the continuously humid *selvas* climate or the wet–dry savanna climates. *Selvas* rainforest occupies the Caribbean side of lowland Central America, the Colombian and Ecuadorean Pacific lowlands and the Amazon plains. Savanna climates reach into southern Mexico, up to the Tropic of Cancer and, in South America, flank the Amazon *selvas* on both sides, reaching into Mato Grosso and to the latitude of São Paulo on the coast.

The western mountain belt has rapidly varying climates, soils and vegetation in relation to altitude, the principal controlling factor. In the tropics the high Andes have moderate temperatures throughout the year; in northern Mexico's western Sierra Madre and in the Andes of southern Argentina/Chile the mountain climates restrict vegetation to subarctic or continental forests of conifers over most of the altitude range. Large areas are desert or near desert. Patagonia, itself a large desert, is extended through Argentina's western provinces in an arc round the Pampas to link with the Chaco, the semi-desert shared by Argentina, Paraguay and Bolivia. Between the Patagonian and western Argentine deserts and the Pacific coast desert, the desert zone links across the mountains of northernmost Argentina and southern Bolivia. On the Pacific coast the Atacama desert and its continuation through Peru form a desert reaching from 30°S near Santiago to 3°S in southern Ecuador. Separate dry zones, where rainfall is often quite abundant but may fail at irregular intervals, include the Brazilian Nordeste and, with less variability, the north coast of Venezuela and all of northern Mexico.

Negative and positive environments

Large areas of Latin America offer serious impediments to permanent settlement. Figure 4 does not show these separately according to type of negative factor, but groups together dissimilar factors in order to produce a synthesis of the negative environments (or at least the most important ones). These include, first, the deserts and dry zones just mentioned, which all have possibilities for amelioration by water-transfer schemes; some (such as the Peruvian coast) are more easily improved than others, but all are areas in which difficulties must be overcome before permanent human settlement is possible. Areas of excessive cold and wind exposure include the mountaintops of the Andes, the mountains above 3000 metres in the western Sierra Madre of Mexico, the southern Chilean/Argentine Andes and the exposed coasts of Tierra del Fuego. Major areas of poor soils include, again, the high mountains where soils are incompletely formed, stony deserts such as those of Patagonia and parts of the Pacific coast desert and the saline soils of many desert lands; the largest area of poor soils is the great stretch of oxisols, laterites and latosols in Brazil and parts of adjoining countries, soils which are deeply weathered by high temperatures and heavy precipitation and have very little of the soluble bases necessary to support plant life. In the *selvas* regions these lands may still support an exuberant and diversified vegetation through the continuous recirculation of nutrients from soil to plant roots and from plant back to topsoil, but the underlying soil fertility is low once the cycle

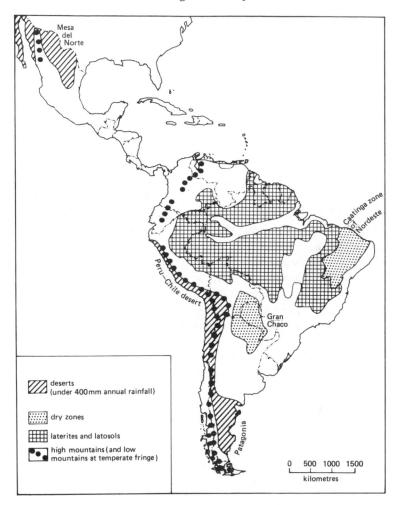

Figure 4 *Negative environments of Latin America. The three main negative regions, those with latosols, dry climates and mountains, occupy over 70 per cent of the total area.*

is broken. Luxuriant forest may also impress travellers through the region because of the better soils present along the floodplains, brought down by the rivers, but beyond the floodplains the vegetation is much more restricted. These oxisols are also found in the wet–dry tropics, in savanna climates (and so, for example, in parts of the Llanos in Colombia), in the savanna of southern Guyana and in the Rio Branco savanna in Brazil (see Figure 4).

By contrast, relatively limited areas of Latin America have acted as positive environments, where man, both in prehistoric and in more recent times, has been able to settle in large numbers and to elaborate more advanced socio-economic structures. Within the Andes the highlands of Bolivia–Peru, in the altitude zone between 4000 and 2500 metres, have provided one such environment. Temperatures at this level rise diurnally to between 20° and 30°C and fall by night to between 10° and 0°C, with little variation from season to season. Rainfall and temperature combined are insufficient to leach out the plant nutrients from the soil but sufficient to allow abundant plant growth through a long growing season – indeed, throughout the year in areas close to the equator. Steep slopes in parts of the region may be countered by terracing and in the drier parts are supplemented by relatively short irrigation canals feeding on the snowmelt from the high Andes. This zone extends north through Ecuador into Colombia and western Venezuela, where a branch of the Andes swings east of the Lake Maracaibo basin at over 3000 metres. In Mexico regions of similar environmental conditions are found on the plateau lands and south of the arid Mesa del Norte; they also reach south in the highland finger through Guatemala and Central America, though the highlands are much reduced in height, and their role as climatic moderators is consequently restricted.

Access and isolation

Most of Latin America's coast has been readily accessible from Europe since colonial times; although distances were greater than those to North America, the sailing conditions were easier, except for those who risked the Cape Horn passage into the Pacific. But even this dangerous route did not deter corsairs seeking to plunder Spanish fleets and the Pacific ports. The Caribbean experiences occasional hurricanes that might destroy shipping, but this sea had the counterbalancing advantage of ready access by water to all land areas and generally good sailing breezes. The most notorious current, the Humboldt or Peruvian current, runs counter to southwards-moving vessels along the Pacific coast, but it could be circumvented by sailing out to sea.

Access to the interior of the continent has been a different matter. Sailors from Europe naturally sought a water access in the early years, and the principal rivers were explored by boat parties. But the River Paraná–Paraguay was found to be shallow, with variable levels and flows and shifting, treacherous sandbanks. Penetration up it to Paraguay and Asunción, the main colonial settlement of the whole basin, was always a slow business: sailors had to fight against current, with only light winds, or were buffeted by the occasional *pampero* wind from the south. Beyond the Paraguay confluence the Paraná has rapids and a gorge section up to the Guayra Falls, making any navigation impossible. The Amazon system appears on the map as an excellent entry to the heart of the continent, but it leads continuously through *selvas* which provide little of direct sustenance to man unless cleared, and it was therefore unattractive. In addition, it allowed no direct access to the Brazilian plateau because its south-bank tributaries, the rivers Tocantins, Xingu and Tapajós, all have rapids sections at the junction of plateau and floodplain, involving difficult portages for canoes and totally preventing the entry of larger wheels.

The São Francisco in north-east Brazil has similar problems in its rapids section, where the Paulo Afonso dam is now placed, not far from the coast. As for the Orinoco, its coastal area is a delta maze which, if negotiated, only allows entry to a deserted savanna plain, the southern part of the Llanos, alternatively flooded and parched in wet and dry seasons.

More important, no river gave direct access to any area of pre-European advanced cultures, either in the Andes or in Mesoamerica. The Magdalena River in Colombia perhaps came closest in reaching to within 100 kilometres of the Chibcha lands around Bogotá, but even it leaves a gap of difficult, steep-sloping mountain country. Indigenous cultures were never dependent on river navigation and sought locations without reference to water-transport possibilities. Thus it may be seen that the dominant power of ships and water transport was lost as soon as the Europeans arrived in America and attempted penetration to the interior.

The topographical isolation of all the west-coast areas by the

Andean chains is another aspect of the overall isolation which was the lot of Latin America. None of the mountain chains is unscalable, but the crossing of many of the Andean ranges over 4000 metres was sufficiently difficult to stimulate the growth of separate administrations and organizations in the west-coast lands (Chile, Peru, Ecuador) and to make a sharp break too between Spanish and Portuguese territories. Colombia is a country split up by separate arms of the Andes and deep intervening valleys. In Central America and Mexico the mountains are lower and form less of a barrier. The topographical barriers of Brazil are notably less of a problem, and the sharp plateau edges of the *Chapadas*, though they may be several hundred metres in height, do not compare with the Andes as isolating elements.

The American Indians

The absolute size of the American Indian (hereafter Indian) population in 1492 is a matter of considerable debate and falls between totals (for all the Americas) of 8.4 million and 75 million (Steward and Faron 1959). Nevertheless, there is fundamental agreement on the relative densities of population in different areas, based on an understanding of the known types of economy and society and the maximum 'carrying capacity' of the different regions, as well as on documentary evidence from the early colonial period and archaeological remains.

Over most of the area there was a very low population density, which contrasts with the many small pockets of high density within the highlands and a few other attractive localities. In Brazil, for example, density was 0.1–1.2 per square kilometre in the non-floodplain *selvas*, 1–2 in the savannas, up to 15 on the Amazon floodplains and 10 on the coast (Denevan 1976, ch. 7, pp. 205–34). Densities of below 10 per square kilometre applied to over 90 per cent of the region under study. In addition to the negative areas described in the previous section, the middle-latitude grasslands of the humid Pampas in Argentina, Uruguay and southernmost Brazil and similar grasslands in the tropical highlands constituted a negative environment for primitive occupation in the absence of powerful ploughing instruments. Steward and Faron (1959, p. 52) for example, placed the density at 0.12 per square mile (0.05 per square kilometre) in the Pampas and Patagonia.

In those environments described above as favourable, the southern Mexico plateau and basin country and the northern Bolivia–Peru–Ecuador–Colombian sierras, there were many small patches of relatively dense settlement. Steward and Faron estimated 10 per square mile (3.9 per square kilometre) in the central Andes as a whole and 6.6 per square mile (2.5 per square kilometre) in upland Colombia, but their totals are perhaps too low (3.5 million inhabitants for the central Andes and 1.5 million for the northern Andes), so that the densities may also be low. The arguments over population size and density in the central Andes are extensive (one writer supporting Steward and Faron's view and reviewing some other contributions is Shea, in Denevan 1976, pp. 151–80). In the Mesoamerican area Sanders (in Denevan 1976, p. 130) estimates for the relatively small basin around Mexico City a population of 1–1.2 million in 1519, a density of 150–70 per square kilometre, which would imply a total of 10–12 million for the Central Mexican area as a whole.

At the time of the Conquest in all of these densely peopled lands settled farmers were living in villages or dispersed settlements of village size, cultivating the land intensively, terracing hillsides to increase the area of flat land, extending irrigation canals where necessary, using an elaborate mixture of crops within individual fields and employing animals for draught work and the provision of meat and skins. Their village communities were also enclosed within larger organizations, chiefdoms or empire-like associations of states, of which the most important in Mesoamerica was the Aztec empire, which had been emerging over the last 200 years and was in active process of expansion at the time of the arrival of Cortés in 1519, and the Inca empire in South America, which had built up over 100 years prior to Pizarro's conquest in 1535 and was similarly active in expansion, reaching south into central Chile, north to Quito in Ecuador. Beyond the empires, chiefdoms or confederacies of chiefdoms formed an aureole of lower-level organization in the area of Colombia, Venezuela and Central America (Figure 5). Beyond these, in Chile and northern Mexico, settled farming communities existed but without an overlying regional organization.

In some cases advanced cultures occupied areas outside the upland oecumene. On the desert coast of Peru man had long used his ingenuity to channel water for irrigation from the forty or more short, snow-fed rivers of the Pacific slope of the Andes and to bring into intensive agriculture the small valleys, with a culture comparable with that of the nearby highlands. The earliest finds of ag-

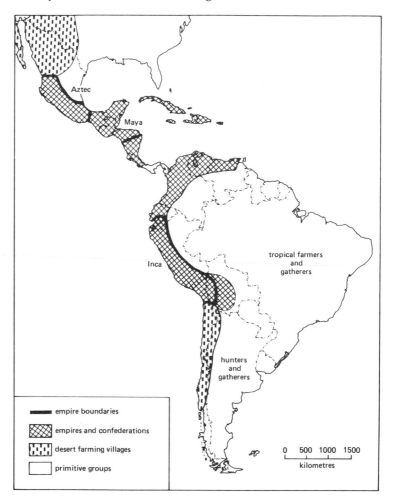

Figure 5　*Native cultures in Latin America at the time of the Conquest (based partially on Steward and Faron 1959). The level of human organization can only be sketched in for the tropical lowlands where drainage earthworks are known but few other indications of civilized life are available.*

riculture and pottery are from the Peruvian north coast, and agriculture seems to date back to 2500 BC in this area.

Another major exception to the geographical determinism which might otherwise seem to apply to pre-European settlement was the Mayan civilization. Although linked to the Mexican area and possibly derived from it, it had a separate life during the last millennium BC and the first AD and occupied the lowlands of Guatemala, British Honduras and, in the final era, the Yucatán peninsula. It is uncertain what density of population was involved, but it was apparently sufficient to support concentrated settlements of urban dwellers at a number of religious and administrative centres. Elsewhere advanced cultures utilized the tropical lowlands for at least several decades at a time. Lowland earthworks are known from the Llanos de Mojos in eastern Bolivia and from lowland Colombia and Venezuela, and they are associated with the agricultural exploitation of seasonally flooded lowlands (Denevan 1966).

Classifications of Indian culture types generally differ from Old World equivalents in not relying on technological differences between bronze, stone, iron and other similar 'ages' but separating different levels of social organization. Sanders and Marino (1970), for example, divide the cultures into empires, chiefdoms and confederacies, settled tribal groups, and nomadic or shifting cultivation groups. For the purposes of the later analysis in this work we may use instead Polanyi's (1977) social division of human groups according to their exchange organization. Taking exchange as the fundamental characteristic of all societies but the forms of exchange as variable, Polanyi separates three types of exchange; market, redistributive and reciprocal. Market organizations are either absent or subsidiary over practically all of the region. Only local trade at small markets was practised in Inca territory (Mason 1957, p. 168) and in Mexico Aztec marketing was similarly limited (Chapman 1957). Trade at open markets seems to have been practised in the Chibcha realm (Eidt 1959), in Nicaragua (Steward and Faron 1959, pp. 212–13, 234) and in the Atacaman region of north Chile (*ibid.*, p. 264). All these areas were peripheral to the large empires.

Within the empires redistributive exchange was more important than open-market trading. Chapman (1957) describes in detail the mechanisms of this trade in the Aztec area of influence. For the Inca area it is less well understood, but the villagers were certainly forced to farm the lands of priesthood and the Incas to produce goods for the royalty and for its armies, which were redistributive mechanisms operated by the autocratic leadership. The *mita*, forced labour used for road building, the postal services, mines and the building of palaces and other public buildings was another element of this system.

Below the empire organization a reciprocity base for the exchange of goods and services was common both in the empires and in the confederations and chiefdoms peripheral to them. It was also present in the dry lands of northern Mexico and northern and central Chile, which Steward and Faron (1959, p. 12) classify as 'desert farm villages'. Throughout these areas village communities shared the work of house building, irrigation, terrace making and harvesting, and these exchanges were directed by the community leaders. In the Andes the rural *ayllu* was both the human community group and its land area in pre-Inca times. This reciprocity system is more important to modern social development than the more impressive empire structures which overlay it, because it has survived in various degrees of decadence, over much of the Latin American area, as in other parts of the world which have not entirely adopted the market exchange system (Erasmus 1965).

The background to colonial occupation

Jointly, the physical environments of the Andean and Mesoamerican highlands, together with those of middle Chile and the Peruvian coast, regions of relatively fertile soil and moderate climate not too different from those of Mediterranean Europe, constituted an attractive resource on which to build empire. Natural advantages were enhanced by the presence in these areas of densely settled and well organized populations. This was an environment of many small, isolated valleys and intermontane basins, with only a few broader areas of easy communications and tillable land; it provided the roots of divisions between regions and, later, between independent republics and regions within them, as Spanish colonization focused on urban centres rather than rural frontiers.

By contrast, Brazilian territory contained initially only limited human or physical resources; nor did it provide automatic foci for human effort, physically separate and distinctive regions that would necessarily move towards independence or separate development paths. The hostility of the physical environment and the lack of tractability of the Indian groups, however, made for a generally coastal concentration of effort in the early period, followed by a loose expansion from the eastern seaboard over the huge expanse of the plateau and river basins of the interior.

Throughout Latin America there were large areas of very sparsely peopled land which resisted weak attempts at colonial settlement and have remained to some extent untouched by modern civilization to the present day, and this has had consequences today in political, social and economic terms. Economically, it reinforced the tendency towards isolation and the separate relations of each area with outside powers and without internal communications in the continent; socially, it promoted distinctions between areas of indigenous culture and those where European efforts have been made against a clean backcloth; politically, it encouraged division and lack of unity in line with economic isolation.

3 The colonial period

Latin America exemplifies, historically as well as at the present day, many of the developmental processes outlined in Chapter 1, and a review of the colonial period, which lasted roughly three centuries, will enable us to see the mechanisms of some of them in more detail. Rather than forward development, much of the movement was one of differentiation, either dependent or disjunctive, for most American territories. In any case, there are only fragmentary statistics against which to gauge any progress in material welfare that might be termed development, and they cannot form the basis for any general conclusions.

As might be expected from a reading of Chapter 2, in which the irregularities of physical and human resources and their structuring into social systems were discussed, there was in AD 1500 a powerful basis for further differentiation during the colonial period; and given the choice open to the Iberians of where their colonizing efforts would be made and which regions should be disregarded or abandoned after fruitless attempts at exploitation, disjunctive processes separating the Europeanized and unaffected areas may be expected. Within the Europeanized area dependent differentiation had a variety of effects which may be studied.

Geographic structures of production, trade and transport, of urban systems, are linked together in a total socio-economic structure that may be studied in its entirety or in terms of its various elements. An attempt is made in what follows to isolate some of these elements before bringing them together in a sketch of the whole. Both processes and resultant geographic patterns are of importance. Settlement processes and structures are a first concern; the organization of production is another; a third is the trading system. These may be brought together by studying the forms of integration of the economy, whether through markets, redistribution or reciprocity.

Settlements and disjunction

The settlement patterns and strategies of the Iberians in Latin America, and their different reactions to different native groups, constitute the first reason for major disjunctions in the colonial period between 'civilized' and 'uncivilized' peoples. Spaniards and Portuguese in the New World, from the time of Columbus's first landfall in the Outer Antilles in 1492 onwards, throughout the first fifty exploratory years, sought instant wealth in the form of gold, silver or jewels rather than any long-term gains through working land or trade. But as they found few regions with ready sources of precious metals, settlement was largely restricted to the areas of permanent agricultural occupation by the natives, who could be induced to work for and support them. This meant that Spanish occupation was limited to the highlands in general, and predominantly to the areas within the two great empires, Aztec and Inca. Portuguese settlers were very few because neither metals nor dense settlement by native groups were to be found in Brazil, and the early colonial period was characterized by coastal plantations, with little attempt at exploring the interior.

In addition, for the purposes of establishing initial control and maintaining it in the early years, the Spaniards needed to concentrate their efforts on usurping the uppermost native echelons of power, so as to be able to employ the same lines of control and methods as had the Incas and Aztecs. It is therefore important to note that the Spanish were very largely urban settlers; they often settled in existing towns and did not destroy the rural settlement pattern or the general structure of rural society.

Pre-Conquest patterns of settlement thus determined in part the post-Conquest patterns, and a disjunction arose because only those limited areas within the hinterland of the colonial towns were incorporated into the effectively occupied colonial territory. In no instance did the Spaniards seek to occupy new lands and to develop their own settlement forms, and the areas of nomadic, hunting or collecting primitives were left severely alone unless specific attractions (such as the mines in northern Mexico) were present. What had been a disjunction between Indian groups with different scales and types of organization became a much deeper division between racially distinct European and *mestizo* groups, with subject populations of settled Indians and the pure Indian groups, mostly primitive, beyond the reach of empire.

Population decline

The division between uplands and lowlands was further sharpened by the population history of the first decades. There is evidence that overall population declined by anything between 25 per cent and 95 per cent (Sanchez-Albornoz 1974), with modern tendencies amongst Latin American demographic historians favouring the higher limits. In the central Andes, for example, Smith (1970) suggests an overall reduction of 88 per cent by the 1560s; Cook and Borah estimated a decline in central Mexico of 89.5 per cent between 1519 and 1568 (Denevan 1976, p. 120). But most authors coincide in finding a much greater rate of decline in the tropical lowlands than in the highlands, Cook and Borah estimating the lowland rates to have been seven times higher than those of the uplands in Mexico, and Smith finding a still greater difference in Peru. In the Peruvian Costa part of the great decline may be attributed to the destruction or deterioration of the irrigation system that was the life support for native populations, but in general the very high rates for the lowlands seem to be due more to the greater virility of some of the introduced European diseases, such as smallpox and measles, or the inherently lower resistance of the tropical populations. That diseases were the main cause of the catastrophic decline of population, rather than war, hard work, or psychological and socio-economic disruption, is agreed in broad measure today, though recent writers have re-emphasized the disruptive effects of the Spanish and Portuguese (see Denevan 1976 for a number of interesting essays on this subject).

As a result of the dramatic lowlands decline, whatever small efforts there had been to develop these lands by the Iberians were largely defeated for want of labour. The lowlands acquired an early and deserved reputation as unhealthy, malarial regions and were left alone by all except those forced to work there in the ports and plantations. The Peruvian coastal region, in place of its pre-Conquest 7.5 million of 1520–5, had perhaps 129,000 in 1571 (Smith 1970), an obvious disincentive to Spanish settlement.

One way round the epidemic disease problem of the lowlands was the importation of slave labour. A central advantage in the use of West African slave labour was its relative immunity to European diseases, which were, after all, Old World diseases, to which all populations of Europe, Asia and Africa had some resistance. Thus in Brazil imports of negroes from West Africa, from the Congo and from Angola, were used along the whole coastal belt, but especially in the plantations of the Nordeste and in the hinterlands of Recife and Bahía. This too may be seen as a disjunctive process, for some few areas became plantation regions and endowed with a human (slave) resource, while others, unoccupied by either Portuguese or Negroes, were left to the small low-density Indian populations. It is true that a few areas of the tropical lowlands had been used intensively in pre-Conquest days, chiefly the seasonally inundated savannas of eastern Bolivia, Colombia and Venezuela (see Denevan 1970, for a summary), but these were abandoned either before or at the time of the Conquest.

Missions

Yet another way in which the territorial separation of groups and the process of disjunction in settlement came into being was through the action of the Church in its missions. In the first hundred years Dominicans and Franciscans were prominent among the religious orders active in America, and they did not practise a forceful policy of independent colonization. But from 1650 to 1750 the Jesuits actively fostered settlements apart from the Spanish-American and Luso-Brazilian communities where the general policy was to foster integration. They created settlements which were intended to preserve native society free from the corruptive influence of Western civilization but to add the Christian faith, under the firm control of Jesuit directors. As Caio Prado says of them (1967, p. 98): 'the Jesuits often acted in manifest opposition not only to the immediate and particular interests of the colonists (and there is no room for argument on this point) but also in opposition to those of the mother country and her colonial policy'.

Mission villages, the *reducciónes* or *reducoes* of Brazil, were set up in Amazonia, in the Upper Paraná plateau on both the Brazilian and the Paraguayan sides, on the Llanos of the Orinoco, the Mojos and Chiquitos areas of Bolivia's Oriente, in Uruguay, everywhere forming a buffer zone between Spanish and Portuguese areas of influence. In all of these areas the Jesuits' gift for practical organization and firm discipline made for a productive economy, with surpluses of cotton cloths, tobacco, dyewoods and sugar from the Bolivian and Paraguayan reductions, and pepper and other spices in the lower Amazon settlements of colonial Maranhão. The very success of these enterprises was in part their downfall; the Jesuits paid no taxes on production or trade, and their organization was often superior to that of the laymen's *haciendas* and plantations, and they were thrown out in the 1760s. But they were also expelled because their policy of isolation ran counter to Iberian designs for an integrative dependency of Latin America on Europe. This isolation was effective, however, for after the Jesuits were expelled from America their territories fell into abandonment and were not linked to the settled areas of civilian rule for the remainder of the colonial period – indeed, until very recently, in the case of some tropical lowland areas where colonization is now proceeding.

General distribution of population

As a result of the factors outlined above, the population map of European settlement in the period 1580–1630 resembles that given in the two maps, Figures 6 and 7. These maps are based on the number of *vecinos* (roughly speaking, the European heads of households or burghers of the colonial towns) and are thus only a crude approximation to the total population or even the European population of the towns. But in the absence of census data and at the macroregional scale used here, they give a good idea of the settlement pattern and stress its confinement to the densely populated Andean highlands as well as a few major ports. Brazil is notably weak in urban structure. Only three cities and fourteen *vilas* (towns) were founded there in the sixteenth century (Hardoy 1975, p. 38).

Dependent structures

Within the colonized area the system described by some historians as dependency, a redistributive system based on Europe, was imposed, and an urban pattern of settlement dominated by a few centres emerged. Some administrative centres were built up from old Indian towns such as Cuzco or Quito. New large towns of rapid growth were the mining towns of Mexico's Mesa del Norte, Durango, Zacatecas, San Luis Potosí or, on the Bolivian *altiplano*, Potosí and Oruro. Potosí achieved spectacular growth, the number of its *vecinos* increasing from 400 to 4000 between 1580 and 1630. Silver mining in the vicinity of these towns created a fairly long-term economic base for growth because it was largely rock mining for ore veins, not the rapid elimination of small pockets of alluvial material

Figure 6   *European settlement pattern around 1580 (based on Hardoy and Aranovich 1969 and Reis Filho 1968).*

Figure 7   *European settlement pattern around 1630 (based on Hardoy and Aranovich 1969 and Reis Filho 1968).*

along stream beds, as in the case of the placer deposits of gold that were scattered throughout America. It is known that the mining towns grew very quickly (Hardoy and Aranovich 1969), although the demographic data are imprecise, to become some of the largest in the empire of Spain. In Brazil the eighteenth-century boom town of Ouro Prêto is a parallel. But all these mining towns were based on a single resource. A more general feature of urbanization was its link with central administration and with trade (which we will treat later in this chapter). Rapid growth was achieved by the leading centres of administration, notably Lima and Mexico City, because of the substantial and increasing centralization of administration over the colonial period of the sixteenth and seventeenth centuries, both in Spanish America (Hardoy and Aranovich 1969) and in Brazil (Reis Filho 1968).

Other rapidly growing towns were the leading ports. Havana, Cartagena, Portobelo and Panama, El Callao and Lima, Veracruz and Acapulco in Mexico all grew rapidly through the trade of the fleets which, after 1561, they dominated. Havana, which grew most rapidly of all, saw a twentyfold increase in the number of its *vecinos*, (officially registered Spanish settlers with land and rights within the city) from 60 to 1200, between 1580 and 1630.

From the data given by Hardoy and Aranovich we may construct rank-size diagrams of the Spanish colonial cities (Figure 8). These data are admitted by the authors to be fragmentary and are not in every case a reliable indication of population size for settlements, but they have the merit of being the best data available and have been estimated on a constant basis at something close to single points in time. In both cases, for the years 1580 and 1630, the sizes are based on the number of *vecinos*. What they suggest is not a standard rank-size progression, but one in which the largest cities are excessively large and there is a lack of smaller centres; in short, a primate city structure. This might be supposed to be a transitory feature, one to be eliminated when the regional hierarchy becomes established and smaller centres become established further away from the main centre of colonization. In fact, the progression between the two dates given is not towards the rank-size structure, but away from it, as we may see in the data for the *audiencia* of Mexico, Bogotá or Charcas. Vapñarsky's (1969) interpretation of this kind of hierarchy is in terms of degree of openness of the regional economy to the exterior; a large metropolitan centre means a region which is relatively open to the exterior, and its size is due to

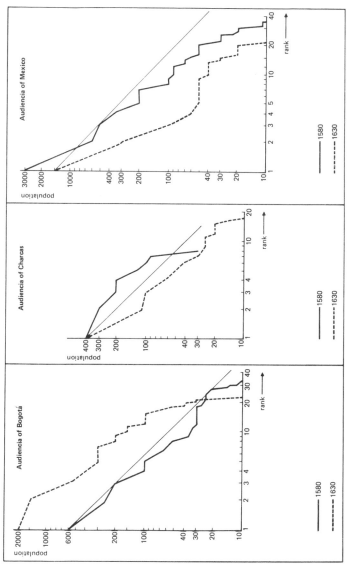

Figure 8   *Rank–size diagrams of the urban structure in three Spanish audiencias (based on Hardoy and Aranovich 1969). The straight line indicates a standard rank–size relation on the log.-log. graph to aid comparison with the actual data portrayed; data for 1630 are reduced by a factor of 10 to make the graph more compact, which is why the population appears larger in 1580.*

trade and other relations with the exterior, which are all channelled through the single centre. It is treading on unsafe ground to infer regional economic structure from city population data, even were they less uncertain than has been indicated for the Spanish colonial ones. What we may suggest, however, is that if such a structure of town sizes does exist, it is by Spanish will. What the number of *vecinos* does measure directly is the administrative importance accorded to each settlement by the mother country, for many of the settlers held some kind of administrative responsibility within the local municipality.

Below the towns rural settlement remained dispersed or in small towns. In general, the *encomienda* system tended to preserve existing Indian towns, as the whole town would be assigned as *encomienda* labour, which it was advantageous to retain in one place (Gibson 1969, p. 227). In many areas the heavy losses among the Indian population after the Conquest meant their villages had become very small hamlets, dispersed over a very wide area. For this reason, and in order to assemble the native populace in places where control and administration might be more easily exerted, Indians were brought in *reducciones,* as in the case of the religious orders, but without the same connotation of isolation. They were introduced formally from the 1570s in Peru under Viceroy Toledo, around 1600 in Mexico under Viceroy Monterrey. Similar grouping movements had been going on unofficially for a long time – even the Laws of Burgos of 1512 recommended a concentration of Indians at the settlement chosen by the Spaniards in Hispaniola, on the idealist grounds that this was necessary to allow proper religious instruction. In all the areas of low-intensity agriculture and in those where no agriculture was practised but only primitive gathering, settlement was very dispersed, with no real concentrations. It should be noted in passing that dispersed settlement is recorded even in some parts of the densely settled areas of upland Mexico in the sixteenth century (Moreno Toscano 1968).

Settlement frontiers

Neatly defined spatial frontiers of settlement that may be drawn on the map are not easy to find in Latin America (Hennessy 1978) but it would seem that some frontier concept is intimately involved in what we have termed disjunctive differentiation. The very term 'frontier' implies a division between settled and unsettled, native and foreign. For this reason it is important to show how little the frontier took on the various positive roles ascribed to it (Miller and Steffen 1976) and to indicate its real role.

First, only in a few areas was there a linear Indian/European frontier of the kind found in North America – principally in south-central Chile and on the Pampas of Argentina (see Figure 9). And in these few areas the frontier was only very sparsely inhabited, and it was not mobile but fixed in one line for the greater part of the colonial period, so that the mechanism of challenge from new environments or societies was not present. The frontier did not teach society because so few people lived on it, and because what they had to impart was nothing new. The Pampas frontier, for example, established in the sixteenth century, only began to move out after 1775, and it was then still virtually a deserted region.

In some areas the geographical zone outside the regions of lay settlement was occupied by the mission – in Bolivia's Oriente, in the Paraná Plateau and on the Amazon (see Figure 9). But mission villages led to no broad process of interchange between cultures and economies; indeed, they were entirely cut off from contact with lay European society in remote interior regions. A lay/religious frontier might have been formed but for the fact that the missionaries' aim was to maintain the isolation of their *protégés* from the corrupting influence of the outside world. Hudson (1976) differentiates two broad types of frontier, those where there is a challenge by nature and those where the challenge is essentially human, whether military, economic or cultural. Neither of these types of challenge was very effective in Latin America. As urban residents with an artificial, man-made environment, and living in any case in the more temperate zones of the region, they experienced little need to cultivate new crops, for example, or to care for new breeds of domestic animals. Instead Indian farm workers worked for them and made modest adjustments to their own agriculture in order to incorporate crops such as wheat, grapes, olives and citrus fruits from the European diet and supply them to new lords. Elsewhere basically European cattle farming systems were established, and the Indians were employed simply as labour in the new *haciendas*.

Similarly, the military threat from the Indians was slight – in the case of Brazil, negligible. European military technology, the horse, firearms, weapons of steel were sufficient to ensure rapid victory in any confrontation, and there was no need to modify methods in any fundamental way. Once the Indians had been conquered, no wholly

Figure 9 *Mission settlements and frontiers. Linear frontiers were compara-tively rare; buffer zones created by missions partially replaced them in some areas.*

new institutions were required to oblige them to work for the Iberian settlers. The *encomienda* and *repartimiento* had been known in medieval Spain before 1492 and could be employed directly to control land and subject peoples, in America as in Andalucia (Diffie 1947, p. 59). Church institutions, urbanistics, administrative structures were brought from Europe with only minor modifications. In Brazil the great land grants or *donatarias* had been employed earlier, in West Africa and in Madeira, as a means of indirect rule.

The Spanish, in occupying the old areas of highest culture, met no effective challenge from the more testing environments of tropical rainforest in the Amazon basin, of the great deserts of northern Mexico or the Chaco, or of the difficult semi-deserts of Brazil's interior Nordeste. Both Spaniards and Portuguese avoided the need to work in tropical climates by employing native or imported slave labour. Their direct experience of tropical conditions was limited to the few who were not urban dwellers but explorers, merchants and farm owners without an urban residence and without a ready labour force.

From these comments on the failure of any frontier to function in a positive way, as has been supposed by most historians of the frontier, we might conclude that there was effectively no frontier. But the frontiers that did exist, between India and white, negro and white, mission and lay territory, settled and unsettled land, did have the negative function of checking or preventing any change in the societies on either side of them; in other words, they helped disjunctive differentiation because of the lack of diffusion between the various human groups. Primitive Indians beyond the frontiers of settlement remained primitive; missions worked towards static ideals over most of the colonial period; class and caste divisions, if we include them as a kind of frontier, worked strongly to separate groups in the areas of European settlement.

The organization of production

A remarkable bias in the treatment of the productive economy of Latin America is evident from the standard texts on the subject. None of these works (Bailey and Nasatir 1960, pp. 166–82; Chaunu 1964; Crow 1946; Diffie 1947, pp. 88–103; Dozer 1962, pp. 151–5; Fagg 1969, pp. 185–201; Haring 1947, pp. 252–73; Herring 1968, pp. 190–203; Worcester and Schaeffer 1956) contains a useful commentary on the subsistence economy of the region, confining themselves to the better-known and more readily studied production of European crops on *haciendas* and plantations. They cover the rapid diffusion of the European crops and animals and the production of these either for local urban markets or for export. Thus silk, tobacco, rice, cotton, cacao, cochineal and indigo are all discussed in some detail as tropical products; wool, leather, hides and tallow, wheat, cattle, horses, wine and olives as temperate latitude items of trade. The texts do not cover maize production, beans, manioc, squash, potatoes, guinea pigs, llama and alpaca in anything more than a perfunctory fashion.

In a typical work on the colonial economy of Chile, Carmagnani (1973) treats agriculture as if it were entirely oriented to the exterior and to trade. According to him (p. 273), the work of the 80 per cent of the work-force engaged in agriculture and mining was exterior-linked, as was that of the 10–15 per cent in services. Only the work of the 5 per cent engaged in crafts is regarded as having been directed towards local consumption. This is obviously incorrect, for most farm production and much service activity must always have been for local markets. The error derives partly from the way in which data for the discussion of trade were gathered (from the records of taxes placed on sales of most goods). Commodities which were not sold for money were omitted, and this probably included a large part of the village economy in which reciprocity relations among groups would ensure a continuous non-market exchange. Subsistence agriculture was important to all districts; even in La Serena, a northern copper-mining district (Carmagnani 1973, p. 173) 64.1 per cent of the active population was engaged in agriculture in 1813 and only 13.1 per cent in mining. No doubt agriculture was in part an adjunct to mining, but at least some of it must have been of an independent subsistence character.

Alongside the commercial market production of agricultural and other raw materials, there remained throughout the colonial period a native sector of subsistence agriculture, just as important to the total economy as the market sector. It is not easily identified or studied because the Spanish and Portuguese settlers came into contact with it only indirectly through their demands on Indian labour, and probably thought it of little importance. Their chroniclers have in consequence little to say about it. Native economies are also ignored because they concerned plants which were unfamiliar to the Europeans and totally excluded the animals which were so important to the Iberians. Farmlands owned by the Indians, under

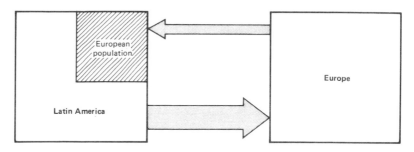

Figure 10   *Market and subsistence socio-economic dualism (based on Morris 1978c).*

the combined pressures of depopulation and the growth of *haciendas* for cattle, were reduced to small and inconspicuous patches, though intensively cultivated and highly productive (Chevalier 1963, pp. 185–226). Indian territorial rights could always be overrun because they were communal rather than individual and were not therefore regarded as legal rights to land. There was thus a disjunction between the native subsistence economy based on traditional products and the 'modern' market production of the *hacienda* or plantation; these two agricultural systems lived in symbiosis – though the market economy was dependent for labour on the subsistence economy – but as social systems, and to some extent as economic systems, they remained apart (see Figure 10). (It is this coexistence of a non-market subsistence economy and a market-oriented export economy that has made Latin America, in historical times, difficult to classify for the neo-Marxists, who would seek to reduce it to 'feudal' or 'capitalist' denominations. See, for example, Cordova 1973, especially pp. 81–93; Bazant 1950; Bagu 1950, p. 13.)

Let us explore briefly the mechanisms of this 'dualism' of colonial agriculture, to use the terms of modern development economists. In the early years the principal institution was the *encomienda*, the 'entrustment' of Indian souls to Spanish lords for their moral care and provision, which also allowed for the use of Indian labour to maintain the new lords. It is almost unnecessary to add that the last function became the major one, and that the *encomenderos* used their dependent Indians as a work-force not only to provide for them but also to produce export goods to be sent to Europe. In this system Indian labour was provided free on the *encomendero*'s land, up to a stipulated number of man days per year. It was a 'dualistic' system, inasmuch as Indians worked on their own land to provide for themselves, the *encomienda* being an extra burden with no real relation to subsistence farming, based on separate products and marketing systems.

The *encomienda* provided a useful alternative to the other basic production methods: slavery, which would have required heavy capital investment in slaves and possibly also in machinery and lands; and modern capitalism with open markets, which could not have succeeded in the social context of Latin America, where no market system was known or sought after by Indian groups.

Not all land was held in *encomienda*. Some lands were held in the form of *repartimientos*, originally large land grants to conquistadors or their families: and some *repartimientos* accompanied *encomiendas*, which did not directly endow their possessor with land at all, though they were often treated as land grants. But *repartimientos* and *mercedes*, also grants of land but for only one lifetime, could not be utilized without human labour, and the *encomienda* was the institution that provided that.

After a few decades the spectacular declines in population made the *encomienda* less useful because the Indians could not be held to one village and might leave the land-owner with no work-force. Their place was assumed by the classical Latin American *hacienda*, fulfilling the same basic function of relating a subsistence community to a capitalist economy. In Mexico, for example, the seventeenth-century *hacienda* was worked by labour that was held effectively to one village by debt-serfdom; both wages and bought goods being controlled by the same *hacienda* owner, company-store prices could always be adjusted to fall short of what might be a level sufficient to pay off debts (Chevalier 1963).

In northern Mexico some colonial *haciendas*, as Chevalier shows, were probably quite self-sufficient, necessarily providing their own food, water, machinery and clothing for want of links to the centre. Elsewhere *hacienda* and village were more interdependent; the village was autarchic but also supplied labour to the *hacienda*, as with traditional *encomiendas*. This is a general picture of the economy of each economic unit, each *hacienda*. From the outside, studying trade and markets, it might appear that the *hacienda* was, at least in average or good years, simply a producer of goods for export (in poor years it might revert to subsistence). But internally dualism was present; there were two economic and social structures. Instead of dependence, we may emphasize disjunction.

Significantly, it is necessary to look hard for a description of Spanish colonial subsistence agriculture, and it is an anthropologist (Service 1951) rather than an historian who provides one. In eastern Paraguay the peculiar conditions of strong racial mixture between European and Indian meant, of course, that native (*mestizo*) agriculture was the dominant type, not one half of a dual system. Sedentary Tupi-Guarani Indians, with a pre-contact farming and fishing economy, maintained this with little change into the colonial period. Although lands were allocated to *encomenderos*, in the sixteenth century the *encomiendas* were rapidly divided up – we exclude here the Chaco territories which have a separate history – and became standard small farms in what was a backwater of the American empire. Service elaborates on the use of traditional digging-stick techniques of cultivation, permanent or shifting plots, the planting of traditional crops of maize, *yuca* (manioc), beans of various types, squashes and gourds, the use of irrigation techniques and of natural fertilizers, and barter exchange.

For Brazil subsistence agriculture is also generally overlooked, perhaps with better reason. On the one hand, large-scale agriculture on the plantations and estates (*fazendas*) was very generally self-sufficient, for slaves and free workers were encouraged to cultivate their own plots of land on the plantations or to grow the subsistence crop (maize and manioc, for example) in the fields with cotton and sugar cane. On the other hand, there was no separate village community or economy which would be drawn on by the planters, as was the case in Spanish America. Indian communities in Brazil were at too low a level of organization and resisted any such assimilation as took place in the area of the old Andean empires. Prado (1967) distinguishes large-scale and subsistence agriculture, but for him (p. 180) the latter is concerned with production of crops for the *colony* (not solely for the local community) and so is of a different nature. We may summarize the position by saying that whereas in Spanish America a dualism between two social organizations and economies was maintained, in Brazil the two economies, subsistence and export, were combined in a single socio-economic unit, that of the great *fazenda* or plantation (*engenho*).

The point is that this simple, basic economy is forgotten or overlooked by the great majority of historians and is treated by Service only because of his anthropological interests. In countries like Bolivia, Peru or Ecuador, where an intensive and productive native agriculture has continued to the present day, it has been ignored except in so far as it has links with commercial production and the outside world – that is, through the *hacienda*. Native intensive agriculture may also have been overlooked because it occupied relatively small areas. Iberian conquerors occupied huge territories and utilized them for livestock production at very low levels of intensity in the Pampas, in interior Brazil, in the Llanos of Venezuela or Colombia, as well as on the Mesa del Norte of Mexico. These areas are impressive in size but they should not blind us to the importance of the small-scale, intensive polyculture of the Indians (Chevalier 1963, pp. 185–226).

Trade

In Latin America long-distance trading had been carried on in pre-Columbian times throughout the empire areas of Maya, Aztec and perhaps also Inca (Chapman 1957), but it was trade of a particular kind, restricted to elite groups in command and taking place in the absence of markets. Apart from this, trade seems to have been very limited in extent throughout the continent, acting through systems of reciprocity and redistribution.

Spanish and Portuguese trade was also naturally a long-distance trade; as opposed to the Christaller–Lösch hypothesis of trade emerging from local demands and building small hinterlands into larger ones, trade was imposed from outside the region, was long-distance before local and specific to some groups in society.

Spanish colonial trade

The outlines of colonial trade are well-known from historical documents. After an early period of exploration up to 1526, ships were required by the Spanish to move in convoy (1526–61) because of the dangers in the Caribbean from buccaneers and the need to avoid the possibility of the Spanish captains indulging in contraband trade.

From 1561 still further control was exercised over Spanish colonial trade by concentrating it at a few major ports, Havana, Cartagena, Lima, Panama. The routes and ports used are indicated in Figure 11. Even at its Spanish base the trade was closely controlled, moving solely through Seville's port of Sanlucar until 1717, when Cadiz replaced it. From Spain the registered merchants could send ships in the organized fleet across the Atlantic, stopping first in the

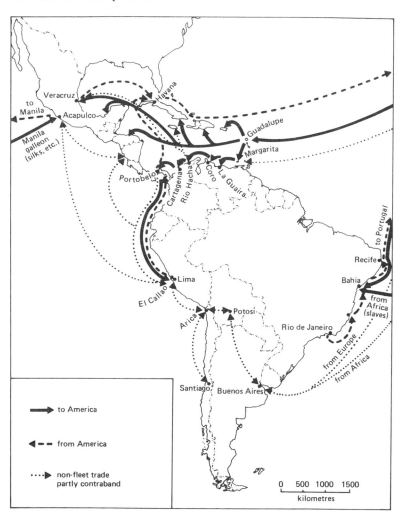

Figure 11   *Colonial trade lines. The ocean lines are indicative of the major flows during the period of the fleet system. Contraband, shown down the Pacific coast and in the River Plate area, was very important in the eighteenth century.*

Outer Antilles for rest and replenishment, at Dominica, Deseada or Guadalupe, and then dispersing. One section went to Tierra Firme, the 'mainland' of northern South America (or the Spanish Main, as the English pirates knew it); it visited the island of Margarita, La Guaira, Coro and Riohacha. Another went to Cartagena and Portobelo, on the Atlantic side of the Panama neck of land. The remainder moved towards Veracruz, port to New Spain, detaching individual ships or small squadrons *en route* for Santo Domingo (Dominican Republic), Puerto Rico and Cuba. A separate structure of long-distance trade on the west coast moved the fleet between El Callao, port of Peru, and Panama, to bring the produce of the Viceroyalty of Peru, and between Manila and Acapulco on the west coast of New Spain (Mexico), controlling the Chinese trade which moved through the Philippines to America.

This standard picture is oversimplified, and there was necessarily regional trade too. In the Caribbean (Ramos 1970), after the first Conquest period when the islands of Hispaniola and Cuba acted as supply sources for expeditions, the area of Venezuela (Tierra Firme) became a sixteenth-century supply source for wheat, cotton, cattle, hides, tallow which were transported to the islands which had growing port and fleet supply functions and could thus absorb these raw materials. The New Spain plateau areas of Puebla and Atlixco also contributed to the supply of the islands. In the seventeenth century there was specialization in cocoa production in Venezuela's lowlands, but it remained a largely regional trade, five-sixths going to Mexico and only one-sixth to Spain (Ramos 1970, pp. 176–80). Tobacco became another regional export. In this way the mainland territories, with abundant land and more labour than the islands, whose native population had been literally decimated, became suppliers of raw materials to the urban populations and the traders of the islands (see Figure 12).

On the Pacific coast inter-regional trade structures were also necessary to establish, for example, the Guayaquil (Ecuador) centre of shipbuilding. Its timber was local, but tar for caulking came from the Santa Elena peninsula west of the Guayas estuary, while cordage, nails and sails came from Panama and were paid for with silver earned from timber exports to Peru, and cocoa exports to Mexico after 1580. Settlements in the west coast tropical areas were supplied with wheat, wine, olives, and textiles from Peru, from the coastal valleys both north and south, and in the case of cloths, from the factories at Cuzco and Cajamarca in the Sierra.

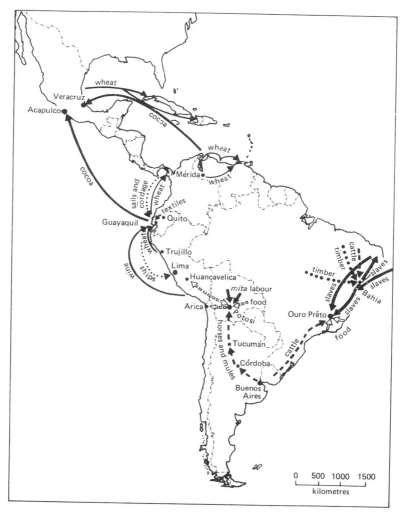

Figure 12   *Regional trade structure, 1600–1700. This map shows only the most important of the inter-regional trading linkages.*

Chinese articles, mostly fine cloths and porcelain, also moved out from Acapulco along the west coast, despite various degrees of prohibition by Spain on trade from Manila to Lima. The conjuncture of abundant Chinese goods and abundant Peruvian silver to pay for them provided too much of an attraction and much illicit trading by vessels engaged in trade on the west coast went on (Borah, 1954).

Potosí

These inter-regional links were largely coastal or maritime (see Figure 12). There is evidence that a few major centres also developed an interior hinterland as a consequence of their need for raw materials. The most spectacular example is the mine of Potosí in Alto Peru (Bolivia). Potosí's supply hinterland reached south into the Pampas, east into the Chaco, north over the uplands of Peru. From the humid Pampas came horses and mules for work in the mine, as the Potosí region, arid and cold at over 4500 metres could produce neither from its bunch-grass vegetation. The animals were driven north to Córdoba, then to the market towns of Tucumán and Salta for sale and fattening prior to their march up the pass of Humahuaca to the high *altiplano* at 4000 metres.

A major labour-supply network had also to be set up because of the high rates of disease and disablement in the mine, where respiratory diseases were common as a result of mine dust and the great difference in temperature between the mine and the outside air. Mine accidents and overwork seem to have killed many (Hanke 1956). Replacement labour came in the form of the *mita*, a pre-Conquest device used by the Incas for supplying public labour for building and maintaining bridges, roads and agricultural terraces and also for mining (Mason 1957, p. 179). A period of labour service in the mine might be required of any able-bodied young man in the area of the empire, though it was only rational to supply such labour from distances of under 800 kilometres (that is, generally from the densely populated Sierra).

Some of Potosí's food supplies came from the north, from nearby lowland valleys (Cobb 1949) and from the Oriente, the eastern lowlands where mission villages produced tropical fruits, cotton, tobacco, cassava and spices for sale. From this region also came pit-props and wood for fuel. One long-distance link of 1500 kilometres was to Huancavelica, the mercury mine in northern

Peru; mercury was needed to extract the silver from its ore. Finally, the finished products had their market links out to the west; not principally to Lima, but to the west coast more directly, first at Arequipa and after 1572 at Arica (Cobb 1949, p. 35), from which they could be taken more cheaply by sea. Mercury from Huancavelica and local dried fish and dried fruit also moved in from Arica to Potosí.

Other mine economies with long-distance linkages were in northern New Spain (Mexico), the second important silver-producing region of America. Its agricultural support area was the Bajío, on the northern fringe of central Mexico, where rainfall was sufficient to produce good grain crops. Mines at Zacatecas, Durango and San Luis were supplied from here.

Regional structures such as these were exceptional rather than the rule in Spanish America. Instead of an integrated modern market structure, the trade links were more as described by Vance (1970), with long-distance penetration lines from coast to interior, collection centres and few other settlements of note. This spatial model, taken beyond the economic dimension in which Vance discusses it, is that of a redistributive economy, drawing supplies from its periphery and not developing linkages among them on any important scale. The interregional links described so enthusiastically by Ramos (1970) as confounding the classic image of narrowly restricted colonial trade were, for the most part, only coastal links between a few of the more important centres, not a complete trading system.

The nature of trade

In its spatial as in its organizational structure the trade system approaches that of a redistributive rather than a market society (the reader is referred to Chapter 1, pp. 38–45, for a discussion of Polanyi's division into reciprocity, redistribution and market systems). Large amounts of various raw materials taken out of the colonial territories are to be seen effectively as tribute in a redistributive system, collected either directly, as in the case of the royal fifth levied on precious metal production both in Brazil and in Spanish America, or indirectly through the use of servile labour to produce raw materials for export to Europe at lower than market prices. Redistribution *from* the centre was more limited in this exploitative scheme, but examples are the *situados*, grants to help maintain various outposts of empire (see p. 85), and the limited efforts made by Spain and Portugal to promote urban construction, road building or education. The use of money in transactions between European merchants and their New World customers should not close our eyes to the redistributive essence of the relation, for although prices were fixed – at the great fairs of Portobelo or Cartagena, for example, when the fleets brought their European goods and took away gold, silver, cotton or cocoa, as the merchants were monopsonists of colonial produce and (apart from contraband) monopoly suppliers – they were established by a few agents in a non-market context.

Under such a trade structure there were elements of dependent and disjunctive differentiation. Dependency on Spain of each colonial area meant the tying in of each territory to the metropolitan economy and some specialization in the production of specific export items for the metropolis, each colony becoming known for its distinctive specialities. But as each colony was linked separately with Europe, and as large areas were not incorporated into the trade structure at all, there was a disjunction between each colony and between colonized and non-colonized lands. This fact is overlooked by those who have attempted to examine the spatial implications of dependency theory. Rofman (1975) for example, characterizes colonial regional structure as entirely dominated by mother-country links with colonial capital and main port. He fails to consider the effect of the lack of contact among the colonies or the regional structures resulting from their positive existence.

Brazil and Portugal

A similar concentration of trade was not possible in Brazil for both technical and societal reasons. Lacking the easily transportable, high value-to-weight-ratio products, gold and silver, at least until the eighteenth century, and producing instead sugar cane, cotton and brazilwood (bulky products which it would be expensive to transport far overland), the ports had to scatter along the whole occupied area of the coast of Brazil. There was also a less dense concentration of trade because Portugal adopted the convoy system between 1649 and 1765, a fleet moving between Lisbon and Bahia under an escort of three or four warships. A separate fleet, the Carreira das Indias, linked Portugal with the Far East and was officially prevented from trading with Brazil, because this would destroy Portugal's monopolist position, and the higher prices offered in Brazil would have diverted much of the traffic destined for Europe. Many ships from the Far East fleet did arrive at Bahia, but it seems largely as carriers of contraband (Lapa 1968).

As in Spanish America, one or two exceptional cases of regional integration are to be found in colonial Brazil. Parallel to the silver mines of New Spain and Alto Peru, the diamond mines of Diamantina and the gold mines of Ouro Prêto and elsewhere in the interior brought goods from a broad hinterland during the eighteenth century – foods from the coast of São Paulo and Rio, slave labour supplies from the Nordeste and cattle from the Pampas fringe territory of Uruguay. A port which developed a regional supply economy around it was Bahia (Salvador), colonial capital of Brazil until 1760. In its heyday it was known as 'the port of Brazil', as though there were no other, and it certainly supplied all the central part of the Brazilian coast with imported goods, primarily slaves from Africa. These were of great significance to the import trade and represented over a quarter of import value in the later colonial period (Prado 1967, p. 270). Bahia also collected goods for export from a wide area – tobacco, wood, spices, sugar and tropical fibres. It had a still wider hinterland as a shipbuilding centre (Lapa 1968), with access to timber resources in the hardwood forest of northern Brazil and other supplies from Amazonas in the north, Maranhão and Pernambuco in the north-east and northern Ilhéus to the south. This timber was used both for local building and for export to the shipyards of Lisbon, Portugal insisting on timber being used as ballast in ships returning to Lisbon in the seventeenth century. Its shipbuilding function was assured by Portuguese decrees which made it the official dockyard for their navy. In addition to shipbuilding and repairing, Lapa has shown that as an urban centre Bahia drew on the whole fertile lowland of the Reconcavo for food supplies and on the whole *sertao*, the interior backlands of the Nordeste, for cattle.

Plantation economies also gather resources from supply areas around them, though only to a moderate degree, as even with their concentration on monoculture (of cane or cocoa or cotton), some subsistence production by the slaves was frequently allowed. Cattle were perhaps the product brought from the greatest distances, and salt meat might come in from as far away as the River Plate (Giberti 1961).

Complex regional structures of trade were not the norm in Brazil, however, any more than in Spanish America. Instead the radial lines around a few major ports which had access to Portugal through Bahia and Recife, and a trade organized outside the context of a free market, were the most important features.

Eighteenth-century changes in trade and administration

In Spanish America some changes in trading controls were made under the Bourbon rulers, who came into possession of Spain from the beginning of the eighteenth century. These changes were due partially to a more enlightened view of colonial administration; they were also a response to the contraband problem which arose because the prices of goods carried by the Iberian fleets were constantly undercut by contraband traders, who paid none of the multiplicity of taxes imposed on all commercial transactions by both Spain and Portugal.

England was the main agent of contraband, with substantial and growing sea power to back her actions. Having imposed on Spain her control of the slave trade to America in 1713, England used slaving ships to bring not only slaves but also all kinds of contraband to America. Villalobos (1968) shows that the fleet supplies to the Pacific and to the Caribbean declined because the colonies were replete with European goods that they were unable to sell. The last Pacific fleet sailed in 1726, and the last to Venezuela in 1737; New Spain, less plagued by contraband, continued to be a partner in the fleet system until 1776.

The decline of the fleet or convoy system and the subdivision of the great viceroyalties inevitably meant some loosening of trade ties, reducing the hegemony in foreign trade of such places as Lima, Panama and Portobelo, Veracruz and Havana. Second-level ports came into greater prominence, feeding their own hinterlands with shorter supply lines. Buenos Aires benefited from the legalization of its extensive contraband trade, a gradual process sanctioned by various decrees over the period 1750–1800 and allied to the creation of its separate viceroyalty of the River Plate in 1776. Valparaiso grew similarly and acquired great importance in the trade of Chile, Guayaquil in Ecuador and La Guaira in the Captaincy-General of Venezuela, created in 1777. In Colombia Cartagena was important as the main outlet to the viceroyalty of New Granada (Colombia, Ecuador and Venezuela), created in 1717.

Rather than produce a market economy with extensive interconnections between all the colonies, however, the eighteenth-century commercial and administrative reforms encouraged the continuation of the existing dependency structure, except that the geographic scale was reduced and the lines of movement were consequently shortened. Ramos (1970) has demonstrated that the sending of individual authorized ships (the *navíos de registro*) to many different ports tended to break up those regional interconnections that did exist between major regions, so that each small colony now looked only to Spain. Further focusing occurred because of the institution of the monopoly trading companies. These, created to fight contraband trade as well as to promote export trade, concentrated their action on a few ports and their hinterlands. In the southern Caribbean, where Curaçao and Jamaica were major contraband centres, the Compañía Guipuzcoana, or Caracas Company, was set up in 1728 and successfully developed the Venezuelan cocoa industry and trade during the eighteenth century. It also promoted the export of cotton, tobacco and timber and brought in European goods for sale. Other companies in Spanish America organized on a similar basis were the Honduras Company, founded in 1714; the Havana Company from 1740; and the Barcelona Company, working with Santo Domingo and Puerto Rico, from 1755. In Brazil the eighteenth-century reforms of the Marquis of Pombal included the establishment of similar companies which operated between 1750 and 1778; the Maranhão – Grão Para and the Pernambuco – Paraiba companies. Each of these organizations tended to create islands of commercial activity with single links to the exterior, though the tendency was always moderated by the ever-present contraband trade.

Inland, some large regional structures were also disrupted by the new administrative and trading arrangements, notably Potosi (Ramos 1970, pp. 287–9). In the late eighteenth century, of Potosi's import trade under 1 per cent was from Lima, 1.6 per cent from Chile, 10 per cent from Cuzco, 21 per cent from the local hinterland, Alto Peru, 40 per cent from the nearby coast and 21 per cent from the River Plate. Lima's hinterland had effectively been reduced, and Potosi, now administratively under Buenos Aires, had been reoriented to the south-east. Chile, too, formerly subject to Lima, now traded largely over the Andes to Buenos Aires.

A major administrative structure of subsidies to special regions, that of the *situados*, always existed under the Spanish colonial regime and might be supposed to have counteracted the disjunctive tendencies of the eighteenth century. *Situados* were sums of money sent from some colonial territories to others either to cover more or less permanent gaps between governmental earnings (mostly from taxes) and expenses (mostly official salaries and wages) or for temporary purposes, such as military expenses or the purchase of state-monopoly goods (tobacco and salt, for example) from their producers. In the eighteenth century the *situados* were all sent from a few *Cajas de Réal Hacienda*, royal Exchequer Offices, situated primarily in New Spain for the Caribbean area and in Lima for most of South America. Considerable volumes of money were transferred in this way: in 1771 2.3 million pesos were transferred from Lima to the River Plate area (a figure approximating the total volume of imports to Potosí annually at this period, which was 2.8 million pesos) (Ramos 1970, pp. 287–8) and in 1791 1.5 million pesos, a sum greater than the total imports of Chile. *Situados* were maintained, and even increased, after the establishment of the Plate viceroyalty. New Spain's largest outlay was for Havana, which received 2.1 million pesos in 1796.

All these massive subsidies did little to encourage the growth of dependent relationships among the colonies, however; they were not payments for goods delivered or credits for encouraging future production or trade, but simply funds to cover unmet public expenditure, and for that reason must have had very few multiplier effects, either within the colonies or between them. They reinforced the disjunctive process which other colonial policies had engendered, while retaining dependency on Spain. Regional differences in wealth may have been reduced by the *situados*, but as they applied very largely to the small administrative elite and to a few special purposes, there could be no general effect of this kind.

Urban size distributions

We have argued above that there were no major changes in the organization of Latin American society or economy over the eighteenth-century period of colonial rule, though some spatial rearrangements did take place. The distribution of town sizes reflects this continuity of process. For the earlier periods it has been indicated that a primate-city type of structure appeared and was

Table 3 *Capital and next several cities as percentage of national population, 1742–1827*

Country	Year	Capital (%)	Next cities (%)	
Argentine	1778	13	11	(Catamarca, Córdoba, Mendoza)
	1800	12	8	(Catamarca, Córdoba, Mendoza)
	1817	10	4	(Córdoba, Salta, Santa Fé)
Brazil	1777	3	5	(Ouro Prêto, Salvador, São Paulo)
	1808	2	4	(Recife, Salvador, São Paulo)
	1819	2	3	(Recife, Salvador, São Paulo)
Chile	1758	11	5	(Concepción, Talca)
	1791	8	3	(Concepción, Talca)
	1813	6	3	(Concepción, Talca)
Colombia	1772	2		
	1825	3		
Cuba	1792	19	15	(Puerto Principe: Camagucy, Santiago de Cuba, Trinidad)
	1827	13	9	(Puerto Principe: Camagucy, Santiago de Cuba, Trinidad)
Mexico	1742	3		
	1803	2	3	(Guanajuato, Puebla, Zacatecas)
	1823	2	2	(Guadalajara, Guanajuato, Puebla)
Peru	1791	5	8	(Arequipa, Ayacucho, Cuzco)
Venezuela	1772	7	8	(Barquisimeto, Maracaibo, Valencia)
	1800	4	5	(Barquisimeto, Maracaibo, Valencia)
	1810	5	5	(Barquisimeto, Maracaibo, Valencia)

Source: Morse (1971a), p. 5a.

typical of all of Spanish America at least. In the period from 1750 onwards, when something approaching modern census data are for the first time available, the distribution of city sizes seems to indicate strong primacy (see Table 3).

This finding can only be tentative because city numbers and population figures are too limited to show details for this period, and it must be admitted that it runs counter to the two views (themselves contradictory) given in the text which has most directly concerned itself with this subject (Morse 1971a). On the one hand, Morse himself, as editor and contributor to the discussion on city sizes, claims that there was a 'primacy dip' in the period around 1800, that large cities did not grow because of war destruction, the colonization of new areas, the reorganization of the economy and the disruption of the primary export sectors (Morse 1971a, p. 5). In opposition to this view (although, curiously enough, without acknowledging their difference of opinion), McGreevey (1971, pp. 116–29) states and shows statistically, using *chi*-square tests of difference from long-normal distributions, that all countries for which he has data exhibit an increase of primacy, having started in 1800 at a position close to log-normality – that is, a city size distribution following Zipf's rank-size rule (1949).

Here neither of these views can be supported. Morse's view of declining primacy is based on the statistics showing that the towns in his lists had a declining proportion of total national population; but primacy or normality refer to urban, not total, populations, and what Morse has really identified is a ruralization of the population, which did indeed take place for most countries and for the reasons he adduces: the disturbances of war and the growth of rural economies in newly occupied areas unlinked as yet to export markets.

McGreevey's own estimate of normality up to 1800 followed by a continuous rise of primacy is correct if we accept its assumptions of a single urban structure for the whole nation. But a national urban system was not really in being at this time, for each region had its own structure. In the large countries like Argentina, instead of a single urban structure centred on Buenos Aires, the isolation of the interior meant that there were several urban structures for different regions, notably in the north-west centred on Tucumán, in the Cuyo area centred on Mendoza, and in the Pampas with Buenos Aires as centre. These, because of the various disjunctive effects outlined earlier in this chapter, were only loosely linked together, and a national urban structure would have to await the arrival of a rail network, which only reached Mendoza and Tucumán, for example, in the 1880s. In Brazil there were similarly loosely connected regional economies and, presumably, corresponding regional urban structures around Rio, Bahia and Recife at the minimum.

Within each of these smaller-than-nation regions a single town was dominant, and a primate structure is likely to have existed; it is only by amalgamating them that the artificial appearance of a national log-normal distribution appears. Since the urban pyramid virtually ends with the towns listed in Table 3, if we separate out these towns and make them the leading centres for individual regions, the lack of lesser centres – most smaller places were effectively villages, places of residence for agriculturalists – gives each region a primate structure, dominated by a single town. For the smaller countries this reasoning is not as plausible for separate regional structures are not as likely, but in these cases, as in some of the larger countries, the number of towns entering is so small that a significant difference from log-normality is difficult to prove statistically in the test mentioned because of the increasing margins for variability that are inherent in F-numbers for small groups.

The socio-economic structure

The facets which have been covered so far may be brought together in terms of the form or forms of exchange integration employed. In pre-Conquest times this integration had largely been in terms of reciprocity relations or, within the great empires, redistribution. It may be asked here what kind of structure is proposed for the colonial period; the answer seems to be that, despite the advent of money and markets, the older systems of interrelationship were adopted and adapted by the new men.

Reciprocity and the primitive groups

A large part of Latin America remained totally outside the colonial format of occupation and for that reason remained, as it had long been, subject only to systems of reciprocity. Goods or services entered into exchange through kinship bonds, the blood relationships of each man determining his rights and obligations. Such a system must have been found in large parts of the Amazon rainforest, Pampas and Llanos, and in the dry areas of Brazil and

Mexico. The geographical landscape corresponding to this social structure is one without urban concentrations, production specialization or long-distance trading links. Reciprocity survived also within the areas endowed with the large-scale organization implied by redistributive systems, but as a minor or subordinate element. The Inca, Aztec and Maya empires did not destroy the basic structure of the villages they absorbed.

Redistribution

Pre-Conquest empires had been built in the areas of more dense population – in Central America under Maya, Aztec and perhaps earlier leaders, and in the Andes under the Tiahuanaco people and their successors, the Incas. These empires were destroyed by the Spanish, but their organizational structure was maintained in large measure. This organization was one of redistribution, with strong leader groups, clans or individuals at the centres, who controlled both the productive and the trading aspects of the economy. Exchange for them was through a centripetal concentration of tribute and some centrifugal redistribution. Foreign trade seems to have been conducted as an institution of the central government rather than on open markets (Chapman 1957). In large measure, the Spanish structures of labour and goods taxes simply replaced existing structures, and all went to maintain large Spanish holdings of land and other forms of wealth, both in America and Europe. Not that the pre-Conquest structures of society and economy predetermined the colonial structure. In Brazil, without any forceful precedent, the Portuguese established a quite similar structure in their own territories, with the necessary modifications to allow for the greater poverty of the area and the almost complete lack of servile labour in the land. What we may say is that the old empires gave a readily adopted example that could be followed with the least amount of effort.

Within the empire areas the reciprocity systems – the *ayllu* of the Inca lands and the *calpulli* of New Spain both refer to a set of blood relations, to a social and economic community and to an area of land – that survived were utilized, as explained above, through the exploitation of community labour for production of an exportable surplus; instead of paying for the labour in money or kind, the community was allowed to maintain its traditional self-sufficient food-producing system. Despite the heavy depopulation of the whole continent in the sixteenth and seventeenth centuries, the group systems survived with remarkable resilience and could be continuously exploited for export production by the arrangements described, those of *encomienda, repartimiento, hacienda*.

As a spatial structure, Figure 14 (page 120) shows a diagrammatic form the lineaments of the colonial redistributive society. Instead of the old centres of empire at Cuzco or Tenochtitlan, the new effective centres of the redistributive systems are now overseas, in Europe. This does not affect the basic structure of routes and settlements, except that a port is now frequently the major centre; this is in practice always the case for colonial Brazil, but Spanish centres such as Quito, Bogotá, Mexico City and Santiago show interest in centrality within the most productive and densely settled provinces of the old empires. In Figure 14 the trade lines are generally radial around the ports which extract the raw-material surpluses obtained from the dualist agricultural systems of the interior. There is no network of communications between the various smaller centres – indeed, there are few small centres, and certainly no second-line centres after the main, primate city. A primate urban structure reflects both the trade organization and the social structure of the colonial period.

Some interior centres of specialized or particularly intensive activity might develop, however, and are shown in the diagram – they modify but do not destroy the basic pattern. Potosí, Bahia, the Mexican mines of Durango or Zacatecas are of this nature. Beyond the frontiers of European influence separate systems of human organization are found, and they inevitably become increasingly differentiated from the Europeanized areas of more accessible or more desirable regions.

4 The neo-colonial period

Political events and regional structure

It has been indicated that the change from colony to independent republic did not imply a sudden or revolutionary change as far as Latin American economy and society were concerned. Prior to the independence wars of 1810–25, Spain had long been in the process of relaxing trade restrictions (which were in any case not observed), and at the time of independence the whole cumbersome machinery of trade regulation had been opened up and made a much less onerous burden than it had traditionally been. Brazil, politically separated from Portugal under a young monarch in 1822, underwent a long economic transition which had started in the eighteenth century and went on through the nineteenth. In neither Spanish nor Portuguese America did independence imply a major social revolution, because those who had spearheaded the independence movements, their intellectual leaders, were the middle-class and upper-class *criollos*, American-born but of European blood and kept out of power by the *peninsulares*, the European-born bureaucrats who took nearly all the top administrative posts. Having achieved the revolution, the *criollos* had no real interest in internal social reforms. Economically, the shifts were slight because external relations had been moving away from reliance on Spain and Portugal, since the beginning of the eighteenth century, towards direct relations with northern Europe. Political changes in the nineteenth century merely confirmed what was already an economic fact.

If anything, the political changes seem to have had a negative effect on some areas; some republics in their entirety, and many individual regions, were made more remote and isolated than in colonial days, and this situation was not always overcome in the nineteenth century. Bolivia was created through the will of the local elite of Sucre and La Paz, an ironic fact, since Bolivar the Liberator was opposed to the process of subdivision of South America into a host of mini-republics. Bolivia had been the colonial province of Upper Peru, in close contact with Peru and thus with the outside world. Now it was artificially separated from Peru, and in addition its source of wealth, Potosí, had experienced a long-term decline. As the century wore on, it would seem still more isolated as it became a country without a seaboard, losing its window on the Pacific in the Nitrates War (1879–83) with Chile. Paraguay similarly became an isolated interior state when its access to Europe via the Paraná became an access through foreign territory. It failed to change this situation by going to war (the War of the Triple Alliance) against its neighbours in the 1860s. Further north, Gran Colombia was split in 1830 into the three republics of Venezuela, Colombia and Ecuador, each of them tiny in resources and population, and Ecuador with no front to the Atlantic. A yet more extreme case of balkanization occurred in Central America, where what had been the 'United Provinces of Central America', through internal disagreements and wars, broke up in 1838 into five tiny republics.

At the sub-national level, political boundaries could also serve to isolate. The boundary between north-west Argentina and newly formed Bolivia, which placed an obstacle to a long-standing trade route, isolated not only Bolivia but also Argentina's north-west provinces, Salta, Jujuy and Tucumán, once dependent on the cattle trade to the silver mines of the *altiplano*. Further south the eighteenth-century administrative changes had included the removal of Cuyo, the region comprising the present-day provinces of Mendoza, San Juan and San Luis, from Chile's jurisdiction to that of the Plate in 1776, on the grounds of its greater accessibility from Buenos Aires. But this land was effectively isolated from both east and west, by deserts and by mountains respectively. In general, the effect of the new political divisions may be said to have been a formalization of the existing colonial barriers to trade between the various colonies due to European policy. Trade relations were with European powers and inter-American relations were made more difficult by the new boundaries.

The new export economies

In the following sections nineteenth-century socio-economic struc-tures are examined in terms of production, trade and settlement. In spite of the obvious changes in political status, a considerable continuity from colonial to post-colonial eras is apparent; although the locational arrangements (the macrogeography) of economic patterns were changed by new alliances and new technology, the internal structures of social and economic relations in each region, and even the small-scale geographic patterns, were comparable with those of colonial times.

A break with the past, it is generally agreed by economic historians, seems to have affected most of Latin America at some time during the nineteenth century. In terms of social and economic structures, we will wish to challenge such a view. The break is apparently provided by the opening up, usually through foreign enterprise and capital, of new areas of production and new resources, which were fed as exports of raw materials to the developing industrial countries of Europe and North America. In Peru, long in depression because of her declining role in trade and the decline of the silver trade, the new export economy was in guano, the organic fertilizer composed of the slowly accumulated deposits of seabirds' excrement on the little islands along the coast, whose aridity was such that the deposits were not subject to natural erosion and could accumulate in thick beds. These exports lasted from 1840 to 1880 before becoming largely exhausted, and in any case they were replaced by the mineral nitrates (*caliche*) of the north Chilean deserts. In Cuba the modernizing export resource was cane sugar, dominant from 1850 among that country's exports, and from 1880 under predominantly foreign control. In this case the export base was more permanent, though whether this was an advantage to the country might be disputed.

Argentina's export economy was also built up from the 1850s, after the fall of Rosas and the move away from limited exports of hides, tallow, horse hair and jerked meat to massive wool, meat and grain exports. For Mexico the transition was apparently less abrupt, as silver and other metal exports maintained some vitality throughout the nineteenth century: but under Porfirio Diaz (1876–1911) a much more effective opening to the exterior, to export raw materials on the new railways, was accomplished. Some countries were opened up still later, as in the case of Bolivia, where tin mining became important in the 1890s, or Venezuela, whose oil was exported from 1917. Yet another group of countries, which includes Ecuador, Paraguay, the Guianas, Central America and most Caribbean islands, experienced little of this opening effect at all.

The challenge to this conventional view of profound change under the new export economies of the nineteenth century is simply stated: it is that although there were new products and areas of production, the development structures were not greatly dissimilar to those of colonial time. Production in colonial time was of a dual nature, feeding local and overseas markets, and it continued to be so in the neo-colonial nineteenth century, for although slavery was progressively restricted and finally banned in the course of the century, serfdom of various kinds was not restricted and indeed expanded in many countries through the growth of large estates at the expense of or alongside the surviving Indian communities. What did change was the market for Latin American products and the ability or willingness of that market to intervene directly in the productive process. In place of Spain and Portugal, the north European powers now acted directly as partners with Latin American countries; they had always had an indirect influence, using Iberia as middleman for their commerce, but now with direct access the links were expanded and intensified.

Northern Europe also contributed something to development – investment of some capital, entrepreneurship and migrants to organize and undertake production in some areas. Their technology brought rapid transport systems to extract raw materials from distant interior regions and to take them away across oceans with minimum spoilage, and they organized modern large-scale mining and plantations or farms using the more productive and efficient new types of machinery, animals and plant stocks.

Throughout, however, this amounted to maintenance of a similar colony–mother country relationship, one of dependent development of the export economy. It may seem, in retrospect, like a revolutionary change because the late colonial and early post-colonial time was one of economic depression and few exports of any kind, which was suddenly followed by a dramatic opening of the export economy. The point to be made here is that there was fundamental change not in qualitative but in quantitative terms; the new economy was one of much more massive exports (or at least of exports after a phase of self-sufficiency), organized in a more efficient manner.

Areal spread of the new export economy – a frontier?

From the point of view of the geography (in the simplest, location sense of the word) of production, there was, of course, change. Large new areas were necessarily incorporated in the productive process for existing or new products in demand by the industrial world – a set of new frontiers, of coffee production in Colombia or Brazil, of wheat maize in the Pampas, of nitrate extraction in the Chilean deserts, came into being – but this should not delude us into seeing a transformation of society and economy as a result. It is perhaps useful to interpret the lack of any radical social restructuring as a result of the non-operation of the frontier functions recognized by Hudson (1976). The expansion of production took place without the erection of a frontier.

Hudson's scheme classifies frontiers according to source of innovation (frontier or heartland) and the presence or absence of intergroup conflicts, as shown below:

Human conflict	Type of frontier Source of innovation	
	Heartland	Frontier
One group (no conflict)	Adapted spread	Environmental conflict
Several groups (conflict)	Stages of occupance	Modification through conflict

In most of the Latin American cases if there was any frontier effect at all, it was a modest one of the first type, 'adapted spread'. There was little conflict with other groups, and the ideas adopted in the new areas were not frontier inventions but imports from other areas.

On several of the expanding frontiers primitive American Indian groups were encountered, and the frontier experience might be thought to be one of major conflict. But the Indian groups were small and scattered and could not present any great resistance to the white man. In the southern Pampas and Patagonia, for example, their numbers may have been only 200,000, spread over a huge territory in tiny bands of hunters, and when an organized campaign against them was mounted in 1879–83, the so-called 'Conquest of the Desert' under General Roca, they were quickly pushed back. No cultural effects on Argentine society were passed on by them, for they were entirely exterminated before any solid contacts could be made.

We may follow through in a little more detail the incorporation of the Pampas lands to show the essentially adaptive mechanisms used in the spread of the effective political and economic frontier and the lack of any fundamental changes in technology or social relations. *Estancias* had been established as the common type of unit for cattle management in the eighteenth century (Giberti 1961) and had proved useful because of their simplicity and flexibility. Few or no permanent buildings were erected; a bend in a river or some other natural enclosure was used to herd together the animals at night; and the whole unit could be moved on to a new area with minimum difficulty. The products were hides and tallow or, in a few cases, *charqui*, salt meat. These *estancias* were extended when the frontier was moved, between 1770 and 1880, from the Rio Salado just south of the Plate, to encompass finally the whole of present-day Argentina. Land-ownership patterns were not changed because the existing land-owners were given rights to most of the frontier lands, often in advance of its survey or even its acquisition from the Indians!

Rosas, dictator–governor of Buenos Aires province from 1829 to 1853, was particularly responsible for many large land grants to his political supporters, and later nineteenth-century governments that followed him made great land sales of the Pampas lands, mostly to existing large land-owners, at ridiculously low prices, to finance their railway-building plans in the absence of a proper tax system that should have been used for this purpose. In no instance was there a positive incentive to change. The frontier itself was in any case a near-desert in demographic terms, for the Indian groups were scanty and in retreat, and the tiny numbers of *gaucho* cowboys – one *gaucho* per 1000 hectares was a figure given by Felix de Azara in 1780 – meant no real chance for pacific contacts. The few contacts that took place, as had been true since the 1530s, were hostile and led to death on at least one side, and no positive learning progress could result from the frontier contact.

Later in the century some changes were made to the economy, but without changing social structures. Foreign technology improved steamships and refrigeration to the point where meat could be shipped frozen to Europe, and mass textile manufacturing created a demand for great quantities of wool. To improve both meat and wool supplies, pedigree stocks of Lincoln sheep were introduced from England in the 1850s, and later the Hereford, Shorthorn and Aberdeen Angus breeds of cattle were incorporated into herds. To meet the needs of these improved breeds, various technical changes – fencing to protect stock and crops, the rotation of crops to include new feed crops for fattening cattle, better control of breeding and pasture rotation – were adopted, and immigrant farmers from Italy and Spain came to operate the tenant grain farms. But for the most part, with the notable exception of some *colonias agrícolas* in Santa Fé, where small owner-operator farms were established, a pattern of a few large land-owners and many small tenant farmers was the norm. Ownership patterns did not change from those of colonial days, and the result was a lack of incentive to adapt and change and none of the markets or entrepreneurial atmosphere necessary to development oriented to the interior of the region rather than to Europe. The occupation of the humid Pampas was thus an exercise which involved no cultural change and little technological innovation – certainly none of local origin. It constituted an areal expansion of the system of economic dependence, with a strengthening of the links to the new centres of European and North American power, but did not basically change the character of dependence.

In Brazil the expansion of the coffee frontier was of a similar character (Hennessy 1978). Introduced in the eighteenth century to Rio de Janeiro, in the 1830s a rising world demand allowed this crop to spread rapidly up the Paraiba valley on slave plantations in the immediate hinterland of Rio, moving west towards São Paulo. When the railway was built across the difficult Sierra do Mar from Santos to São Paulo in the 1860s, expansion could proceed west through the state, finally reaching into northern Paraná in the present century. This spread was across a land with only a tiny Indian population of primitive collectors and cultivators, reduced over colonial time by European disease and slave-catching expeditions by the *bandeirantes* of São Paulo. Little was learnt from contact with these people. Plantation-type farm units with slaves, and then increasingly small farms operated by ex-slaves or immigrants, were characteristic, so that an old-established pattern of *latifundio–minifundio* was carried forward into the coffee lands. Farming techniques were simple in the extreme, involving cutting and clearing, planting and harvesting, with only a minimum of cultivation before abandoning the land when erosion and the depletion of fertility of the soil necessitated it. Plantation operations were modified only in this century by the adoption of the colonization-company kind of development in northern Paraná, from the 1920s. As in the humid Pampas of Argentina and Uruguay, this was a process of areal expansion, of growth in the dimensions of the economy, but not of development in the sense of structural change.

In the far north-west of Brazil, along a number of tributaries of the upper Amazon, as well as in the Acre territory of Bolivia and adjacent provinces of Peru, another kind of raw material was exploited from the 1870s to the beginning of the First World War: rubber. It also involved a very simple technology, for rubber was produced here entirely by collection from wild trees. A small force of rubber tappers was collected together at the main merchant centre, Manáus, and sent upstream in canoes to tap the trees in territory which would be defined for each *seringueiro* or rubber collector. Although a new product, the extraction was controlled from Europe through its demand, and more locally and directly through the Manáus merchants who dominated the marketing and the supply of credit to the *seringueiro*. In the Bolivian sector of the Madeira river drainage and in the Putumayo and neighbouring Amazon headstreams in Peru, a similar development took place in the 1880s. In each case, exploitation of the rubber trees extended the modern world's influence further, reducing the areas still occupied by primitive peoples, though leaving large areas untouched and so continuing the processes of both dependent and disjunctive development.

Examples of Hudson's other types of frontier are not easy to identify. Environmental conflicts were limited for reasons that are fairly clear; the new frontiers were either in the temperate lands, Mexico, Chile, Uruguay, Argentina, where the environment presented no obstacle, or they were in the humid tropics, where the adjustments were minimized because Europeans did not themselves work the land, leaving it to slaves or poor *mestizo* peoples. And many of the adjustments for tropical production had already been made in the course of the 300 years of colonial rule.

Possibly the Brazilian and certainly all tropical agricultural frontiers exhibit one important adaptation to environment – shifting cultivation. Brazil's westward-shifting coffee frontier, and the small-farmer frontier of the southern panhandle states – Rio Grande do Sul, Santa Catarina and Paraná – in the nineteenth century, involved cultivation or cropping for a few years, followed by farm abandonment because of declining fertility. Primitive Indians had long practised shifting cultivation (the *roça*), and the European and *mestizo* population early learnt to adopt this ecologically sound land-use form (Henshall and Momsen 1974).

But even this break with European tradition, which had its effects in, for example, the loosening of the population's ties to the soil in any particular area, did not create a new society of economy. Coffee still had to be exported, and the coffee merchants of São Paulo still effectively controlled production on the moving frontier.

As to the two other frontier types, the 'stages of occupance' type, whereby successive waves moving out from a heartland push each other further west, as in Turner's (1893) thesis on western North America, is not operative for several reasons. Turner's scheme was for a pattern of successively lower-intensity land uses at varying distances from the market, which could not hold for Latin America because a subsistence economy prevailed in many parts; the market itself was also distant, in Europe and North America, making the whole Latin American area peripheral. A few hundred kilometres more or less could not change the facts of peripherality. Human conflicts, as in Hudson's fourth category, were limited in scale in the region, short-lived and one-sided for the most part, with few cases of a mixed culture emanating from the selection of the better elements of each one.

Relating the kind of frontier experience to the various categories of growth of Chapter 1, it would seem to have been a process of simple growth rather than development, and the expansion of a known technology and a set of social interrelations from other areas. No doubt this is in part because we are looking at one piece in a much larger system which extends out to Europe, and if the whole were to be studied, we could see processes of differentiation between the colonial peripheries, with their various raw material specializations, and the mother country with its manufacturing, commercial and administrative roles. The individual innovations (coffee, cotton, wheat growing, new breeds of animals, even new farm technologies in their entirety) spread relatively unchanged across a landscape; the changes in technology occurred in the advanced countries, and the process is one of differentiation between these and a world-wide economic empire being built to produce export commodities.

Independent development

In a few exceptional cases this dependent, outward-oriented development was replaced by a different, autonomous one because social structures were more amenable, more democratic, because dominant centres of power were too distant to challenge such development. In Antioquia, the district around Medellín in Colombia, for example, local merchants in the successful coffee-exporting industry, farmers turned merchants, mine owners and workers, separate groups competing in a relatively open society where traditional landlords had not been able to exert control invested their earnings in textile factories (Parsons 1968) and thereby set up a chain of local earnings and re-investment that has culminated in the rise of modern industrial Medellín. Although the technology of the first mills in the 1890s and the machinery itself was all imported, there were largely intra-regional multiplier effects from then on because the market for cotton goods, as well as the raw material for the factories, was local or regional.

In Argentina the exception was the Santa Fé central district, where European colonization had broken the standard *estancia* pattern of large ranches with a network of small farms with mixed arable, dairy and other products. A denser population, the marketing of farm goods, and some processing (for example, of dairy produce) gave a kind of development separate from that of the deserted humid Pampas in general (Balan 1976; Sternberg 1972). This latter region reflected solely the influence of world markets and the world designation of the Pampas as a producer of raw materials, first hides and salt meat, then wool, meat and grain.

Another such case seems to have been São Paulo, where a typical raw-material export economy based on coffee was converted through local investment into a diversified industrial economy with local multiplier effects. A coffee frontier has been described above, and its lack of any permanent effect on the societies involved in its movement west through the nineteenth century; but the investment of coffee money in the commercial capital, São Paulo City, did have an effect on the urban region. Some of the investments were made by *comissários,* the intermediaries who provided credit to the planners when needed and who also marketed the coffee crop (Morse 1974, p. 140), and some directly by planters who, with the advent of railways, could live in the city and still retain control of large and distant *fazendas*. Using local raw materials, pottery making, cotton textiles, furniture and other wood products, cement and food processing industries were prominent from the early days of growth in the last quarter of the century. Labour was provided by the abundant flow of European immigrants (Italians outnumbered Brazilians by two to one in São Paulo by 1897, according to Morse,

1974, p. 175), but a crucial role seems to have been that of the independent, locally accruing capital of planters and *comissários* that sought local outlets for investment and did not automatically flow to Europe or North America.

Monterrey in north-east Mexico also achieved industrial development of a semi-independent character. In this city the chance factor of its location near the international frontier with the United States at a key time, that of the North American Civil War, seems to have sparked off industrial growth, again using funds derived from commerce as trading profits (Mauro, in Barkin 1972) to prime the industrial pump. As the direct route out for wool and cotton from the South, through the Gulf of Mexico ports of the USA, had become impossible because of the Northerners' blockade, textile industries were founded in Monterrey to use the available raw materials, followed by a beer factory and several foundries during the 1890s. Regional isolation from Mexico City also aided this separate development in the far north-east, but once set going, the momentum of industrialization has been maintained up to the present day. In this instance, capital and entrepreneurship were in part North American, so that to speak of an independent process of industrialization is not strictly accurate; nevertheless, the new industries established were certainly geared less to the exterior than any previous raw-material export economy. Markets within the country, and raw-material sources too, gave a set of internal linkages which contrast with the largely external linkages of raw-material exports. In addition, there were various linkages among the industries themselves, glass-container manufacture, for example, relating to the manufacture of beer and to fuel supplies.

Transportation and trade

If what has been said about the expansion of production is extended to trade and transportation lines, a net of centripetal lines focusing on the major ports should be expected. Such a pattern is evident, in which large regions are connected to the main cities, and it is the more prominent because a new form of land transport, the railway, by its nature tended to focus traffic. Suited to concentrated, massive loads and regular, continuous use, railways were not designed to serve large, thinly populated areas that might only generate an irregular or light traffic. They therefore tended to provide only mainline through routes, without many branches or alternative lines, in the thinly peopled hinterland of most Latin American ports: large blocks of country were entirely neglected. Railways were needed because the development of the interior regions could not rely on road provision – the regions were dependent on the action of regional governments whose funds were always insufficient to maintain existing poor tracks, let alone build new roads – nor could the river network be used for modern transport. In the absence of dredging, the Paraná and Orinoco were inaccessible to all except light craft, whose captains would know the varying location of sandbanks; the Amazon, at least in its main channel, was used to provide access to Manáus for ocean-going vessels, but it lacked resources other than rubber.

The growth of the rail linkages may be illustrated by examples. São Paulo had a major rail system by 1897, with thirteen different profitable companies operating very largely between the state capital and its hinterland. The linkages were, however, of a special kind. They did not constitute a network, for they were not built according to any overall state plan, were unconnected to each other because they belonged to different companies and often even had different gauges. Only three of them had more than 1000 kilometres of track. Two had a 1.6-metre gauge, one a 0.75-metre gauge and the rest a 1.0-metre gauge (Zalduendo 1975, p. 240). The railways connected parts of the hinterland to São Paulo but not to each other. There was, of course, a link between the rise of the coffee economy and the rail net, the latter coming to serve as means of evacuation for the coffee crop, though the frontier coffee farms could be well forward of the railhead. A centripetal set of lines was therefore representative of the kind of links the economy was

Table 4   *São Paulo in the nineteenth century: population, rail network, freight*

Year	Population of city (000)	Rail network of state (km)	Freight carried (000 tonnes)
1855	15.5	—	—
1870	—	139	106.5
1872	27.6	—	—
1880	—	1212	312.0
1884	35.0	—	—
1890	64.9	2425	1049.4

Source: Morse (1951).

developing. The city grew in conjunction with its transport links and the freight that they carried. Foreign capital was employed to build these railways, attracted to Brazil by the grants commonly made of land lying adjacent to the track, by the monopoly of rail provision within certain zones and by guaranteed interest rates for invested capital. In 1870 three-quarters of the capital and 72 per cent of the rail track built was financed to British firms (Zalduendo 1975, p. 220). This was obviously a dependent form of development, relying on outside interest for the initial investment and knowledge and on the same outsiders for finished-product markets.

Beyond the rail hinterlands of São Paulo and Rio, different processes ensued from the dawn of the railway age. The Nordeste, now a poor backwater of Brazil well past the glory of its plantation prime, had by 1892 a series of very small rail lines, linking tiny hinterlands to individual ports without important connections between them. There, it would seem, the railway brought a disjunctive development, islands of export-related economic activity separated by many kilometres of economic desert as far as the market economy was concerned. From north to south, Belém, São Luis de Maranhão, Parnaiba, Camocim, Fortaleza, Natal, João, Pessoa, Recife, Maceió each had its own strip of backcountry, producing a little cotton, sugar cane or vegetable oil and exporting them by way of a narrow-gauge railway to the coast (see Figure 13). Typical were the Pernambuco Great Western with 141 kilometres of 1-metre track, or the Alagoas Central of Maceió with 150 kilometres of 1-metre track. Between these the less accessible coastal areas relapsed into relative obscurity. The interior regions which were beyond the reach of railways and would remain so into the twentieth century were still more inaccessible. The interior of the Nordeste, including most of Maranhão, the middle São Francisco valley, most of Piauí, were never served by rail; and yet greater isolation was found in the Centre West – that is, the states of Mato Grosso and Goiás – and the whole Amazon region of the north. In sum, the Brazilian railways provided for and encouraged different processes, a dependent integration of the major city regions with export-providing hinterlands and a disjunctive development elsewhere, railways linking neither with their neighbours nor with more distant areas which remained totally unserved by modern means of communication.

The growth of the export economy provided a similar impetus to a radial system in Argentina, through the extension of numerous

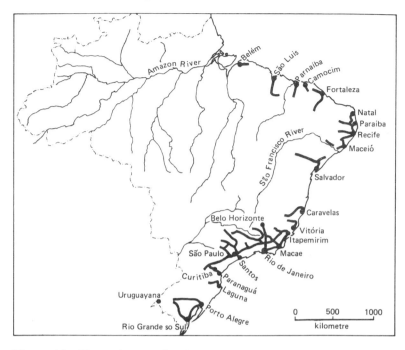

Figure 13   *The rail network of Brazil around 1880 (based partly on Zalduendo 1975).*

individual lines from Buenos Aires out into the wheatlands of the northern humid Pampas. A slightly different historical backcloth for rail development did exist, in that before the advent of the railways there had been major development in some interior regions of Argentina, the north-west and Cuyo, which had indeed been more densely peopled and productive than the Pampas in the period prior to 1850. This provided a better reason for a good long-distance network linking the interior and the Pampas with Buenos Aires.

Steam first reached the River Plate region in the form of propulsion for Paraná river boats, reducing the sailing time between Rosario and Buenos Aires from twenty days to between thirty and forty hours. But the river did not link important resource areas with the coast; this function was left to the railways. Steam railways were adopted from 1857. Initially the capital was provided by Buenos Aires merchants supported by the province government. Wool was the first major export of the railways, for at this time improved breeds of sheep were introduced from Britain to the northern

Buenos Aires province section of the Pampas (Morris 1977). Railways centred on Buenos Aires City both because their construction had begun there and because of a viable freight item available to them. Wool was later followed by wheat and maize as a more complex cattle-fattening and grain-production system took over the best lands.

From 1866 a competing rail line was built from Rosario towards Córdoba, which it reached in 1870. This line was built with the inducement of major land grants and was guaranteed a 7 per cent interest on investments. But the line did not expand after 1870, and Buenos Aires, better situated as an export port and already the commercial centre of the country, reinforced its hegemony, the whole south of Buenos Aires province entering into the city's hinterland by 1888. Up to the 1880s the railways served to link the Pampas lands with the principal ports, and the Pampas export economy was built up while other regions remained in a near-subsistence condition. In Cuyo, the provinces of Mendoza, San Luis and San Juan were cut off by desert and distance from Buenos Aires and by mountains from Chile, so that an isolated, self-sufficient economy and society prevailed. Some linkages to the exterior were present in the old-established livestock trade, whereby store cattle and mules were moved west from the Pampas to irrigated alfalfa in Cuyo, then on to Chile for sale. Dried fruit and wine were also sent to Buenos Aires on a small scale from the 2500 hectares of vineyards in 1881. But there was local self-sufficiency in the production of grains (wheat and maize) and other foodstuffs, and regional craft industries producing carts, saddles and leather goods, candles and soap, farm tools and rough furniture were predominant.

In the north-west the relations of a similarly isolated economy with the outside world were based on livestock. Something of the old cattle trade to Bolivia and Peru was maintained and extended also to northern Chile, where nitrates attracted a mining populace in the second half of the century. Mules and horses moved from the Pampas through the region to Bolivia by a trade system independent of railways or paved roads. Maize, wheat and a whole assemblance of traditional Indian crops such as beans and squashes fed the still dense local population. A modest specialization in the production of wine, tobacco and sugar had been established, but monoculture of sugar in Tucumán had to await the arrival of the railway in 1884, just as vineyard specialization in Mendoza came only with the railway, also in 1884. Artisan industries of many kinds survived from colonial times and would survive into the twentieth century. As in interior Brazil, a separate development pattern had been followed, but in this case it was that of a peasant rather than a primitive society and economy.

The Argentine rail net penetrated much deeper than the Brazilian or other South American nets. By 1884 Mendoza and Tucumán had been reached by rail; the effects included the conversion of Mendoza into a commercial vine producer and Tucumán into a sugar producer, both for national markets. Craft industries and subsistence agriculture now underwent a gradual decline. In the interior provinces, however, the railways did not form a network, and large areas were left outside the influence of rail connections, including the whole province of Catamarca and much of Santiago del Estero in the north-west, and the Argentine section of the Gran Chaco in the north, plus virtually all of Patagonia in the south. Table 5 shows the regional bias of the network, which was not corrected by 1900 and indeed never altered substantially thereafter.

The Brazilian process of the division of the rail network into a series of single penetration lines reaching a short distance from the coast was not followed, but the wide gaps in the Argentine network and the lack of cross-links between the interior provinces, heightened by railway pricing policy (Scalabrini Ortiz 1958), effectively isolated these provinces, apart from areas directly on or near the rail lines. For the Pampas and for those other points in the space economy linked effectively with export or national markets, the geographical dependency was as it was in Brazil and similarly supported by a financial dependence on Britain, which in 1900 operated and administered fifteen of the railway companies, with 77

Table 5 *Argentina: rail network, 1890 and 1900*

| Region | 1890 | | 1900 | |
	Extent of track (km)	Percentage of total	Extent of track (km)	Percentage of total
Pampas	6444	68.6	10,435	62.8
Mesopotamia	532	5.7	1285	7.7
North-west	1700	18.1	3618	21.8
Cuyo	654	7.0	801	4.8
Patagonia	70	0.6	470	2.8

Source: Zalduendo (1975), p. 310.

per cent of the national track, and indirectly controlled, through renting or financial supervision, part of the remainder (Zalduendo 1975, p. 370).

Over Latin America generally, the relatively disconnected Brazilian pattern was more common than the Argentine one. Individual small regions became linked with small ports through single-purpose railways developed by private firms in the absence of any general planning of network integration – usually with varying gauges and with terminals in different cities. In Peru, for example, the Central Railway and the Southern Railway, built in the 1860s and 1870s, though the two principal lines, were never connected one to another, nor to the other much smaller lines which ran in from the coast further north to sugar plantations or mines. Competition from coastal sea traffic was blamed for the lack of an integrated line, but in reality the very nature of rail development, either by government seeking the prestige of the railway or by private firms concerned only with the movement of individual bulk products such as sugar cane and sugar in the west and wool and copper from the Sierra, was not one that would lead to integration. Again, as elsewhere, the lines were foreign-owned, not from the first because guano profits had been used by the government for rail construction, but from 1890, when enormous Peruvian debts to the outside world were taken over by a British company, the Peruvian Corporation, in exchange for railway and other transport control.

Argentina's and Brazil's isolation was partially broken from the 1850s. Mexico remained an isolated nation till the 1880s, when Porfirio Diaz opened the country to North American influence and achieved some large-scale regional integration, as had been proposed, but never achieved, under the 1857 Constitution. Up to this time the country had retained a large measure of regional, even local, self-sufficiency (Cortes Conde 1974, p. 80; Chevalier 1963). Both the great *haciendas* and the Indian *comunidades* remained autarchic institutions. Indeed, society and economy had gone through a process of involution because of the decline in silver mining and the civil wars up to 1870. Self-sufficiency was encouraged by the inter-state customs duties and by the survival of slavery and feudal serfdom.

Under Diaz, from 1876 to 1910, Mexican railways expanded from 645 kilometres to over 2400 kilometres. A set of east–west links had been advocated by politicians who still remembered the military threat from the northern neighbour, but the main lines finally built were primarily north-south links, opening the country to its logical trading partner. The Central Mexico was finished by 1880, linking Mexico City with El Paso and thus with Chicago. East of this line the Nacional Mexicano linked the capital with Monterrey and Laredo in 1888.

The breakdown of regional isolation stressed by Cortes Conde (1974) was still not complete, however. Some regions of northern Mexico were certainly incorporated into a national scheme, and a diversified export economy was set in motion. In addition to silver, the north now produced zinc, lead and copper, using new technology for extraction and transport and feeding a new, foreign market. Capital was invested directly by foreign firms in the development of railways, under the stimulus of a subsidy to constructors. Besides investment in the railway infrastructure, foreign investments, chiefly from France, went directly into textile industries; from both North America and Britain into oil wells; and from many countries into public utilities, urban transport, water and power supply.

As in the other countries mentioned in this section, the new Mexican transport net had a complex effect in helping concentration in the major cities and a few selected resource areas related to them, where foreign investment was concentrated. By contrast with the well-connected areas of the north, the densely peopled areas of traditional society and economy in the southern uplands (Oaxaca, Guerrero, Chiapas) were still isolated and little affected by new development. Even some parts of the centre, relatively close to Mexico City, were still in the world of the great *hacienda*. In 1910 in Mexico state, where 84 per cent of the people were involved in farming, 99.5 per cent were landless and sixty-four *haciendas* monopolized the best lands (Herring 1968, p. 334). In the south this was a standard situation, which resisted the 'modernizing' effect of the railways and discouraged their promoters from even attempting construction.

Transport and economic development

There are insufficient data to give a precise quantitative picture of the changes in regional fortunes due to transport improvement. But it is evident that two major categories of region are present – those affected and those unaffected by new means of transport. In the former two effects were possible: either 'spread' effects (the diffusion of modern technology and the diversification of the regional economy, as in regions like Antioquia, São Paulo or Monterrey) or 'backwash' effects (as in most other regions, where development meant concentration on single crops and the concentration of ownership of economic activities in a few hands). Beyond the influence of the rail lines the traditional, isolated regions remained static, undermined only marginally by the competition of new economic forms. And the presence alone of the rail line was insufficient to ensure 'modernization'; in the Peruvian Sierra, north-west Argentina and elsewhere in the Andes traditional communities were little affected by modern transport when their labour was not called into use for work in mines or ranches. There was thus a continuous differentiation between traditional and 'modernizing' regions, a process separate from those going on within the modern, market-oriented system.

Urban structures

In the last sections a process of opening up to the exterior, at different rates in various countries and regions, has been described in terms of the inputs of new land, labour and capital and the building of transport links between some regions and ports linking them with the outside world. Other regions have been seen to stagnate outside the new export economies.

A view of the urban hierarchy suggests a similar overall process and adds further aspects to it. If, as has been suggested and as would seem logical, a strongly organized export economy is reflected in a primate-city type of urban hierarchy, then we may relate the two in Latin America. Berry (1961) discovered no general relation between city primacy and economic development, and later writers (for instance, Gilbert 1976) have found difficulty in enunciating any general tendencies to be discovered; McGreevey (1971, pp. 116–29), however, found a positive statistical relation between urban primacy and the volume of exports per capita.

This reduction of the explanation for city size to economic arguments need not concern us for the moment, but the finding of high primacy is certainly valid and of importance. Even measured in a simplistic way, using only the top end of the urban hierarchy, primate structure may be seen to be strong *throughout the period*. It does decline after the late eighteenth century, as all Latin America was disturbed by war and changes in allegiance and then recovered towards the end of the century as major cities again become the foci for movement outwards of new raw-material exports. But primacy throughout is the more significant element – indeed, it is stronger than is suggested by the data because the *real regions* to which urban structure is related are smaller than the political units which are used as the measuring units in Tables 3 and 6. If we consider Recife, for example, not as one town in a Brazilian system, but as a regional centre for a north-eastern system, its primacy is immediately enhanced.

In Argentina the pattern is straightforward; a decline in primacy of Buenos Aires until mid-century and a rise thereafter. Those cities following Buenos Aires stagnate and do not recover during the century, however. These apparently simple changes do, of course, cover a more complex inter-regional shift between the north-west and the Pampas. In the eighteenth century the interior centres in the densely peopled irrigated oases of the north-west were dominant, and each city was important as centre to its own intensively farmed and irrigated area. Catamarca, Mendoza, Salta, Santiago del Estero were comparatively important urban centres. Later, as the Pampas developed, these cities were replaced by the second-line cities of the Pampas, Córdoba, Santa Fé, Rosario and La Plata.

Table 6, which extends the information given in Table 3 (page 86), is incomplete, for it does not show what happened to whole regions which had no important towns, regions of rural economy suffering from outmigration. Those areas away from the main rail lines and not producing for export markets were inevitably left to

Table 6 *Capital and next several cities as percentage of national population, 1835–1921*

Country	Year	Capital (%)	Next cities (%)
Argentina	1839	8	4 (Córdoba, Santa Fé, Tucumán)
	1857	7	3 (Córdoba, Santa Fé, Tucumán)
	1869	10	4 (Córdoba, Rosario, Tucumán)
	1895	17	5 (Córdoba, La Plata, Rosario)
	1914	20	5 (Córdoba, Rosario, Tucumán)
Brazil	1854	2	3 (Belém, Recife, Salvador)
	1872	3	3 (Belém, Recife, Salvador)
	1890	4	3 (Belém, Recife, Salvador)
	1900	4	3 (Belém, Salvador, São Paulo)
	1920	4	4 (Recife, Salvador, São Paulo)

Table 6 *Continued*

Country	Year	Capital (%)	Next cities (%)	
Chile	1835	7	4	(Talca, Valparaiso)
	1865	6	5	(Talca, Valparaiso)
	1875	7	6	(Concepción, Valparaiso)
	1885	7	5	(Concepción, Valparaiso)
	1895	9	6	(Concepción, Valparaiso)
	1907	10	7	(Concepción, Valparaiso)
	1920	14	7	(Concepción, Valparaiso)
Colombia	1851	2	2	(Bucaramanga, Cali, Medellín)
	1870	1	2	(Barranquilla, Cali, Medellín)
	1905	2	3	(Barranquilla, Medellín, Pasto)
	1918	2	3	(Barranquilla, Cali, Medellín)
Cuba	1841	12	7	(Matanzas, Puerto Principe, Santiago de Cuba)
	1861	14	7	(Matanzas, Puerto Principe, Santiago de Cuba)
	1899	16	7	(Cienfuegos, Matanzas, Santiago de Cuba)
	1907	14	5	(Cienfuegos, Matanzas, Santiago de Cuba)
	1919	14	5	(Matanzas, Puerto Principe, Santiago de Cuba)
Mexico	1877	2	2	(Guadalajara, Guanajuato, Puebla)
	1910	3	2	(Guadalajara, Monterrey, Puebla)
	1921	4	2	(Guadalajara, Monterrey, Puebla)
Peru	1862	4	3	(Arequipa, Ayacucho, Cuzco)
	1876	4	3	(Arequipa, Caballo, Cuzco)
	1908	3	3	(Arequipa, Caballo, Cuzco)
	1920	5	3	(Arequipa, Caballo, Cuzco)
Venezuela	1873	3	5	(Barquisimeto, Maracaibo, Valencia)
	1881	3	5	(Barquisimeto, Maracaibo, Valencia)
	1891	3	5	(Barquisimeto, Maracaibo, Valencia)
	1920	4	4	(Barquisimeto, Maracaibo, Valencia)

Source: Morse (1971a), p. 5a.

stagnate and are generally undocumented in the statistics. The dominance of Buenos Aires is the natural reflection of its success in attracting and retaining the rail lines in a country with no natural waterways into its most important interior regions – success which was followed by its growth as port and commercial centre as well as administrative heart of the country.

Brazil's pattern is similar, though less marked in its ups and downs. In this case interregional changes in economic importance are less significant, the major centres of Rio, Recife, São Paulo and Salvador retaining their centrality to large regions. Nineteenth-century Brazil may indeed be regarded as a series of countries, not one, at least in economic terms, and the low percentage of national population represented by the cities reflects this economic structure – Brazilian writers have referred to the country as an economic and cultural archipelago, not a subcontinent. If the big Brazilian cities are viewed as central to the large regions such as the Nordeste, the Amazon and the south-east of the South, they have quite large portions of the relevant populations and are primate in relation to other urban centres.

Mexico exhibits something of the same pattern – a small percentage of total population in the big cities and a nineteenth-century decline in primacy. Wibel and de la Cruz (in Morse 1971, p. 97) claim that Mexico City retained its level of primacy throughout the colonial and post-colonial periods; it certainly surpassed the next competitor by a fair margin, but this next city itself changed from one period to another. In the eighteenth century it was Guanajuato, leading silver-mining town of the viceroyalty, but this town's economy slumped with Independence, its wars and destruction, and was replaced first by Puebla, then by Guadalajara to the west, new industrial and agricultural centres. As with Brazil, the major towns represent only a tiny proportion of national population and should be viewed as a series of metropolises to regions within Mexico until well into the present century. Even the civilizing rails failed to join up all Mexico, linking only selected points or small regions within it with the capital and the outside world. By 1921, as Table 6 shows, Mexico City still contained only 4 per cent of national population, despite a long period of relative growth, and some of the regional capitals, Mérida, Guanajuato, Monterrey, Puebla, Zacatecas, were small towns. Mexico City's population in that year was 615,000; that of Guadalajara 143,000; Puebla 96,000; Monterrey 88,000; Mérida 79,000; San Luis Potosí 57,000; Veracruz, the main port,

54,000; and Guanajuato 19,000. But this left some large regions in the densely peopled south of the country with no important cities and no regional structure to support them. The picture is one, again, of the partial integration of some regions with the national centre, leaving others, which experienced no real change, to stagnate. The term 'hierarchy of towns' and the underlying concept, that of a network of mutually adjusted and related towns, a city system, are inappropriate to this situation, in which the various regional economies were not integrated.

Venezuela's urban growth patterns during the century exhibit considerable stability in the relative placing of the larger towns. Valencia, Barquisimeto and Maracaibo were the main centres throughout the period and have remained so up to the present. This stability cannot be seen as indicative of close-knit relations among various members of an urban hierarchy, but of the regional-centre function which each fulfilled, over most of the period, independently of national growth. Venezuela was an even more backward and remote area than those described so far, and interregional links were very poor until the motor car age (Santos 1973). Valencia, within 160 kilometres of Caracas, had no rail link until 1912, and most of the country was unconnected, as it remains, by rail lines. The Caracas region focused on the metropolis and had a port at La Guaira; the Aragua Valley basin looked towards Valencia and its port outlet at Puerto Cabello; the northern part of the Andes centred on Barquisimeto, with a rail line out to Tucacas and Puerto Cabello; while the whole enclosed Lake Maracaibo basin focused on Maracaibo City. In the interior the Llanos and the Orinoco system centred on the little town of Angostura (Ciudad Bolivar); to the south were the Indian territories of Guyana. As in Brazil, we may conclude that if a primate *national* urban structure was not to be found, it was because the nation was not a single urban system but a number of isolated, regional ones.

Concentration in national capitals and the role of government and commerce

The growth rates of the main cities of Latin America were the same as, or even less than, the national population growth rate until 1850, but in the late nineteenth century they moved ahead. This new growth is attributable partially to exports growth, as indicated above. But it must be remembered too that these exports were generally raw materials, derived from regions far away from the capitals, and often not even exported, in a geographical sense, through them. Although Buenos Aires and Montevideo could act physically as outlets to the Pampas, São Paulo to the coffee lands of southern Brazil, Georgetown to the sugar plantations of Guiana, Havana to those of Cuba, many capitals were not major ports for the new exports. In Chile Santiago could grow on the basis of nitrates from 1860 to the end of the century, followed by copper, and in both cases the far north was the producing and exporting region. Venezuela's export-led growth in the early twentieth century was based on oil from Maracaibo in the far west and Anzoategui in the Oriente, but the main visible result was the expansion of Caracus, neatly placed between the two. Even bogotá, slow-growing and little related to the outside world when coffee and textile manufactures were already stimulating the Antioqueño economy centred on Medellín, grew rapidly after 1870, though producing little itself. Capital-city growth throughout Latin America is thus due in general to the export trade but does not depend on the region.

A Latin American economist, Cordova (1973), attributed the growth of national capitals in this way to the introduction of a money economy, which permitted a physical separation between production and consumption zones. The profits on crude oil produced at Maracaibo and exported from there could thus be consumed at Caracas, through the operation of monetary chains linking the two. This explanation seems necessary but not sufficient; a money economy had been introduced long before, in the sense that some form of money had been used for payments, especially international payments, since the early colonial period, and money was certainly in use throughout the colonial period. Cordova seems to confuse here the survival of a feudal form, the use of tokens on *haciendas* for payment of workers (a system which allowed debt serfdom because the tokens could only be exchanged at the *haciendas'* own stores) with the existence of a generally non-monetary economy, a mistake he is forced into by his attempt to define capitalism and feudalism in narrowly monetary terms.

Reasons for the concentration of population in capital cities not involved in exporting are, of course, much more complex and too numerous to enumerate completely here. They include the growing role of administration and management in the more complex economy of modern times; the growing size of effective economic units, and thus of economic regions, linked to the birth and development of transport systems; the 'push' effects in rural areas, notably in the slave countries Cuba and Brazil, where free slaves moved into the cities, and in countries which received large numbers of immigrants, such as Argentina, where the migrants also ended up in big cities; and the rise of manufacturing industry.

It is not the purpose here to investigate all these aspects; they are common to most parts of the world. An important Latin American feature, however, would seem to be the role of government and commerce as opposed to industry. It has been shown already that foreign capital was essential to the development of the new export economies in the absence of sophisticated local money markets. Capital from Britain was essential to the development of guano in Peru and thus to the development of railways, which were built on the same financial foundations. British capital was also dominant in railway construction in Brazil, Argentina and most other South American countries. In Central America north American capital was most prominent in the later stages of concentration in the sugar-cane estates and mills of Cuba, and in mining in Chile or Mexico.

Governments and merchants were drawn inexorably into the production process and thus helped the emphasis on capital cities, as government agencies managed the investment of money and also regulated the consumption of revenue, all from capital cities. In Argentina the national government at Buenos Aires was implicated during the 1850s because of potential competition from the interior provinces and had actively to seek foreign funds, as did its competitor at Paraná, the government of the Confederation. Thereafter the national government was constantly involved in railway financing through its guarantee of interest rates on invested capital, its offer of land grants on the first lines and even, as on the Southern Railway to Bahia Blanca, its subsidy of £500 per kilometre built. Indubitably, all these were necessary financial operations in order to attract British railway builders, who had the safer options of Indian or European investment to take up if not attracted by high returns. The point is that the operation converted Argentina and other Latin governments into important economic–financial agents, and so also the capital cities into what Scobie (1972) calls 'commercial–bureaucratic cities'. In the case of Buenos Aires, employment measures are inadequate to demonstrate this, but Scobie shows that even on the basis of capital invested, which under-represents com-

Table 7 *Buenos Aires: distribution of capital investment in industry, by percentages, 1895–1914*

Year	Industry	Commerce	Industry as percentage of commerce
1895	95	167	56.7
1904	—	521	—
1909	324	724	44.8
1914	548	996	55.0

Source: Scobie (1972), p. 1070.

merce because it needs relatively little investment per unit of turnover, the city was commercial, not industrial. In 1895 capital in industry was 56.7 per cent that in commerce; in 1909, 44.8 per cent; in 1914, 55 per cent. Furthermore, 31.7 per cent of those industries which had developed were directly related to the agricultural export-oriented economy, and the remainder were very largely consumer industries easily introduced into any developing economy.

But Buenos Aires's growth, and that of Montevideo, which was similar, is to be explained by their position as gateways to the huge, fertile plains of the humid Pampas, as commercial and processing centres and ports. A better case for the involvement of government without any necessary regional associations is that of Peru in relation to guano. Here the resource exploited was on the tiny offshore Chinchas and Lobos Islands, in the period 1840–80. Ships could carry the guano, unprocessed, directly to foreign ports, without involving Lima–El Callao in any physical way. But as soon as the government had assessed the potential profit from export of guano, it took over the management of the resource (albeit unskilfully). In considerable need of revenue to pay for slave liberation

Table 8 *Chile: total and metropolitan population, 1865 and 1907*

Year	Total (000)	Santiago	+	Valparaíso	=	metropolis (000)
1865	1918	115		70		185
1907	3249	333		162		495
Increase	69%					168%

Source: Adapted from Morse (1971b), p. 54.

and war reparations, it sold concessions for guano extraction first to Peruvian entrepreneurs, then (inevitably) to British firms, since the Peruvian government had already indebted itself to Britain and had no other financial security to offer. We should not confuse metropolitan growth and national integration – Lima's growth from 56,000 in 1836 to 100,000 (or 134,000 including El Callao) in 1876, did not involve any real linking of the huge Sierran Indian population to the national capital or indeed any other major region. Chile's urban growth in the late nineteenth century was highly concentrated in the capital. If we include with Santiago its port, Valparaíso, at 97 kilometres' distance, metropolitan size far exceeds that of any competitor. And in the later decades of the century this metropolis grew at a rate more than double that of the country as a whole (see Table 8). Exports were primarily nitrates and copper (mine products were 78 per cent of exports in 1881) from the Norte Grande; but the control of these mines and their administration (as well as the administration of the war that secured the nitrate region for Chile) was at Santiago. It is, of course, true that Santiago benefited from the reorganization of agriculture, from export-trade orientation to production for internal markets, principally in the capital, which had built rail links with both the far north and the far south. But the key to Chilean wealth was nitrate exports. Government involvement in that industry was considerable up to the time of the Jorge Montt government of 1891–1901, which denationalized mines, most of the investments being taken up by British investors. But until 1920 the government received 29.4 per cent of earnings from nitrate exploitation as tax.

Small towns

The other side of the coin of great-city growth and dominance is the lack of a solid mass of small towns at the base of the urban hierarchy. Some of the reasons for this lack are the same as those for growth of the large city. Migrations from rural areas draining small towns go to fill large cities. But some additional points may be made, especially concerning the nature of rural production systems and societies. Under the impetus of the expansion of the primary sector for exports, production for markets was extended over scantily peopled areas such as the Argentine Pampas. But the technology of cattle ranching was extremely simple and, in the absence of a dense pre-existing population, evolved without the need for any of the urban functions of small towns. Cortes Conde (1968) has commented extensively on the slight population and lack of urban centres associated with expansion in Buenos Aires province during the nineteenth century, given the almost total self-sufficiency of the *gaucho*'s way of life and his independence of transport means, processing plants and land management of any kind in the traditional *estancia*. This *estancia* pattern may be contrasted with that established in the few areas of intensive cultivation and small farms which grew up in areas such as central Santa Fé and generally adjacent to the rail lines. Intensive farming created needs for urban services such as schools, churches and markets for the produce and for consumer goods, all of which were to be supplied from a network of small towns. In Santa Fé a fine net of *poblados*, between 500 and 5000 inhabitants in size, grew up after 1870. Whereas these settlements had comprised 3.5 per cent of the total population in 1858, they formed 16.0 per cent in 1895 (Balan 1976, p. 154). Balan similarly contrasts the urban experience in São Paulo's coffee areas. In the Paraíba valley, the early area of expansion in 1850–70, slave production involved a self-sufficient kind of unit, the plantation, with no need for towns. Later expansion in the west of the state and in Paraná state, was based on free farming and brought into being many small towns. Elsewhere the other export crops, rubber, sugar, cotton and cocoa, failed to stimulate towns because of their peculiar production systems, and in general the plantation type of unit, with its self-sufficiency and lack of need for any outside services or linked processing, meant a corresponding lack of small towns.

Growth and development processes and structures

We may classify the economic and social processes of the period in terms of the categories outlined in Chapter 1. In doing so, it will become apparent, if it is not already, that the neo-colonial phase is little different from the colonial one, either in its developmental processes or in the structures resulting from these. These latter may be given a spatial representation which is only a variant on that for the colonial period (see Figure 2, p. 34). The expansion of the agricultural area used for commercial export crops and the expansion of mining and other extractive activities, such as the mining of guano or collection of rubber, may be seen as simple growth processes. They spread unchallenged and without change across broad territories. Along with this growth of production there was the closely related spread of modern transport facilities, notably the railway, serving to carry the raw-material exports out to the coastal ports. Urban growth was itself relatively simple and undifferentiated, for most towns had the same local gathering and marketing functions, as well as administration, as they had in colonial times. There are more of them, but the qualitative differences are small.

Differentiation

These simple expansions of production, trade and marketing can be seen as a more complex growth-plus-differentiation process of development only if we look at them as part of a world process, with centres in Europe and the United States. Within such a scheme the ex-colonial areas are ones of dependent development – development which is induced and maintained by an outside country or set of countries. They are also to be seen as areas experiencing technological differentiation processes if we compare them one with another in terms of actual products and associated technology; thus the Pampas obviously becomes different from the north Chilean deserts because it extracts wheat and maize and cattle instead of nitrate deposits and uses a totally different set of tools to do so. But, underlying these differences, both areas exhibit a similar broad set of relations between producing peripheries raw materials and a single mother-country/market area which absorbs raw materials and exchanges them for its own manufactures. Both north Chile and the Pampas become, during the nineteenth century, part of the dependent periphery.

Complex growth and epigenesis — the regional industrialization areas

Within a few of the countries of Latin America a process of differentiation and development goes on at the level of individual country or region. In these cases the rise of manufacturing industry produces changes in the role of agriculture, trade and transport linkages and urban centres, which all now become more closely interrelated with one another than with distant European or North American market countries. Agriculture starts to feed local manufacturing labour forces; major trade links are now between the

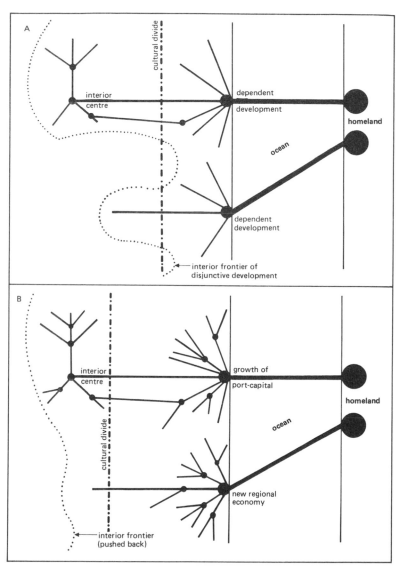

Figure 14   *Colonial (A) and neo-colonial (B) socio-economic structure.
Near the coast dependent development and some technological differentiation
are found. Beyond the cultural divide disjunctive development or differentiation is more common. Beyond the frontier a totally independent path is
followed by non-Europeanized groups. The neo-colonial period makes a
more powerful dependent development and extends its effects inland, but it
allows the continuation of disjunctive development and differentiation.*

towns of a region or between town and hinterland; and manufacturing comes to assume a more important role than administration and commerce. Instead of dependent development, this is a
semi-independent development process, with some (especially
initial) stimuli from the exterior but thereafter largely self-impelled
growth and differentiation.

Disjunctive differentiation

As in the colonial period, there is a continuing disjunctive differentiation between the export economy areas and others left
behind in the 'development' race. First, there remain large areas
beyond the frontier, occupied by primitive tribal peoples for the
most part. Second, there are cultural enclaves, largely in the Andean
area, where a social disjunction between market or redistributive
societies and the reciprocity and communal structure of simple
communities remain. Some of these enclaves may be isolated by the
lack of transport and communications, but these are not essential for
their survival. Roads, rails and cities have developed in upland Peru,
Bolivia and Ecuador without destroying old cultures.

These various facets of development may be portrayed in a
diagram which shows the different types of area in a schematic
manner (see Figure 14). Rather than any simple process of forward
development, or any classification depending on the specific technology of production or the final product, the diagram focuses on
the various degrees of dependence or independence from the
advanced countries and on differentiation processes. Only a schema
of the geographical patterns can be provided, for to give more detail
would require many specific models based on the production technology and forms of trade and marketing appropriate to each
product. As already stated, beneath all such specific variations a
broad general model may be perceived.

In the diagram the changes from the colonial model may be
summarized thus: the pushing back of spatial frontiers as new areas
are incorporated into commercial production; the growth of urban
places, especially the ports and major cities; the reinforcement of
transport links, but without changing their fundamental character,
that of radial patterns focused on the primate city.

5 The modern period

Rather than a new phase of development beginning with the twentieth century, new processes appear to take their place alongside older ones or only partially to replace or modify them. Centralization, a long-established tendency, is not superseded as a spatial–geographic structure, though it now operates at new scales and there are new factors to help explain its persistence. Traditional social structures survive along with the modern ones which are introduced into the more advanced regions, posing the problem of social differentiation.

Two of the central facts in this modern period, not new but presenting themselves with an unprecedented force, seem worth focusing on. One is the growth and spatial mobility of population. Absolute growth is due to improved sanitary and health conditions, which have had the same effects in Latin America as in the rest of the underdeveloped world, raising the survival rates for infants and thus diminishing the death rate without any corresponding effect on the birth rate for an interval which is, commonly, at least one generation. Demographers see this growth as a limited phase of transition before birth rates fall to match death rates, but during the transition there is heavy demographic pressure on finite resources in both rural and urban areas. Migration of people to new rural areas and especially to towns is related to population growth but can scarcely be seen as its sole cause. Industrialization is another major trend of the present century, closely associated with changes in urban function and rural economic activity, usually with overseas sources of technological advance and industrial ownership and with the demographic movements already noted.

These trends may now be examined in more detail, but alongside them we shall have cause to cite again the disjunction associated with primitive and traditional socio-economic structures. And even within the modern economy there are disjunctive elements which it

Table 9 *Urban and rural population, by country, 1960 and 1978*

Country	1960 Urban (000)	Rural (000)	Urban (%)	1978 Urban (000)	Rural (000)	Urban (%)
Argentina	15,172	5439	73.6	22,261	4128	84.4
Bolivia	887	2426	26.8	1545	3312	31.8
Brazil	32,598	38,160	46.1	72,277	44,116	62.1
Chile	5222	2479	67.8	8682	2175	80.0
Colombia	7420	7977	48.2	18,165	7299	71.3
Costa Rica	410	844	32.7	957	1197	44.4
Ecuador	1515	2821	34.9	3248	4213	43.5
El Salvador	935	1498	38.4	1763	2634	40.1
Guatemala	1332	2633	33.6	2050	4572	31.0
Guyana	164	414	28.4	359	466	43.5
Honduras	438	1457	23.1	1183	2256	34.4
Mexico	17,705	17,218	50.7	42,574	24,370	63.6
Nicaragua	545	875	38.4	1327	1066	55.5
Panama	441	621	41.5	957	868	52.4
Paraguay	605	1105	35.4	1047	1841	36.3
Peru	4630	5392	46.2	11,384	5452	67.6
Uruguay	2006	477	80.8	2304	548	80.8
Venezuela	4901	2451	66.7	10,060	3095	76.5
Latin America	99,285	101,334	49.5	208,014	121,431	63.1

Sources: Inter-American Development Bank 1978 Report (Washington 1979), p. 415; Stöhr (1975), p. 49.

is worth exploring, even if they may be regarded as local and temporary dysfunctions of the capitalist system.

Population growth and migration

Throughout Latin America the growth of population places a strain directly on rural resources and indirectly, through migration, on urban places as well. Population increases (Table 9) are currently lower than their peak in recent years, which was generally above 3 per cent per annum. But Mexico, the Central American countries and a few others maintain a very high rate of over 3 per cent annually, and only Argentina at 1.4 per cent, Chile at 1.9 per cent and Uruguay at 0.8 per cent have achieved levels comparable with those of Western Europe.

It is of interest to examine the relationship between absolute population growth and a major interregional process of this century, migration. In the densely peopled uplands of the Andean countries, in the Caribbean, in Mexico and generally in those areas where high rural population densities are already found rural–urban migration may be seen as a reaction to rising population pressure. This last term is a slippery one, but we may regard it, from an economic standpoint, as unemployment and poverty resulting from inadequate local resources. Migration would thus be an economic response to this poverty and, following neoclassical economic principles, would move labour from low- to high-wage regions – that is, to the towns.

Table 10 would seem to corroborate such ideas, for it shows that urban wages are consistently higher, by a substantial margin, than agricultural, and that they are possibly higher in buying capacity even after allowance for the urban cost of living and rural non-money incomes has been made. Certainly, if we regard population pressure as related direct to physical resources, no sense can be made of the migration pattern, for Table 9 shows rural–urban migration to be high in Argentina, where effective out-migration of 5 per cent per annum is the interpretation of a − 1.5 per cent growth of rural population. In this country and in many others with marked rural–urban migration, there is an abundance of land for settlers, if this were the only or the main factor involved.

Moving at once to more sophisticated models of migration, the standard neoclassical economics version is exemplified by Herrick (1972). He begins by rejecting a gravity-model formulation of

Table 10 *Wages in agriculture and manufacturing, 1963–75*

Country	Year									
	1963	1967	1968	1969	1970	1971	1972	1973	1974	1975
Argentina[a]										
Agriculture	0.19	0.76	0.82	0.91	1.14	1.75	2.5	3.74	6.41	16.83
Manufacturing	0.40	1.22	1.27	1.40	1.65	2.27	3.31	5.82	7.49	20.33
Chile[b]										
Agriculture	35.8	134.4	156.2	209.4	336	560	840	1773.2	23,035	123.2[c]
Manufacturing	100.1	391.5	525.2	722.4	1042	1481	2408	7265.0	45,766	205.5[c]
Mexico[c]										
Agriculture	305.8	440.2	513	513	593.6	593.6	698.3	767.2	1058.1	1290.8
Manufacturing	1135.0	1468.0	1544	1621	1703.0	1851.0	1956.0	2202.0	2815.0	3424.0

[a] Pesos per hour; 1963–9 converted to new pesos to make uniform series. The differences agriculture/manufacture are greater than those shown because agricultural rates are the average and manufacturing are minimum rates.

[b] Monthly rates; for agriculture the calculation is an estimate from day rates, multiplying by 28, which probably exaggerates real wages.

[c] In 1975 the currency was changed; one peso = 1000 old escudos.

Source: Calculated from data given in *Statistical Abstract of Latin America*, vol. 19 (1979), pp. 170–2.

migration, which seems a dangerous start in view of the number of good approximations which have been made to migration processes with such models. Instead it is proposed that the difference in returns in economic terms will explain migration patterns. Migration is the function of three variables: the difference in returns before and after migration, the difference in costs before and after and the length of time the prospective migrant will expect to spend at his destination. The first two are economic variables, the last a potentially non-economic one, though Herrick sees it in an economic light – that is, he proposes that net returns from the decision to migrate will depend on the length of time the migrant expects to stay, and thus the extra wages that the migrant may receive, at his new, urban, higher-paying job. Major features such as the age selectivity of migration can thus be explained by the long prospective life in the towns for these migrants. Female migration and the migration of the skilled are explained in terms of higher differences in wage. Some characteristics are not readily explained in these terms, however. Much migration is of a gradual nature, a movement of rural people into small towns, and of townsfolk into large cities, up to the metropolis level. For any family this may occur either in one lifetime or over several generations (Gilbert and Sollis 1979), but in either case it reflects not a simple appraisal of differences in economic returns but a pattern of widening horizons of knowledge. Information about, and a positive perception of, urban conditions and opportunities diffuse out only slowly from towns to their hinterlands, and in isolated areas only the opportunities available in the nearest town are understood and considered. As the migrants move up the urban hierarchy, their information and their ability to assess the information they receive is improved, and they may move on to the places of greater opportunity, the large cities.

Another information-related characteristic is apparently the declining selectivity of migrants through time. Cardona and Simmons (1975) report, on the basis of several Latin American studies in different countries, that in early stages those with more initiative, education or wealth move out, while at a later point in time migration becomes generalized in all segments of society in the rural source areas. It is not easy to interpret such moves as purely economic, especially as this latter-day mass migration often comes when the metropolitan city has insufficient jobs to provide for the huge increases of population and must place migrants in the informal urban sector, without capital investment or firm organization. What seems to happen is a change in perception of the large city so as to discount initial hardships, perhaps to an excessive extent. If income differentials were the principal factor at work in promoting migration, there would, in fact, have to be a reversal of the current order, for the differences of income at the higher levels of urban and rural income are much smaller than those at the bottom, according to Colombian data (Berry and Urrutia 1976).

Even within the destination city, movement may be understood partially as a pattern of improvements of information and perception. Migrants are found to move first to the central-city slums (for example, Bogotá; see Flinn 1971) and then out to the shanty towns surrounding the city. As initial migrants, without much knowledge of or contacts in the city, they are forced to accept the central city's rented accommodation. Later they acquire information, perhaps join a social group and move to a squatter zone as a group. There may, in addition, be important psychological elements in migration behaviour, so that the early migrants are from among the more adventurous, enterprising or optimistic types (Cardona and Simmons 1975, pp. 31–2). But these factors are not commonly thought of as operating in any regionally biased manner, and their effect must, for the purposes of this exposition, be overlooked.

The urban network has been emphasized in migration studies. There are other types of movement, including the rural–rural type, the movements of colonization towards unoccupied or thinly settled land, but these are much smaller. There is nothing comparable with the late nineteenth-century/early twentieth-century colonization, when, for example (Bourde 1974), two-thirds of a net 3.5 million migrants to Argentina in the period 1857–1941 moved out into the provinces, to rural areas and small towns, and similar movements occurred in southern Brazil and Uruguay. In modern times the rural colonists are relatively insignificant, despite government schemes for the purpose. In Peru, for example, the 1940–60 migration gain of the eastern *selvas* provinces, Loreto, San Martín and Amazonas, was about 100,000, but most of this (69,000) went to Loreto and thus probably to Iquitos (Dollfus 1973, p. 229) rather than to rural areas. This slight colonization compares with a migration gain of probably 600,000 by Lima in the same period.

As for the international flows, the period of massive intercontinental movements is past, and the only country to have accepted important numbers of Europeans since World War II is Venezuela,

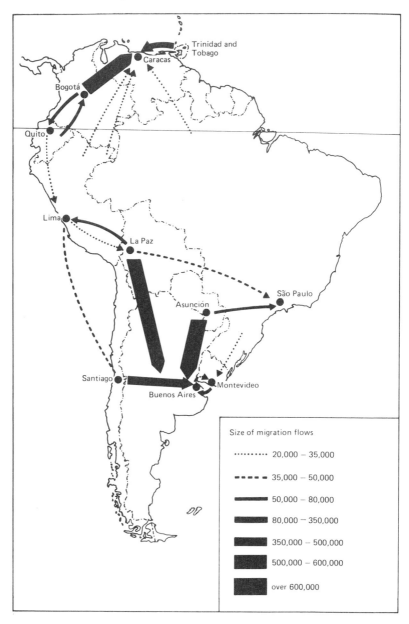

Figure 15   *International migration flows in South America, 1975 (based on International Labour Organization data). Migration fields focusing on Buenos Aires and Caracas are the most notable features.*

where 350,000 entered in the period 1950–60. Of these 190,000 went to Caracas (Arriaga 1968). In recent years even this flow has declined, and now international movements are mostly between neighbour countries, forming a network which is effectually only an extension of the regional and interregional migration nets which focus on big cities. International migration leads from the poor, more rural countries towards the metropolises of the more wealthy countries, so that, for example, Argentina is a major recipient of migrants from Chile, Bolivia, Paraguay, Uruguay and parts of Brazil, while Venezuela is a recipient of Colombians, Trinidadians and other West Indies people. A macroregional structure emerges (Figure 15) focusing on Buenos Aires, São Paulo and Rio (though in Brazil the network is largely internal to the country), Caracas and Mexico City, with hinterlands many hundreds of kilometres in radius.

Migration and the regions

For the most part migration may be seen as a movement draining rural regions of resources and centralizing development in towns. As the migratory movement siphons off skilled sections of the community from the earliest stages, it drains the community of leaders and innovators and makes change or adaptation difficult. It is thus a contributor to the 'backwash' effects identified by Myrdal (1957) and others who regard economic development as an inherently unbalancing process.

It might be supposed that there would be backflows from the migrants, through their return to the community with new skills, through their transmission of funds to the village and family or through the provision of information to help the farmer improve his lot. In fact, such flows are minimal in effect. Most migrants do not return; those who do are often the failed migrants who have learned least of value from their urban experience, and they generally move out of agriculture into commerce or other fields, passing on little new knowledge about agriculture. As to remittances, in money or in kind, the evidence (Connell *et al*. 1976, ch. 5) is that the flows are slight and often the net flow is outwards from village to town, so that the village, despite its poverty, is subsidizing the city, especially the new migrants without full employment and the students. Doughty (1968) describes the case of Huaylas, a small Peruvian town with a strong community spirit, where the migrants to Lima have an organization that contributes regularly to home-town public funds. Browning and Feindt (1971, ch. 3) show predominantly outflows from Monterrey, Mexico. But such organizations and flows cannot be found widely in Latin America. Migration does not even seem to release land for the village because many migrants, both to new rural areas and to the city, retain their farms after moving away, in the first case because they may choose to operate farms in several different areas at once (Stearman 1978) and, in the second, simply because the farms provide insurance against misfortune and the migrants have emotional ties to the land.

For the large city the migration flows are obviously important, as they bring in a new, young labour force to match new capital investment in the city. Something of a controversy has surrounded the demographic contribution of rural migrants to city growth (see Weller, Macisco and Martine 1971), but the consensus of opinion now is that rural–urban migration is a large component, larger than natural increase in urban growth. An estimate for Rio de Janeiro, for example, is that in-migration accounted for 66.7 per cent of its 1940–50 increase and 45 per cent in 1950–60. Buenos Aires's growth was 72 per cent as a result of net in-migration in the 1950s. The role of this massive contribution to industrialization cannot be overestimated.

Migration and involution

Clifford Geertz (1963) describes a process, for Indonesia, of change induced in agriculture of the *sawah* (wet rice) type by continued population pressure insufficiently relieved by either migration or growth of the cultivated area. This kind of agriculture was able to absorb large amounts of extra labour by making economic life more complex, by using more assiduous hand labour in cultivation and irrigation and by developing more complicated, inter-meshed land-tenure forms, a series of measures he calls involution. This is a non-growth, non-development form of adjustment to the pressure of rising population and diminishing land resources. In Latin America this kind of response is less evident, at least at the present day, perhaps because of land availability and the possibility of migration to towns; though in some areas of strong community organization and intensive irrigation agriculture, as in upland Andean America, it may well be operative. (See below, pp. 139–44. Land availability may be less important than social structure; in Indonesia

Outer Indonesia presents abundant land resources for the colonist, but there is a great reluctance to take it up. The large areas of tropical lowland America have similarly been of slight attraction to upland villagers in most countries.)

What is more obvious is a parallel to this in the urban scene, where large numbers of migrants accumulate, seeking work and without any immediate possibility of absorption into the 'formal' urban sector (into modern industries, that is, and services run by firms with capital). Instead it is forced into an 'informal' sector of family business, using large inputs of labour and virtually none of capital, mostly in the tertiary sector but also in craft manufactures and transport, and this may be regarded as a process of urban involution in order to survive (McGee 1971). The production of cheap clothes and furniture, the sale of all kinds of convenience goods from the streets without permanent shops, the service industries of haircutting, general jobbing, house construction or repair in the shanty zones all come into this sector. Although no precise measure of its extent has been made, this urban involution is particularly apparent in the largest cities, and as the informal sector relies heavily on in-migrants, it may be seen as in part a function of the modernization of industry and migration movements.

Industrialization

In considering Latin American development in this century some writers have focused less on demographic change than on the modernization of industry. Giving a tag to the age, the twentieth century is a period of manufacturing or of import substitution, to specify the usual mechanism of industrialization. For most countries there has been a change in their economic role, as seen from the West, from producers of primary commodities for export to partially industrialized states with diversified economies.

The general picture of a gross economic change might be challenged in terms of some kinds of statistical indices. Table 11 shows that although specific products change, the leading exports are still primary products for the majority of countries. It is significant that only the largest countries, Mexico, Argentina and Brazil, have a diversified export structure, including many manufactures. As a proportion of Gross Domestic Product (GDP), however, manufacturing is much more important, reaching over 50 per cent in Argentina and falling below 25 per cent only in Guatemala, Para-

Table 11   *Two leading exports: share of total export value*

Country	1955 Exports	% of total	1975 Exports	% of total
Argentina	Cereals	27.4	Corn	17.5
	Meats	26.3	Wheat	10.2
Bolivia	Tin	54.9	Tin	41.1
	Wolframite	13.4	Petroleum	25.8
Brazil	Coffee	60.8	Sugar	11.2
	Cacao	5.0	Iron ore	10.6
Chile	Metal and ores	85.6	Copper	66.6[b]
	Iron	3.8	Nitrates	20.0[b]
Colombia	Coffee	76.7	Coffee	41.4[b]
	Petroleum	14.9	Petroleum	2[b]
Costa Rica	Coffee	48.6	Bananas	27.1
	Bananas	38.7	Coffee	19.8
Cuba	Sugar	81.2	Sugar	74.6[a]
	Tobacco	5.9	Nickel cobalt	14.7[a]
Ecuador	Bananas	35.6	Petroleum	56.6
	Coffee	30.4	Bananas	17.0
El Salvador	Coffee	78.2	Coffee	32.7
	Cotton	15.6	Cotton	14.8
Guatemala	Coffee	79.0	Coffee	25.0
	Bananas	8.0	Sugar	17.8
Honduras	Bananas	61.1	Coffee	20.1
	Coffee	19.0	Bananas	15.9
Mexico	Cotton	14.5	Coffee	6.3
	Coffee	13.2	Cotton	5.9
Nicaragua	Coffee	34.4	Cotton	25.4
	Cotton	30.6	Coffee	12.8
Panama	Bananas	64.0	Ref. petroleum	45.5
	Shrimp	25.8	Bananas	21.0
Paraguay	Woods	37.2	Meat	18.2
	Quebracho extract	20.4	Timber	16.0
Peru	Cotton	25.1	Copper	23.2[b]
	Lead	11.9	Fishmeal	13.0[b]
Uruguay	Wool	51.0	Wool	22.5
	Meat	19.7	Meat	19.1
Venezuela	Petroleum	91.9	Petroleum	95.2
	Iron ore	4.8	Iron ore	2.4[b]
United States	Manufactured goods	54.8	Machinery	39.3
	Semi-manufactured goods	15.6	Food, live animals	14.4

Notes: [a] = 1972; [b] = 1974.

Source: Inter-American Development Bank 1978 Report (Washington 1979), p. 466.

guay and Haiti in the 1970–4 period. Despite recent rises in raw-material prices, the drift of their contribution to exports and to GDP is downwards relative to a growing manufacturing and service sector.

Import substitution

Most countries of the region had only a very modest manufacturing establishment at the beginning of the century. Primary-goods exports required few industrial inputs in order to extract or process them; items such as cane crushers, mining machinery and railways from mine to port were complicated items needed in small quantities at irregular intervals and it was not worth establishing local industries to cater to demand. But a number of factors – including the increased contact with Europe and North America which fostered demand for new goods, then war isolation from supplies in 1914–18 – combined with growing urban concentrations of demand, which now passed the threshold size for the establishment of many light industries in countries such as Mexico, Chile, Argentina and Peru, to produce beer, matches or glass bottles.

In the case of Chile, isolated by the Andes and by distance from Europe, industry had built up at the time of the War of the Pacific (1879–84) to meet government demands for war material. Manufacturing growth was also related to the growth of nitrate exports, which provided good government revenues up to 1914. It was also related, as Kirsch (1973) shows, to the same group which managed the import–export business and the country's great estates, a small social elite, partly immigrant, which effectively controlled the country. In other words – and this is true for other industrializing countries – manufacturing came as an extension of commercial interests developed in the period of primary-export economy, not as a new, hostile or competitive interest. Since the same power group was involved and the same interests were represented, neither the pattern of economic activity nor the process of centralization was severely disrupted – considerable continuity was provided by the entrepreneurs.

For Peru industrial expansion began in the 1890s in relatively prosperous times and was based on substantial profits from cotton and sugar, reinvested by the local elite in cotton- and wool-textile manufacturing, flour milling, brewing and other light consumer-goods industry. Peruvian industry failed to expand after 1910, when effective tariff protection declined and capital moved back into primary export production where the profit margins were more attractive. As in Chile, the links were with the existing commercial interests, but in this case industry failed to expand because these interests moved back into primary exports when manufacturing became less profitable. World War I failed to stimulate manufactures, as Peru was never isolated from a supplier, the United States (Thorp and Bertram 1975). A similar relation to commercial enterprise is evident in Brazil, where from the late nineteenth century (Morse 1971a) the coffee merchants and plantation aristocracy saw possibilities for investment based on São Paulo's centrality in a transport network linking it to many prosperous small towns and a hinterland which provided both materials and markets for new products.

Stimuli to industrial growth came with the Depression years, then with World War II, cutting off supplies from overseas; and in two major countries, Argentina and Brazil, the populist government under Perón (1945–55) and Vargas (1930–45) promoted industrial and infrastructural growth at the expense of agriculture.

The principal state mechanism aiding industrialization was the erection of tariff barriers against imports, making them more expensive and thus less desirable than new local substitutes or equivalents. As imports were already mostly consumer goods, it was these kinds of goods which were encouraged as local products. Imports of capital or intermediate goods were not important for several reasons. First, there were few existing manufacturers of a modern description to form a demand for machinery to use in factories. Manufacture of such items as rails or wagons would not be undertaken for the internal market because demand was so irregular and so unpredictable. In addition, as already noted, the manufacturing sector was controlled by a small elite with capital that had no absolute commitment to industry and could fairly readily switch its investments into urban speculation, farming or other activities. Heavy capital investment in manufacturing would have compromised this mobility.

Consumer-goods imports were thus dominant, and as the governmental aim was usually to promote revenues rather than to protect infant industry, tariffs were placed on most current imports, and protection of consumer goods manufacturing was the effective result. The smaller capital requirements of these industries were a positive attraction – capital was a difficulty in the absence of a fluid capital market. Modern banks were in existence by 1900 but did not cater effectively for industries except through rather cumbersome mortgage loans. Yet another consumer-industry link was that the merchants, who initiated manufacturing in many republics, were most familiar with, and interested in handling, those consumer goods which they were already importing. They saw the possibility of replacing such imports with local manufactures and knew the channels by which the products could be marketed, as shown for Chile by Kirsch (1973).

Utilities and capital-goods industries

Another quite distinct route towards industrialization has been adopted with respect to some kinds of manufacture. For the public utilities such as telephone and telecommunications, railways and tramlines, power and light companies, and for some heavy industries such as steel, chemicals and ore refining, concentrating the use of import tariffs was not effective because of the large scale of capital inputs and the advanced technology they required. These industries had to be set up either as branches or subsidiaries of foreign firms or by national governments. In the case of many such industries the public 'visibility' of the foreign companies and their obvious links with the exterior were strong incentives for movements to expropriate them.

In Argentina the telephone system was acquired from International Telephone and Telegraph in 1946 to form a state agency; the railways followed in 1948. In Chile the copper industry was progressively taken over under Frei between 1964 and 1970, then fully expropriated under Allende. Railways in Mexico were nationalized in 1937 and petroleum production in 1938. In 1960–1 the electric power utilities were taken over. In Guyana (formerly British Guiana) bauxite mining and alumina manufacture have been expropriated, and in 1976 the country's major industrial firm, based on sugar-cane production and milling but with ramifications in all sectors, was taken over from Booker McConnell. In Peru the 1968 military government assumed direct control of oil refining and petrochemicals, cement, paper, fertilizers and fishmeal, as well as taking over the public utilities in their entirety. The list could be extended considerably, but the pattern is similar in other countries.

Nationalization is not, of course, the only means of acquiring heavy industries. Political factors have favoured the growth of an integrated iron and steel industry in Argentina, Chile, Peru, Venezuela and Brazil through direct state investment in these industries, although the market in these countries is not large enough to support the most economic size of unit for this industry, which now approaches 10 million tonnes of crude-steel output per annum. With the advantage of a long and increasingly important flow of oil royalties to the state, Venezuela has long been able to afford state ownership of industries. Apart from the nationalization, with full compensation, of the oil industry in 1977 and the iron-ore industry in 1976, she has set up sugar and rice-milling industries and hydroelectric power installations and is rapidly building up steel industries and heavy engineering. During World War II Brazil too set up steel-making works at Volta Redonda, alkali factories, lorry-making plants and iron ore mines (Dickenson 1978, p. 10).

Foreign ownership has not been reduced to low levels for industry in many countries, and industrial growth spurred by foreign investment is still particularly strong in a few. An example is Venezuela, where Caracas has a substantial pharmaceuticals and fine-chemicals industry (detergents, soap powders, photographic materials, paints), built up on the basis of bulk concentrate imports, which are only subdivided and packaged in the country, no real processing taking place. In vehicle assembly, in Caracas, Barcelona and Valencia, a further stage is reached because parts are imported which must be assembled into the finished vehicle. But in these industries the major link remains that with the exterior; they are little more than devices for crossing the high tariff wall on finished goods. Brito Figueroa (1975, p. 772) reports a study in Venezuela in which 430 major firms which collectively dominate the nation's industry were found to have foreign mother companies. Of these, 104 were in commerce, most of the rest having manufacturing plants of the assembly type, notably cars, chemicals and foodstuffs.

In Brazil the 'economic miracle' of the 1960s is no doubt ascribable to foreign investment, and multinationals have had here the best investment climate in Latin America. They account for a third of the invested capital (Cunningham 1979, p. 219) and, in selected sectors, even more – in pharmaceuticals 86 per cent, motor vehicles 100 per cent, rubber goods 100 per cent, glass 90 per cent and vehicle components 62 per cent. Heavy industries such as iron and steel or petroleum have been placed in the hands of state firms.

Separate origins are thus apparent for the consumer and capital-goods industries. In view of the difference in their evolution, it might be anticipated that there would be few linkages between them, and this is indeed the case. Most consumer industries are set up in relation to labour supplies and to final markets – in the large towns – but not to their inputs of capital goods. Conversely, the great public enterprises (steel works, refineries, power plants) are not set up with particular regard to local consumer industries and are indeed often oriented, especially those under or formerly under foreign control, to overseas markets.

This structure is made still more disconnected by the way in which individual entrepreneurs have built up their industrial empires. There is no quantitative information on this point, and an example must suffice. Torcuato di Tella was born in Italy in 1892 and migrated as a boy to Argentina to begin manufacturing with a bread-kneading machine patented in 1911 (Cochran and Reina 1962). He then expanded into petrol-pump manufacture in the 1920s and from there built up the SIAM–Di Tella industrial empire, with products as varied as service-station equipment, steel storage tanks and motor-vehicle assembly, predominantly through a process of horizontal expansion into the manufacture of already known products by well-established methods, rather than by slowly creating the home-grown technology needed for vertical integration (Cochran and Reina 1962, p. 91). Capital needs for these additions to the empire were also much lower than large-scale investments in backwards vertical linkage.

In sum, the consumer-goods orientation of much industry, the lack of vertical linkages in industry and the links with overseas investment and entrepreneurship are seen as a set of historical factors promoting a strong central concentration of manufacturing. Another set may be regarded as more directly economic and are commonly grouped together as the 'urban agglomeration' factor. This is a compound of the various kinds of external economy available to the manufacturer in the big city: a large labour pool, its high level and variety of skills, infrastructure such as power, light, water and transport, even buildings, and the ready availability of capital, management, advertising and other services.

This 'agglomeration' factor is difficult to tie down, although its elements are readily identified. One attempt to measure its *effects* has been made for Brazil (Boisier, Smolka and Barros 1973). In this study of manufacturing employment and productivity the separate effects on productivity of sectoral concentration, size of firm and city size are calculated from official data, and although these elements work together – in the sense that more productive industrial sectors, with larger and more efficient plant, concentrate in the cities, where 'agglomeration' economies are also at work – city size alone (the 'agglomeration factor') is found to have a separate, identifiable effect. Table 12 illustrates the constant finding of higher indices in larger urban centres.

The largest cities, Rio and São Paulo, attracting the largest industrial establishments and the most productive industrial sectors, have an immense advantage in industrial productivity in this way, and the productivity effect is also found to be regional in character, the Sudeste region (Rio, São Paulo and Minas) having a productivity double that of the Norte region (Pará and Amazonas). A second group of factors may thus be agreed to be 'agglomerational'. But a third set seems to be related to information and perception of information by the entrepreneur as decision-maker. This also acts as a strong centralizing factor because of the limited field of knowledge and biased perceptions of the decision-makers. Part of the reason for concentration of go-ahead, productive types of manufacturing and of larger plants in the big cities are the decision-making processes of the industrialist rather than objective advantages. Explaining, for example, the overwhelming concentration of industry in metropolitan centres, Browning (1975) notes, first, knowledge of the major city as an industrial location as opposed to ignorance about provincial towns; second, the role of contacts with the government which may help establishment and growth of the industry; and third, the 1945–70 immigration, which principally helped one country and city, Caracas in Venezuela, but to a lesser degree also other cities and other countries, in bringing in new skills and information from abroad.

Table 12 *Productivity indices for different city sizes, 1969*

| Establishments | Urban centres | | | |
	Small	Medium	Large	Total
Small	11.34	14.36	15.69	14.58
Medium	11.82	15.03	17.08	15.42
Large	13.35	16.95	22.66	19.72
Total	12.70	16.28	20.83	18.28

Source: Boisier *et al.* (1973), p. 131.

Inductive studies of specific industries or countries to back up this behavioural interpretation of industrial location are not easy to find. One study of the entrepreneurs themselves is that by Gilbert (1974a), who sought to explain the increasing predominance of the four major cities of Colombia, Cali, Bogotá, Medellín and Barranquilla, by urban and industrial growth during recent decades. His explanation is twofold, based partly on hypothesized urban economies of scale and 'agglomeration' and partly (and more specifically) on the presence of government agencies with which the industrialist had particular need to deal in the big cities. A need to negotiate with the official for import licences was a specific feature of the Colombian scene.

These remarks do not add up to a model of industrial location for Latin America, and it is not the purpose of this work to provide one. But the important components of such a model may be enumerated. They include (a) purely economic factors, such as the cost of raw materials and other inputs, size and distribution of market, and transportation costs; (b) urban 'agglomeration' factors, including the access to many external economies (this factor may be regarded as one of *availability* rather than access to such facilities, for outside the cities such economies may be simply absent, not just more expensive as a result of greater distances); (c) structural factors due to historical evolution – lack of vertical integration, consumer-goods orientation, overseas ties; (d) the environment for decision-makers, which really includes all elements from (a), (b) and (c), but particularly the geography of the industrialist's information field and his perception of this information.

Agriculture

It may seem unfair to leave the description of agricultural change to follow that of demographic and industrial change; many writers would regard agriculture as the central theme in modern Latin America. But agricultural change may also be seen as deriving in great measure from other important trends, and in many of the republics it is closely associated with the demographic and manufacturing evolution (in a passive sense, not as a lead sector). Agricultural growth has been mostly in the form of area expansion, to meet two kinds of demand. First, population increases have created a demand for land to feed the national population, as in the colonization areas in Paraguay, Peru, Bolivia, Ecuador, Colombia and Brazil around the rim of the Amazon Basin, whether spontaneous or under government supervision. Second, some areas of commercial-crop monoculture have expanded to meet foreign demand, perhaps aided by increases in local demand.

Table 13 shows the growth of production to be a matter more of expanding area than of increasing yields. The maize area, for example, has expanded in almost every country of Latin America, very largely to meet domestic needs. But yield increases are substantially smaller, except in Mexico where 'Green Revolution' technology was applied principally and most successfully to the large commercial farms of the north, and where a very low yield (0.75 tons per hectare) in the base period meant a massive yield increase by 1976. In some countries (Chile, Colombia, Ecuador, Peru, Venezuela) the wheat-growing area is contracting, and this has encouraged some increase in yields, as when area is reduced only the better suited and most profitable areas are left in production. For sugar cane and beans areal expansions are, again, far larger than rises in yield, and the expansion of the area of beans in Brazil, Chile, Ecuador, Paraguay has been at the expense of yields. This pattern could be extended by reference to other crops and products, but the message is clear. Only countries like El Salvador, with a high pressure of population on the land resource, or Mexico, with special access to technology, have achieved both yield and area expansion for most major crops.

Table 13 *Agricultural expansion: percentage increase in area and yield (over 1948–52 average) for selected crops, 1976*

Country	Crop			
	Maize (% increase)	*Wheat* (% increase)	*Sugar cane** (% increase)	*Dry bean* (% increase)
Argentina				
Area	58.9	59.9	49.8	35.8
Yield	30.1	35.7	−6.0	25.0
Bolivia				
Area	96.6	37.7	138.0	200.0
Yield	−6.5	36.7	28.2	0.0
Brazil				
Area	140.1	426.5	48.1	239.1
Yield	27.8	21.6	6.2	−29.4

Table 13 *Continued*

Country	Maize (% increase)	Wheat (% increase)	Crop Sugar cane* (% increase)	Dry bean (% increase)
Chile				
Area	122.9	−11.1	—	5.2
Yield	79.6	2.5	—	−5.4
Colombia				
Area	−11.4	−71.1	28.6	7.4
Yield	32.0	69.0	12.4	26.4
Costa Rica				
Area	12.0	—	66.7	29.6
Yield	12.1	—	32.4	21.9
Ecuador				
Area	136	−1.8	28.2	215
Yield	33.3	104.8	−24.0	−51.7
El Salvador				
Area	26.4	—	48.0	41.7
Yield	92.7	—	77.1	1.2
Mexico				
Area	70.7	31.9	17.4	100
Yield	70.7	378.4	14.8	142
Paraguay				
Area	236.9	1650	75.0	215
Yield	−1.0	28.4	1.5	−8.5
Peru				
Area	109.4	−11.4	7.5	103
Yield	15.9	10.4	9.0	−18
Venezuela				
Area	54.8	−80.0	34.5	−3.6
Yield	13.3	−29.0	18.9	−30.0

* The sugar cane percentage change is calculated over the 1961–5 average.

Source: Based on statistics in *Statistical Abstract of Latin America 1978* (Los Angeles, Ca.), sect. 15, pp. 178–86.

Such findings may seem surprising in view of the history of 'Green Revolution' farming, which began in Mexico in 1943 and whose results might logically be expected to have diffused to neighbour countries earlier and more effectively than to other parts of the world. In fact, the diffusion to Latin America from Mexico, with the exception of Colombia, was slight; the new dwarf wheat types, for example, were more effectively diffused in the 1960s to India and the Middle East and in the 1970s to North Africa (Jones 1977). But it is understandable in view of the structural difficulties (small farms, lack of capital, poor access to markets) of most Latin American farmers: the use of the new varieties of crops requires heavier inputs of fertilizers, irrigation, more care and expenditure on seed, all capital expenditures which are difficult to justify in countries of the region.

Most countries have a large unused land reserve and have been able to draw freely on it for the expansion of production. In Mexico, for example, there has been active colonization, under government guidance, of three north-western river basins, the Yaqui, the Mayo and the Fuerte, since 1951 (Dozier 1963). These desert valleys have been used to expand the areas under rice, sugar cane, cotton and vegetables as part of a regional development scheme involving also industrial development and power production. Similarly, plans for the improvement of the basin of the Tepalcatepec tributary of the Balsas were approved in 1938 and later expanded into a scheme for the whole of the Balsas; and in the south-east the Papaloapan (1947) and Grijalvas basins were colonized in the post-war era. Thus Mexico's increases in production have not been the product solely of a 'Green Revolution' in productivity, using new strains of seed, higher inputs of fertilizer and so on but also of expanding farmland, with a 28 per cent increase from 1960 to 1975.

Mexican agricultural expansion has been a response to the needs of a rapidly growing population and (especially) growing urban markets. It has seen, in consequence, the development of a wide variety of food and industrial crops, a diversified agriculture not dominated by one crop or by a few producers. Agricultural expansion of a somewhat different kind, relating back to an older pattern described in the last chapter, may be cited from some countries, where commercial agriculture expands onto new lands for export markets. For example, until after 1900 Honduras in Central America had nearly all its scanty population in the central and southern highlands, centred on Tegucigalpa, the capital. Since then another economic focus has emerged in the banana plantations area around the town of San Pedro Sula, in the Ulua river basin. A whole new market-oriented agricultural region has come into being for the purpose of producing exportable bananas – a region, culturally and economically distinct from the interior, where a traditional Indian population lives at subsistence levels on *minifundio*-type holdings in symbiosis with the traditional great cattle ranches, the *latifundios*. The coast has a large Negro element; its farms are largely geared for commercial production; and it is oriented outwards, especially to the dominant United States market.

Such cases may be viewed not as expanding farmlands related to domestic markets, as in Mexico, but as new additions to the examples of nineteenth-century-style development based on one or two primary commodities. Following Honduras's colonial and post-colonial dependence on mining in the interior (West and Augelli 1966), bananas were exported from the 1860s and soon came under the control of the United Fruit Company in the Ulua valley and under Standard Fruit on the coastal plain further east. These two foreign companies became responsible for all development, constructing ports and railways and other infrastructure for the export economy and providing the main source of Honduran government funds. In more recent decades old plantations have been affected by disease, abandoned and put to subsistence farming or converted to oil-palm or sugar-cane production, but the neo-colonial or primary-export-based economy remains. At present coffee, bananas and timber between them account for 63 per cent (in 1975–7) of Honduran exports, and the links are primarily to the United States and Western Europe. The staple export development of the other Central American republics is similar in many ways to that of Honduras, especially Costa Rica's with its banana lands around Limon on the Caribbean and, more recently, also on the Pacific lowlands, and Guatemala's, with banana, cotton and rice production on the lowland areas of the Pacific slopes and coffee on the intermediate slopes.

It has been claimed above that agricultural trends were stimulated by population and industrial change. In the case of these export economies growth is obviously not locally inspired, but a response to demographic and industrial change in the developed countries of the West. In geographic terms, the difference is important: rather than centring entirely on the burgeoning capital city, completely separate growth areas have developed, with links outwards. Although money transfers and economic and political control from the capital are likely, regional dualism is found between the traditional rural regions and the modern plantation. Like Honduras and most of Central America, we may cite Ecuador, with its coastal plains put to commercial banana production while its Sierra remains near subsistence levels. Peru has its coastal, export-oriented valleys contrasting with interior regions of traditional subsistence agriculture. Extractive industries, which will not be examined here, only extend this pattern, forming isolated, outward-looking regions poorly linked with the capital and central regions, although economic transfers may ensure regional poverty.

Developmental processes

Inter-regional migration and industrial centralization, together with agricultural expansion, form regional patterns of development and differentiation which are evident on both international and national scales. Internationally, for some countries there is a forward development with positive steps into manufacturing and a more productive agriculture, whose products can also (though more dubiously) be added to the national product. But as other countries stagnate or achieve only negligible advances, there is a more powerful process of international differentiation in levels of income and economic structure (see Table 14).

To what extent is this development dependent on foreign capital and technology? In industry technical dependency on foreign countries is substantial because the research and development for technological advance is undertaken very largely in the industrial nations. This dependency is not diminished by the most recent nationalization of capital goods and other industries, for in high-technology industries such as petrochemicals, nationalization of the local industry (as in Venezuela in 1977) results in local ownership but also in a continued need to purchase technical assistance from abroad both to maintain and to update local installations with the frequent advances of this industry's technology. As the markets are overseas, it is necessary to be competitive at international levels which cannot be achieved without the latest equipment and techniques. In some industries, such as the motor car industry throughout the continent, there is a dependency not only on foreign design and components but also on imports of sheet steel suitable for the industry, demand being insufficient to warrant Latin American sheet-steel production.

Table 14 *Gross Domestic Product, total and per capita, by country, 1960, 1974–8*

Country	Total (millions of 1976 dollars)		Per capita (1976 dollars)	
	1960	1974–8*	1960	1974–8*
Argentina	24,055.2	42,938.7	1167.1	1627.1
Bolivia	937.5	2331.0	283.0	479.9
Brazil	35,815.4	130,568.6	506.2	1121.8
Chile	8200.7	14,774.5	1064.9	1360.8
Colombia	6130.6	16,224.3	398.2	637.1
Ecuador	1354.6	4679.1	312.4	627.1
El Salvador	1048.5	2703.4	431.0	613.8
Guatemala	2124.3	5830.8	535.8	880.5
Guyana	279.9	456.7	484.3	553.6
Honduras	694.4	2472.4	931.2	1174.0
Mexico	23,451.1	68,015.3	671.5	1016.0
Nicaragua	692.0	1980.8	487.3	778.9
Panama	809.9	2288.8	762.6	1254.1
Paraguay	601.6	1662.7	351.8	575.7
Peru	6361.9	14,277.5	634.8	848.0
Uruguay	2948.9	3870.5	1187.6	1357.1
Venezuela	10,122.9	27,985.9	1376.9	2127.3
Latin America	131,016.6	354,748.6	653.1	1076.8

* Preliminary estimate.

Source: Inter-American Development Bank 1978 Report (Washington 1979), p. 420.

The political or control dependency asserted by critics of the present economic world order is more difficult to ascertain. In some industries and some countries (the copper industry in Chile, the pharmaceuticals industry of most countries) it is very real, through financial manipulation of product and input costs, control of markets and so on. In general, though, it is scarcely a realistic model. In agriculture national technical dependency is less strong. In so far as production has been increased through areal expansion to meet domestic demand, it is an autonomous growth. Only where there are powerful yield increases, as with Mexican crop production, does the expansion have dependent aspects because increases are continuously dependent on imported fertilizers, machinery or technology. Of course, the growth of plantation agriculture for foreign markets has a stronger element of dependency, through market and technological links.

Internal processes

Internally, the pattern is one of powerful differentiation. Migration, it has been noted above, leads to inter-regional differences in the labour pool of skills, age groups and perhaps even psychological types. The migration process may be seen as a national centripetal movement dependent on the centre, working dendritically in from rural areas, through the urban hierarchy, to the largest towns. There are return movements and migration circuits, it is true, but the net movement which has an effect on regional futures is this drain to the centre. This movement links centre and region but at the expense of the latter; instead of acting as a balancing operation, as envisaged by neoclassical economic theory, through labour movements towards higher wage areas, migration divides by its selectivity, sending the most highly qualified and most strongly motivated of rural dwellers to the city and fostering the development of modern industry there. Diminishing social returns, in the form of higher pollution and congestion costs, are not a sufficient barrier to individual movement because the individual pays not the marginal social costs of extra congestion but the average; and even this average cost he may be only dimly aware of, in diminished health, stress, lack of fresh air and other factors which he himself finds difficult to evaluate.

Migration has been found to be less selective over time so that a view of it as a differentiation factor might be challenged (if all segments of society move, the country areas are not disadvantaged).

But even allowing this diminished selectivity, the simple loss of population is itself a factor. Rural areas suffer a constant break-up of communities or of families through losses, thus experiencing a social disruption and the unresearched factor of a demonstration effect, the migrants being effective demonstrations of no confidence in the rural home regions.

Industrial change has been a concentration of growth at the centre – not a movement inwards from the periphery except in so far as modern, central manufacturing facilities replace peripheral craft industry, but certainly a highly centralizing factor for economic activity. In Brazil value added in manufacturing was concentrated to the extent of 75 per cent in the states of Rio de Janeiro, Guanabara and São Paulo in 1969. In Peru Jameson (1976) notes a rise in Lima's share of manufacturing gross value from 59 per cent in 1955 to 73.2 per cent in 1972.

In some cases an absolute drain on provincial industries can be seen, as in the case of Huancayo, cited by Roberts (in Portes and Browning 1976, pp. 99–131). In this region of the Sierra behind Lima, he contends, the small towns did not become integrated into a modern production system because mining and large estates allowed temporary work and the retaining of small farms by workers. Modern industries were built up in Huancayo from the 1940s, principally textiles, but in the 1960s and 70s de-industrialization took place, with a loss of the textile industry to larger factories using newer technology in Lima. This has caused a reversion to a bazaar economy in Huancayo itself, with small-scale household enterprises coming to the fore, family units and flexibility featuring strongly. This kind of industrial centralization means too a concentration of high incomes in the large cities and an increase in regional imbalances of income.

Beside the powerful centralizing movements of industry and population movement, agricultural growth is scarcely effective as a counterweight. The areal expansion in many crops already noted does not necessarily embrace totally new areas of occupation and is often merely the conversion of natural pasture to arable land; but in any case the commercial systems associated with agricultural expansion remain centred on the large cities. Even where relatively thorough agrarian reforms have been attempted, as in Peru, Chile and Mexico, regional structure and relations with the capital city have generally remained unaltered.

In contrast to the pattern of inter-regional dependency, the disjunctive patterns of various kinds, continuing the processes mentioned for earlier historical periods, are harder to discern. Independent development was cited for the nineteenth century in the Argentine Pampas, in Antioquia within Colombia and in São Paulo. These are examples of what Richardson (1973a) terms 'generative growth', a growth which is either independent of, or at least not at the expense of, growth in other regions and which may be contrasted with the competitive growth implied by dependent development, in which growth at one centre makes it difficult for others to develop.

In the Pampas region Santa Fé's early diversification and relative advance was checked by the redefinition of this region as a relatively poor periphery of the larger humid Pampas, dominated by the regional and national market of Buenos Aires and by land tenure and productive systems based on livestock farming, to which intensive arable was subsidiary. The whole Pampas system was itself subsidiary to the larger market system centred on Britain. Antioquia's early advance was also checked by this region's incorporation into a national system centred on Bogotá, although agriculture has remained relatively prosperous in the region and Medellín and Cali have become separate regional centres of considerable power in western Colombia.

Peru's development in the 1890s, and again in the 1930s and 1940s, has been characterized as autonomous by Thorp and Bertram (1978) during periods when exports were reviving from previous crises but foreign intervention was slight because of distrust of Peru as a defaulter on international payments commitments. In these periods exports were rising and were controlled by native entrepreneurs. In addition, the lead sectors, sugar and mining, with linkages to local firms such as foundries, and the export entrepreneurs, also invested in industries for the local market. During the 1890s Peru was the only country to establish Peruvian-owned public utilities, producing electricity, running trams, the ports and a water supply. Thorp and Bertram also claim that there was a relative dispersal of modern economic growth too, with sugar and cotton on the coast, rubber, coffee and cocoa in the Montana and Selvas, silver, copper and wool in the Sierra. But there are no data to show the degree of spread effects, and these industries, geared to exports and big Lima or foreign firms, can have had few multiplier effects among the Indian communities of subsistence farmers.

Probably the autonomy achieved was greatest for the Peruvian nation, and for the Lima region, which acquired many industries through import substitution and the processing of export goods. In 1902 about 60 per cent of the industrial firms had been established since 1890, a veritable industrial revolution, which meant a better-rounded economy for Peru (and especially for the Lima area); but this industrial expansion could not provide regional autonomy for interior raw-material-producing regions which were serving Lima or the export markets, except in the limited sense that control was predominantly in the hands of Peruvians rather than foreigners.

Perhaps the best example of a region which retained autonomy in its industrial drive is São Paulo, where the entrepreneurship of the Paulista coffee merchants and planters has been noted by Morse (1974), and the difference in social structure due to free labour as opposed to a slave labour system is emphasized by Balan (1976). Industries such as textiles, principally cotton, here encouraged a backwards vertical integration to produce textile-mill machinery at São Paulo and then machinery for other kinds of mills, feeding back still further into a demand for steel made locally in non-integrated steel mills. Brazil's (and São Paulo's) relative isolation from world capital and lack of the strong commercial links present, for example, in the River Plate area may be one reason for the evident willingness to integrate vertically here.

In recent decades the early manufacturing advance was followed by Vargas's emphasis on capital goods industries and infrastructure, and since World War II by the car-manufacturing industry, developed first as an assembly-plant type of operation up to 1955, then becoming an industry making over 90 per cent of its components locally by 1966 (Gwynne 1978). These component industries were naturally located, for the most part, in the south-east, by the Rio–São Paulo axial region. Here import substitution reached back behind the consumer product to its inputs, and the process has extended still further with the construction of two new models of Brazilian design as well as manufacture.

The degree of autonomy in this kind of development should not be overstated. Ultimate ownership, research and administration functions for the car companies, as for the other multinational companies, are still foreign, and foreign penetration has extended particularly since the 1964 military takeover in Brazil, which was followed by a rapid improvement in national growth rates, the so-called 'economic miracle', dependent on foreign investment under attractive terms. What we may say is that the relative self-sufficiency within the country of the south-east region, for inputs of materials and labour and for markets, and its relatively diversified structure of industry, make it a less dependent *region* than some *countries* of the continent which lack the markets to warrant investment in heavy industries of any kind and whose industrial structure is therefore weak and unbalanced. This kind of definition of autonomy follows and extends that of Utria (1972), which is defined solely on the basis of markets and would make every metropolitan region autonomous.

Rio–São Paulo is itself a central metropolitan region, so that its relative independence has not helped to establish endogenous growth processes in other regions, which latter exhibit a considerable dependence on it. The exploitation of the Amazon Basin in recent years, for example, undertaken by private firms at a very rapid pace under the aegis of the central government through its regional agencies, has depended greatly on the stimulus of demand for raw materials from the south-east region, and ownership of these firms is either in the latter region or overseas (Cardoso and Müller 1978). A general conclusion, though tentative, is that the process of import substitution and the growth of manufacturing led to a degree of autonomy for some *nations* but did not produce regional autonomies, since the regions now became tied to dominant national markets and centres of power. In the terms of the models of growth processes illustrated in Chapter 1, from a single model, the Western world's economic system, there is a partial splitting up into a large number of semi-autonomous systems (the republics of Latin America and elsewhere), but within each of these smaller systems there is an evolution comparable with that of Figure 1 which leaves the peripheral regions to enjoy only a dependent kind of development through the expansion of their national system. The regional process is not comparable with that of Figure 2 or Figure 3 (pages 34 and 36).

Disjunctive differentiation

Apart from the semi-independent growth some favoured regions may achieve, there are areas of substantial differentiation due to the operation of a disjunctive process between the modern and the traditional. In these areas development may be said to follow the pattern of Figure 3 in Chapter 1, though forward development is not implied but an ever-increasing separation between static, traditional regions and those achieving positive development. One view of this, that of some economists, is in terms of dualism. Agriculture is flexible and capable of absorbing almost infinite additions of labour while maintaining a positive economic return, if not to the individual at least to the community, in areas of traditional intensive agriculture. Industry has fixed capital/labour ratios and is not able to absorb extra labour beyond that needed to expand overall output. Thus a result of population increase is labour's absorption by agriculture, which cannot be modernized because it would not then be able to absorb more labour, while industry absorbs labour either at the rate of increase of production or at a lower rate reflecting its continuous advances in mechanization and displacement of labour. The model is widely criticized today (see Brookfield 1975 for a review) but the criticisms seem unsatisfactory because they are in purely economic terms. It is easy to show that industry does, in fact, absorb labour, that agriculture cannot always take on more workers and that there is an interpenetration of modern and traditional in both industry and agriculture (or in town and countryside if we take these to be the categories of dualism). But the dual process is not wholly economic, and different economic reactions can only be understood by considering the different social contexts of the economy in traditional and modern regions.

One kind of dualism has already been mentioned above (pages 130–1), that described by Geertz (1963) for rural Indonesia and by McGee (1971) for urban places of South-East Asia; modern capital-intensive industry or agriculture spreads out and displaces traditional economy, so that an increase of population and a declining resource base for the remnants of traditional societies result in involution. In general, involution results from an excess of popula-

Table 15 *Underemployment in some countries of Latin America*

Country	Agriculture (%)	Other (%)	Total (%)
Chile	30	28	—
Peru	13	29	
Paraguay	40		
Uruguay	20	—	20
Venezuela	—	—	50
Central America	30	—	—
Colombia	25	14	

Source: Lederman (1969), p. 13.

tion in relation to available work, either in rural or in urban areas. That this is a real problem is shown by the figures in Table 15, based on estimates of various kinds and representing the position of the 1960s.

Unemployment in 1965 was estimated at only 11.1 per cent for Latin America as a whole, but these high estimates for underemployment are a more impressive indicator of the dualist pressures in the economy. The agricultural population in Latin America, although it has been far outstripped by urban population, has increased and is increasing still in most countries. In Argentina it declined after 1950, as in Peru, but in Brazil, Chile, Colombia, Panama, Venezuela and most other countries of the region it increased at least into the 1960s.

Rural underemployment and population growth are reflected in two kinds of farming, a dualism within the agricultural sector between large-scale *latifundia* and small-scale intensive *minifundia*. The *latifundio* can control its work-force as can any firm; the *minifundio* must needs support all its dependent population. There is no possibility of 'dismissing' surplus labour because the *minifundio* is not an isolated economic enterprise but an element in a closely knit community. These differences are reflected in the different intensities of land use as between large and small farms. High inputs of labour per unit of land (ratio of column 1 and column 2 in Table 16) characterize the family- and sub-family-sized farms and the high value of output per hectare (column 3), although the value of product per worker is lower so that larger farmers and labourers are collectively richer than small farmers.

Table 16 is a measure of the economic aspects of agricultural

Table 16 *Agricultural productivity in some countries of Latin America*

Country and group size	% of total national production value (index; sub-family = 100)			
	Agricultural land	Agricultural labour force	Per hectare of agric. land	Per farm worker
Argentina, 1960				
Sub-familiar	3	30	100	100
Familiar	46	49	30	250
Multi-familiar (medium)	15	15	50	470
Multi-familiar (large)	36	6	12	620
Total	*100*	*100*	*30*	*260*

Table 16 *Continued*

Country and group size	% of total national production value (index: sub-family = 100)			
	Agricultural land	Agricultural labour force	Per hectare of agric. land	Per farm worker
Brazil, 1950				
Sub-familiar	0	11	100	100
Familiar	6	26	80	290
Multi-familiar (medium)	34	42	53	420
Multi-familiar (large)	60	21	11	690
Total	*100*	*100*	*19*	*410*
Chile, 1955				
Sub-familiar	0	13	100	100
Familiar	8	28	14	170
Multi-familiar (medium)	13	21	12	310
Multi-familiar (large)	79	38	5	440
Total	*100*	*100*	*7*	*290*
Colombia, 1960				
Sub-familiar	5	58	100	100
Familiar	25	31	48	418
Multi-familiar (medium)	25	7	19	753
Multi-familiar (large)	45	4	9	995
Total	*100*	*100*	*26*	*281*
Ecuador, 1954				
Sub-familiar	20		100	
Familiar	19		85	
Multi-familiar (medium)	19		54	
Multi-familiar (large)	42		37	
Total	*100*		*54*	
Guatemala, 1950				
Sub-familiar	15	68	100	100
Familiar	13	13	56	220
Multi-familiar (medium)	32	12	54	670
Multi-familiar (large)	40	7	25	710
Total	*100*	*100*	*48*	*220*

Source: Domike and Barraclough (1965), pp. 14–15.

involution and dualism. Small farmers operate with a totally different structure of input factors, with little land and much labour, from that of large farmers. This regrettable situation is a primary focus of attention for those who argue for agrarian reform.

Apart from the agricultural involution suggested above, in the cities there is an evident division between the informal sector, Santos's *circuit inférieur* (Santos 1971) which may occupy over half the urban population, and the formal, organized sector of commerce and industry. This arises from the massive immigrations to Latin American cities of uneducated and temporarily unabsorbable labour, which supports itself by filling holes in the economy where a willingness to work but total lack of capital can be put to good purpose.

In developmental terms this dualism is perhaps a less important one than the rural division, because in the cities a considerable dynamism of society and economy ensures that the new arrivals from the country are soon exposed to modern ways of life, and with the exception of a minority, of which some return to the rural areas, the new urbanites are absorbed into the city.

Another dimension of duality, which appears forcefully only in the rural areas and is gradually lost through the mixing process present in every city, is the cultural one, which serves partially to reinforce the economic and to determine its incidence. Cultural background differences are still large in the Andean countries, and are indexed in language. Rowe (1947) and Cole and Mather (1978) show the continuing importance of the non-Spanish-speaking (principally Quechua) population in the southern Sierra of Peru and, to a lesser extent throughout the Sierra. Over Peru Quechua speakers were 46.5 per cent of the total in the 1940 Census, and in the southern Sierra between 80 and 100 per cent of the population spoke only Quechua (Cole and Mather 1978, p. 42, Fig. 4.4). The 1960 Census does not have such complete tabulations on language but classifies people according to their mother language and shows the same southern Sierra departments, Ayacucho, Huancavelica, Apurimac, Puno and Cuzco, with 10 per cent or less with the Spanish language as mother tongue. This kind of dualism does not depend on an action–reaction relation such as that implied by involution. It reflects geographic isolation and the corresponding cultural isolation of the Andean peoples over a long period.

Geographic patterns

Associated with the developmental processes described, there are geographic patterns, some of which have been hinted at. In some cases physical factors, the Latin American environment of mountains, deserts and forests or the configuration of specific countries and their frontiers come into play so strongly that they obliterate the geographic structure based solely on social and economic factors emphasized in what follows. Mountain and valley relief in Colombia reduces the tendency to urban primacy and the centralization of transport networks and flows in that country. Mountain relief between the export-oriented coastal port, Guayaquil, and the national capital, Quito, give Ecuador a dual rather than a single centre. By contrast, the placing of Buenos Aires in the centre of the most fertile and productive agricultural region, surrounded by less fortunate peripheral regions, has exaggerated trends towards centralization already present from previous historical periods and to be expected from its economic structure. Again, in contrast to this centralization, in the West Indies the subdivision of land into small island units reduces the tendency towards macroregional centralization; each island is a self-contained region firmly bounded on the exterior. Nevertheless, social and economic forces are associated with a 'standard' pattern, which may be outlined.

As previously, it is not the intention to present this pattern either as direct cause or as result of economic or social structure; to do so would be, in the first case, spatial determinism, in the second, socio-economic determinism, not essentially more admirable than the physical determinism prevalent in geographic thinking earlier this century. To some extent the geographic structure is a determinant of economic and social change as well as a resultant. A given geographic concentration of urban population in a single city provides advantages or urban agglomeration that attract further agglomeration of migrants and industries, and this may be further reinforced by a radial transport and communications network. On the other hand, a society and economy dominated by the individual family on the social side, and by large-scale manufacture on the economic side, will itself encourage the growth of great cities with links out from them to less developed peripheries. There is no ultimate separation between form and process.

Urban structures

Most writers have commented on the tendency towards the excessive concentration of population in a few large cities in underdeveloped countries. This feature is present even in large countries such as Argentina and Mexico, although in these countries the tendency should, in theory, be less marked because of the interregional isolation and differentiation described in earlier chapters. Browning (in Unikel and Necochea 1975) uses two methods for measuring primacy: first city/second city, and first city divided by the next three. There is no general agreement on what precisely is meant by primacy, or on whether it involves all urban places or just a few. Intuitively, Browning's first index seems too limited, in that it ignores virtually all the urban hierarchy. At the other extreme, El-Shakhs (1972) seems to have too extensive an index: he takes the average of each city's average-sized ratio to all towns below it in the system. This smooths out the important deviations at the top, which should at least have been given an extra weighting in the index. Using Browning's method of computation, the general tendency, during the present century at least up to 1970, is seen to be the increasing dominance of one city in the urban system (see Table 17; Browning's indices are used here as simple approximations).

Brazil's primacy is less extreme, unless we regard Rio–São Paulo as a single urban complex which acts as metropolis for the country. It may be seen that regional centres such as Recife, Porto Alegre and Belém fall far behind. A similar dual centre in Ecuador has Guayaquil as port, Quito as administrative centre.

What is the present trend of primacy in Latin America? Statistically, as pointed out in the last chapter, there has been a nineteenth- and twentieth-century tendency towards the rising primacy of the metropolitan cities. Rather than changing relationships within an existing network, however, this was interpreted as the emergence of a new national urban network replacing the old regional networks. McGreevey's (1971) study indicates that urban primacy came into existence over this period, first in Mexico, then in Cuba, Chile, Argentina, Brazil, Peru, Venezuela and Colombia. This primacy, and the tendency towards it, he associates with the growth of exports. Both the tendency and the relationship are challengeable; the case was made that primacy was already an old-established feature in the nineteenth century, not on the scale of the new republics but on that of somewhat smaller regions, and the integration of these regional systems into a national urban system produced urban primacy as we know it. This process, given the isolation and lack of integration of some regions in large countries, is still taking place and is producing an apparent increase in primacy. Centralization forces are as strong as ever, but they now operate over a larger spatial framework.

Centralization is more easily achieved in small countries, one of which, Uruguay, has an enormous concentration of urban population in Montevideo; Paraguay and Cuba are similarly top-heavy, whereas Brazil, Mexico and Colombia have a more regionalized structure because of their size (see Table 17). Size of country is, of course, not the only factor determining urban structure, and the role of primary exports, degree of industrialization, ease of transport within the country and distribution of resources all come into play with different force in different countries and interact with the factor we have stressed above, the integration of sub-national regions into a national urban structure.

Transportation networks

An aspect of geographic structure related to urban primacy and to migration and commodity flows dominated by the centre is the development of a single transport net linked radially to the metropolis. To some extent, this is an inheritance of nineteenth-century construction, as with the Uruguayan and Argentine railways. But in other countries, as in Brazil (see Figure 13, page 104), in Venezuela, even in Peru, the railways did not constitute a network at all. That role was reserved for the present century and for roads. After 1920 the introduction of cars and lorry transport induced governments to improve or remake many unsurfaced roads that had previously handled only carts or horse, mule and foot traffic. Given the existing structure of economic and power links, the centripetal pattern was normally followed, as any atlas map will show.

The roads were not put through unpopulated areas as promoters of settlement until relatively recent times, however. In general, up to 1950 roads merely linked existing centres of concentrated settlement, totally avoiding large segments of thinly peopled territory. Thus, for example, Venezuela, acknowledged to have a very advanced road system among South American countries, has still to put road connections into its Guayana territory (apart from the short spurs which reach into the northern fringe to iron ore

Table 17 *Urban primacy in the twentieth century*

Census year	First city	2nd city	3rd city	4th city	Indices	
					4-city	2-city
Argentina						
1895	754,068 Buenos Aires	107,959 Rosario	60,991 La Plata	54,763 Córdoba	3.4	7.0
1970	8,925,000 Buenos Aires	810,840 Rosario	798,663 Córdoba	506,287 La Plata	4.2	11.0
Brazil						
1900	899,294 Rio de Janeiro	243,275 São Paulo	205,813 Salvador	154,849 Recife	1.5	3.7
1970	5,186,752 São Paulo	4,252,009 Rio de Janeiro	1,106,722 Belo Horizonte	1,046,454 Recife	0.8	1.2
Chile						
1907	398,414 Santiago	193,191 Valparaiso–Viña del Mar	92,199 Concepción–Talcahuano	48,186 Iquique	1.2	2.1
1970	2,661,920 Santiago	289,456 Valparaiso–Viña del Mar	191,746 Concepción–Talcahuano	149,344 Viña del Mar	4.2	9.2

	City 1	City 2	City 3	City 4		
Colombia						
1912	133,058 Bogotá	84,444 Medellín	59,579 Barranquilla	36,632 Cali	0.7	1.6
1970	2,818,300 Bogotá	1,207,800 Medellín	1,022,200 Cali	693,900 Barranquilla	1.0	2.3
Mexico						
1900	344,721 Mexico City	101,208 Guadalajara	93,521 Puebla	62,266 Leon	1.3	3.4
1970	10,766,791 Mexico City	1,856,876 Guadalajara	1,154,339 Monterrey	468,887 Leon	4.3	5.8
Peru						
1876	143,688 Lima–Callao	26,958 Arequipa	14,773 Chiclayo	8,372 Trujillo	3.0	5.3
1970	3,158,411 Lima–Callao	296,220 Callao	304,653 Arequipa	241,882 Trujillo	3.7	10.7
Venezuela						
1891	121,634 Caracas	54,387 Maracaibo	34,742 Valencia	27,114 Barquisimeto	1.0	2.2
1970	2,175,400 Caracas	650,002 Maracaibo	366,154 Valencia	334,333 Barquisimeto	1.6	3.3

Sources: Unikel and Necochea (1975), pp. 162–4; *Statistical Yearbook of Latin America*, vol. 18 (1976), pp. 84–5.

deposits); the Llanos region of Apure, south of the River Apure, is similarly without roads, like the adjacent areas of the Colombian Llanos. Only in a few cases, and in recent years, has the role of penetration and long-distance interconnection been recognized, as with the Carretera Marginal de las Selvas in Bolivia, Peru, Ecuador and Colombia (abandoned for want of the international support required by this major road project in the western Amazon Selvas), or the modern Trans-Chaco road now under construction. An important fact of modern development, already hinted at in the last section, which saw inter-regional integration as a continuing process today, is thus the number of large regions remaining marginal to modern civilization or at least physically unlinked to the centre. Brazil's policy of roadbuilding into the Amazon Basin is a movement which is breaking down this isolation and bringing more land into the modern oecumene, and it may be expected that, for whatever reason (Brazil's military government would seem to be more concerned with the strategic control of peripheral areas than with socio-economic development), other countries are likely to develop transport systems in the same way. Most of them have large amounts of virtually uninhabited land, even in small countries such as Guatemala (see Table 18).

Table 18   *Surface of unsettled areas as percentage of total national surface*

Country	Unsettled areas (1 inhabitant/km²) as percentage of national total
Paraguay	65.14
Ecuador	65.11
Bolivia	59.00
Venezuela	49.77
Colombia	44.83
Peru	43.32
Brazil	40.04
Guatemala	32.93
Chile	31.13
Argentina	17.61

Source: Stöhr (1975), p. 50

Flows

To a centripetal structure of transport facilities corresponds a less visible but equally centripetal set of flows. As an example, the inter-state flows of Brazil may be used (see Figure 16). They show a massive concentration on Rio and São Paulo, in terms of the dominant flow lines, though some states lie beyond the whole national circuit of trade. Outside this network only the Nordeste, distant and with an important regional centre at Recife, is separate. The whole country focuses thus on the south-east, major market for the raw materials of the peripheral regions and major provider of the processed goods and manufactures needed in the regions.

This centripetal pattern is maintained over time. Another example which illustrates this is the airway network. Data for 1967 (following Pedersen 1975, p. 55) and for 1979 have been compiled to show the lines used most frequently within the South American continent, excluding international flights in order to emphasize the regional structure. From the thin and incomplete structure of 1967 there is obviously a considerable growth and outwards expansion by 1979 (see Figure 17). Among the Andean countries such centres as Lima and La Paz, expand their influence over national hinterlands, and in Brazil Belém, Manáus, Natal, Brasília and Goiânia all appear for the first time on the map or see major expansion in the time interval used. To Pedersen this transportation structure is both the index and the mechanism of economic development – the main centres have accessibility to modernization influence from overseas, and in turn they influence many lesser centres around them; the 1967–79 growth would be seen by him as a central part of the development process. Here it is seen more as an indicator of the structure of development and its varying impact on different places. The spatial pattern is seen to remain heavily focused on the few major centres; for cities other than the capitals the principal or only link, using the method employed in the map, is always to the capital.

Centripetal flows are also apparent in the movement of capital. Fiscal movements in many countries are probably a major form of transfer to the large cities because of the residence tendencies of the rich. Miller (1971b) cites a study of Brazil's north-east, where the major sugar tax leads to the centralization of regional incomes because it is levied at the administrative centre of the firm and spent there too in proportion to the amount levied, although the economic base for the tax (sugar-cane production) is almost entirely rural.

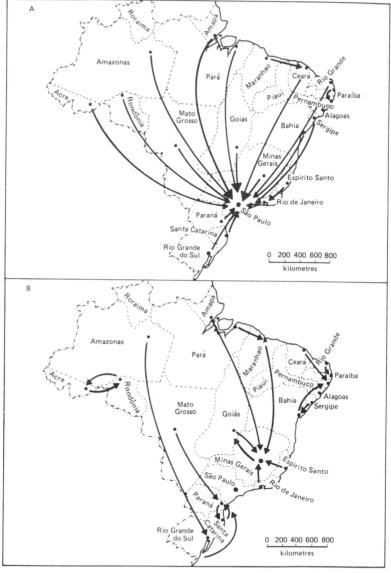

Figure 16   *Inter-state freight flows in Brazil. Diagram A shows the single most important flow in 1973 and indicates the dominance of Rio and especially São Paulo. Diagram B indicates the flow pattern when São Paulo is eliminated from the calculations and shows a more regional structure at this secondary level, with three separate foci in the south (Paraná–Santa Catarina), south-east (Minas) and north-east (Pernambuco).*

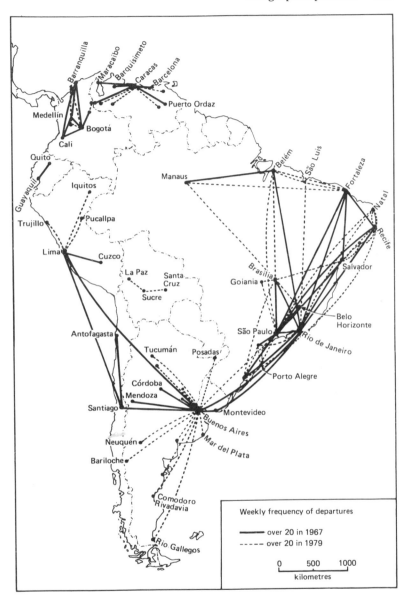

Figure 17 *Airline networks in South America, 1967 and 1979 (based on Pedersen 1975 and the* ABC World Airways Guide *1979). The dotted lines show the important services added during the twelve-year period, which have not affected the centripetal structure, even in relatively advanced countries such as Argentina.*

Personal income taxes in Brazil also favour the centre, as Baer (1965) shows from data on the fiscal burden, which remains a constant proportion in incomes both in the north-east and in other regions, although these latter have become much more wealthy than the north-east over recent years (Baer 1965, pp. 180–1). Exchange rates also provide a net transfer of funds to the south-east because imports to the north-east, largely consumer items, are taxed highly, while capital-goods imports, which mostly go to the south-east, are not subject to high tariffs. The funds accumulated in this way are used to prop up the coffee economy of the south-east.

Bank transfers and movement within the firm are more difficult to trace. Firm capital movements are primarily, in any case, in the form of the relocation or new establishment of factories. One type of financial movement which may be indicative of transfers by private individuals, because of the small amounts that are characteristic and the mechanism used, is that of postal orders. For Venezuela these show a definite inward movement to the capital, in all probability as remittances to new migrant families or individuals, students and other dependents (see Figure 18). Other largely recipient cities are the principal ones of the Andean states, Mérida, Trujillo, San Cristobal, while the more industrially progressive towns, such as Maracaibo, Valencia and Maracay, are providers of funds for other regions. The picture is complex, and the statistics do not tell us the specific city-to-city movement, but the structure is evidently dominated by the inflow to Caracas, representing over 50 per cent of all movements.

Flows of capital in the form of plant are scarcely recognized as flows at all; they are chronologically discontinuous, lumpy movements perhaps best described in terms of their results, which consist of the heavy concentration of manufacturing capital in the largest cities. In Peru, as noted above, the gross value of manufacturing production concentrated in Lima was 59 per cent in 1955, 65.1 per cent in 1963 and 73.2 per cent in 1972. The centralization of manufacturing has been so powerful in recent decades that it has caused an industrial shadow effect that Roberts (in Portes and Browning 1976, pp. 99–131) described for Huancayo in the Sierra. What industries there are in provincial cities are linked by material flows predominantly with Lima and the exterior. Thus Jameson (1976) shows that Arequipa industries are linked, via inputs and outputs, with Lima and overseas, not to its own agricultural and mining hinterland, except for the soft drinks and beer industries.

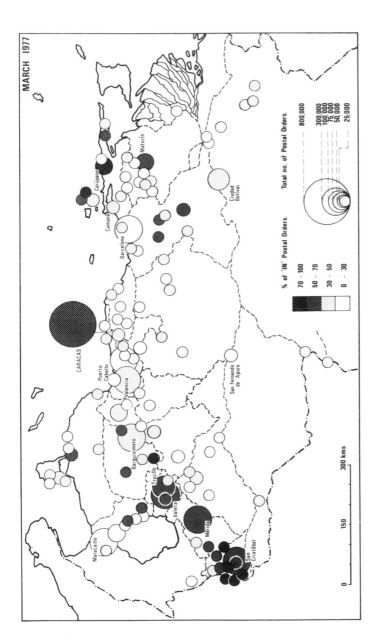

Figure 18 *Postal Order flows in Venezuela (based on data in* Boletin Mensuel, Dirección General de Estadística y Censos, *Caracas, 1976–8).*

Table 19   *Brazil: gross value of industrial production, 1920, 1940, 1960*

Year	All Brazil	São Paulo State	Rio de Janeiro City (Former Federal District, now Guanabara State)
1920	3,200,670 (100%)	1,009,073 (31.53%)	666,276 (20.82%)
1940	17,479,393 (100%)	7,601,721 (43.49%)	3,321,643 (19.00%)
1960	1,194,784,551 (100%)	658,067,422 (55.08%)	114,319,540 (9.57%)

Source: Calculated from *Anuario Estatístico do Brasil* (various dates); data on gross value of industrial production from censuses.

In Brazil, twentieth-century concentration of industry has increased, especially within the Greater São Paulo conurbation, as Table 19 shows. Rio de Janeiro has been the capital over nearly the whole period to which these data refer but has seen its relative importance decline in spite of massive absolute growth in industrial production.

Income distribution

Centralized patterns of population and migration, of resource movements and of fixed and mobile capital all suggest substantial inter-regional differences of income level, whether this is measured in straightforward monetary terms or as some compound of income and welfare and quality-of-life variables. Information on these latter variables is scarce and difficult to compare between countries. Although unreliable, direct income measures are somewhat more standardized and available. Pedersen (1975, Appendix B, pp. 258–9), for example, assembled data on seventy-four large subnational regions covering all South America, standardized according to buying power; when mapped, there is an expectable pattern of inter-regional differences. Data on changes over the 1950s were also assembled and seem to show a process of smoothing of regional differences, but as the data are unreliable, and as many of the regions whose status has improved are still in the process of change from a non-money to a money economy, this conclusion cannot be strongly supported. It can indeed only be agreed, with Pedersen, that the areas of urbanization and industrialization are the principal high-income areas.

The data for changes over a period of time in Argentina are of interest with respect to the processes of income differentiation and convergence (Morris 1975). For this country there is an apparent convergence between 1961 and 1969, which would seem to mark a confirmation of the neoclassical theory of regional convergence in response to differences of wages and interest between regions. In neither year is the pattern one of simple metropolitan dominance; the richest areas include the Patagonian provinces, resource frontier for the national industrial complex with iron ore, petroleum, gas, hydroelectric power and coal. Evidently, a peripheral region is not necessarily a poor one, and this point has to be borne in mind in constructing policy. On the other hand, the northern provinces, despite heavy out-migration over a long period, do have a large population of considerable poverty.

Unfortunately, there is no simple test of the relation between inter-regional migration, capital movement and income distribution in a country. Gauthier (1975) compares the neoclassical and dis-equilibrium theories of migration in their application to Brazil, which achieved some divergence of inter-regional incomes in the 1950s, then convergence in the mid 1960s, followed again by divergence in the late 1960s and early 1970s. During the 1950s there was a rapid industrial–urban expansion related to import substitution programmes and focusing essentially on Rio–São Paulo; this might be held to account for divergence in incomes in a disequilibrating movement, or in one which was neoclassical but much modified to take into account the costs of migration, inter-sectoral shifts in employment among the migrants and other ele-ments (Gauthier 1975, pp. 55–6). At any rate, the build-up in the south-east was associated in time with heavy migration out of the north-east. Divergence of incomes was checked in the mid 1960s. Was this the result of the migration from the north-east, which had by now evened out differences, or was it due to other factors? At this time a mild recession in industrial growth made for lower inter-regional differences in any case, because the recession affected the south-east most strongly. In addition, the influence of regional policy, through the creation of SUDENE in 1959, might be expected to have been felt by this time. In the late 1960s rapid central growth is associated with a rise in income differentials. This divergence might be ascribed to lowered migration from the north-east again, but there is no time-lag effect between the two, as should have occurred, and it seems more likely that the effective decline of regional policy, with SUDENE's being placed under federal control and its reduced functions, together with a massive entry of foreign capital to the south-east, were responsible for this divergence.

Income data are, of course, only an approximate surrogate for the total welfare of the region, which is probably what planners and politicians would like to be informed about when considering regional differences. There is no agreement on what elements go to make up the welfare of a region, so that value judgements must enter. One study (Slater 1975) shows the utility of a single index in demonstrating the high inter-relations of nine separate variables for the twenty-three Peruvian *departamentos* in 1946 and 1955. These variables were the ratios of telegrams, motor vehicles, hospital beds, provincial council expenditure and bank deposits to population, the ratio of private cars to total vehicles, and the ratios of secondary to primary school children, late/early primary, female pupils/all pupils. Despite the variety of these economic and social indicators, they all had strong loadings on a single factor when subjected to factor analysis, except for the female education variable, and thus seem to indicate a common pattern. This first common factor accounted for 74.4 per cent of total variance. The pattern shown is one of high values in the metropolitan area of Lima–El Callao, relatively high values for most coastal *departamentos*, especially Ica, Arequipa and Tacna to the south of Lima, Lambayeque to the north, then intermediate or low values in the Sierra, and low values in the Selvas.

Another study of Peru, focusing on the same topic of income and welfare and using a similar factor analysis method (Cole and Mather 1972), arrived at comparable patterns of economic development, based on income- and employment-related measures, the highest values again being on the coast. This study also revealed other dimensions to development, with quite separate patterns; beside a factor I, which explained 67 per cent of common variance, factors II and III explained 21 per cent and 12 per cent of the common factor structure. Whereas the income measures were in an east–west gradient, cultural differences (as measured by the propor-tion of adults, Spanish-speaking proportion, rate of population increase, coca chewing, percentage eligible to vote, percentage

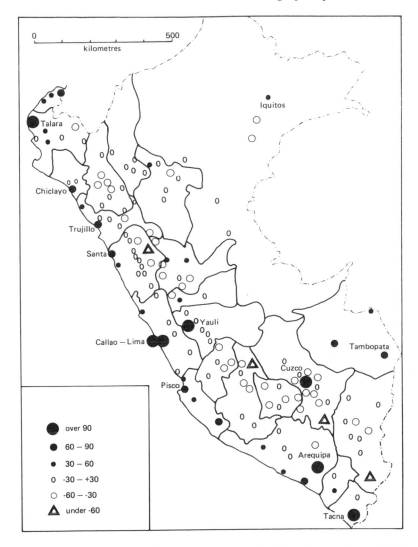

Figure 19 *Multi-factor development scores for Peruvian provinces, 1961 (based on Cole and Mather 1978, p. 53, Fig. 5.6).*

actually voting and literacy rates) were grouped into a second factor, revealing a north–south pattern, with highest levels in the north and lowest in the southern Sierra. Yet other variables, such as the male/female ratio, migration rates and population density, produced a third demographic factor summarizing their collective influence and showed spatial patterns of high values both east and west of the Sierra, which was lower.

A much more sophisticated survey (Cole and Mather 1978), in a series of studies for 1940–70 at department, province and district level, emphasized the Sierra, both north and south, as the most backward region. Figure 19 shows the situation in 1961 at province level, based on a combined score for six factors extracted from thirty-three original variables. This map parallels fairly closely those for 1940 and 1970.

Other data, on a nation-by-nation basis, are coarse but show a very obvious pattern of the same general kind, with the higher-income countries corresponding to urban–industrial growth (see Table 14, page 145). Given the greater friction of the migration of labour and of the movement of capital between these countries, some differences might be expected. But the trend in the differences over the period 1961–77 is towards not convergence but divergence, despite what is probably an increasing volume of international migration. A question mark may thus be placed against the convergence of incomes that Pedersen sees. Countries such as Venezuela or Argentina, which act as migration centres, have also been the ones to achieve higher rates of income growth over the last two decades.

A spatial model of regional development

It is possible to reduce the patterns of development to a geographical model, even if loosely stated. Friedmann's (1966) model provides a starting-point, as it is outlined in both temporal and geographical terms and is more complete than those described by other regional economists such as Boudeville (1966), while remaining less theoretical and less demanding of quantitative data that are hard to come by in the manner of Richardson's (1973a) model.

The time dimension of Friedmann's model is a classification into stages of development which relate to industrialization and urbanization and the processes of concentration and dispersal; as for space, the model is a von Thunen-like set of concentric rings around a centre, each ring having its own kind of developmental and planning problems. We may neglect for the moment the temporal aspects, which fit in only marginally with the historical sequence outlined in previous chapters, and examine the spatial model, making a preliminary classification of Latin American regions. Central and peripheral regions may be identified whether convergence or divergence movements are thought to dominate in the nation. First, within each country there is a central focus of development, a metropolitan city, which experiences industrial development and immigration from rural areas and/or from overseas because of the ready availability of well-paid jobs in its burgeoning economy – or at least the promise of such jobs. The problems are those of urban economic dualism, environmental deterioration and pollution, social adaptation and the provision of service, and infrastructure. These metropolitan centres are very generally capital cities, though in a number of countries (for example, the Guianas, each with under a million inhabitants) there is no effective metropolitan centre because the country, and thus also the city, are too small to generate agglomeration economies through the proximity of other enterprises. Around the metropolis satellite cities may develop, or the metropolitan function may be divided between two or more cities, as at Lima – El Callao or Rio – São Paulo.

In some countries Friedmann's second category of 'upward transitional' areas, which may be thought of here as 'urbanized developing regions', can be identified. These regions feel the spread effects of metropolitan development either because they belong to the urban network headed by the metropolis or because they lie in its immediate hinterland so as to enjoy the effects of some of its special demands for labour (commuters), industrial development land, fresh foods, recreation spaces and to share its external economies in physical and other infrastructure. Such zones would include the River Plate axis from Buenos Aires to Santa Fé, with the steel centre of San Nicolás and the port and industrial centre of Rosario; in the central region of Chile, the Santiago–Rancagua–Valparaiso triangle; in Venezuela, the Caracas–Maracay–Valencia development corridor; and with less definition, because large areas of poor, little-affected agricultural land are included, the triangle of Rio–São Paulo–Belo Horizonte in Brazil. Mexico City's industrial expansion has led to an aureole of lesser industrial centres, notably at nearby Puebla but also further east and west at Veracruz and Guadalajara, in a larger developing zone with some pockets of rural poverty. As admitted by Odell and Preston (1973, p. 210), however, this larger growth zone is still only in embryonic form, and Mexico City itself concentrates 36 per cent of national industrial production. One characteristic of the developed regions, apart from their proximity to metropolitan 'agglomeration' economies, is their large number of lesser urban centres and good access to them. If the development process is seen as an urban–industrial one and reliant on diffusion or spread through an urban hierarchy, then the 'upward transitional' regions must be defined in relation to this urban structure and connections, not simply to distance from the capital. These areas benefit also from another element in regional growth of modern times, the decentralization promoted either as a governmental measure or by private initiatives. Industrial growth at Rancagua, Valparaiso or San Antonio, Chile, at San Nicolás and La Plata in Buenos Aires province, at Valencia and Maracay in Venezuela, may be viewed as partially of this character. These places certainly benefit from the external economies of their central location, but also from lower transport costs, lower levels of various kinds of pollution and a better working environment.

If we accept the argument of this book that modern development is an inherently unbalancing process, then the 'urbanized development regions' must be viewed as simply sharing with the metropolis or centre its positive development as against that of all other regions. Friedmann's (1966) own interpretation, reaffirmed by him (Friedmann 1971a) in an appraisal of the role of cities in development, is different. He sees the cities as providing a network for the transmission of technological innovation, this latter being the key to development, and his 'upward transitional' regions as developing positively because of the outwards transmission of development impulses, following broadly the growth-pole theory.

Large areas come into the category of 'underdeveloped regions', or Friedmann's 'downward transitional' category. As a result of the selective out-migration of their best-qualified elements and the outflow of capital and resources, they are relatively impoverished by comparison with the centre. But the category should be restricted to areas where man/land ratios are unfavourable and where large surpluses of one or another resource are not available for national growth; it should not be applied, as might seem from a reading of Friedmann, to all poor areas outside the centre and its immediate aureole apart from the areas as yet unincorporated into national economic life. Included in the 'underdeveloped' category would be such areas as the Nordeste of Brazil; the north-west of Argentina, with its large population of subsistence farmers and labourers and constant outmigration; central Chile outside the metropolitan influence around Santiago, a region in which a peasant population lives on an insufficient land resource and also suffers heavy outmigration; the north-east and north-west of Venezuela, with a large subsistence farming population; and the south of Mexico beyond Mexico City's direct influence, again with a dense rural population which is not benefiting from the modernization of agricultural technology that is occurring in the north of the country. All of these also suffer dualism between large and small farmers. Following a 'diffusionist' or growth-pole line of regional growth theory, such regions should suffer, by contrast with the 'urbanized developing regions', from the lack of an urban network, a poor transport network, and poor communications and other infrastructure. This, in fact, seems only partially true; there are many small and medium-sized towns in these regions acting as small-region market centres, and there are major transportation arteries running through them. But the towns do not have the function of modernization centres supposed by diffusionists, nor do the roads encourage local, as opposed to national, development. Nor is it apparent how diffusion would solve the dualism of socio-economic structure.

What Friedmann (1966) designated as 'resource frontiers' and thought of as 'underdeveloped' – sparsely peopled areas with resources as yet untapped – may be redesignated into two types (and the object areas shifted somewhat): first, the areas of continuing nineteenth-century-style primary export economy, the 'international export base regions': and second, 'national export base regions' catering to other regions of the country. Friedmann's term 'resource frontier' lays emphasis on features that are not crucial in the consideration of such regions, for although they may lie on physical frontiers, they are often opened up by the most modern and standardized types of exploitation, by large national or foreign companies who wish to exploit mineral ores, timber, hydroelectric power, according to a present international pattern. Nor is it centrally important that they have an economy based on resources – all regions have these, but in the export base regions there is a combination of two features, the dominance of just one or two resources, and their export to other regions. Here we imply the dangers and problems both of monoculture and of dependence on other regions or countries for a market. 'International export base regions' include the plantation lands of both Pacific and Atlantic lowlands in the Central American republics; the Pacific lowlands of Ecuador in the Daule valley hinterland of Guayaquil; the coastal sugar-cane plantation areas of northern Peru, Cuba or the Republic of Guyana; coffee lands in south-east Brazil (in Paraná and São Paulo states) and in Colombia or Central America, successfully oriented to strong export markets. Other examples are the mineral economies of the eastern *altiplano* in Bolivia, the southern and Central Sierra in Peru, the Maracaibo Basin in Venezuela, as well as the Guayana region in that country.

'Resource regions' linked to the national economy are fewer in number and belong principally to the larger countries that have generated enough demand from their metropolitan centres. In Argentine Patagonia has hydroelectricity, oil and gas, coal, forests (as yet an almost untapped resource) and iron ore at Sierra Grande; these resources are used very largely internally, the hydroelectric power in a national grid, coal oil and gas in the central region and iron ore in steel-making at the centre. Some direct export of wool from the great *estancias* occurs from Patagonia, but the overall orientation is internal. Misiones province is similarly a producer of raw materials for domestic industry – tung nuts for oil, yerba maté for tea, timber for paper making and other uses, and power production from the dams on the River Paraná at Yaciretá and Corpus. Mexico's northern regions come into the same category; iron ore and coal from Coahuila serve the steel mills of Monclova and Monterrey in the north-east. Petroleum comes largely from Veracruz and Tamaulipas on the Caribbean coast. Zinc, lead, silver, copper and sulphur are other mineral ores of importance in the north. Agricultural production of surpluses is also concentrated in the north, where cotton is grown on the irrigated lands of the interior and the north-west, as well as fruits and vegetables for Mexico City. The north is, of course, also the principal producer of exports in Mexico, but exports are not a large part of the Gross National Product (GNP) in this country, and a growing population is forcing a diversion into domestic markets for raw materials and foods. Cole (1973, p. 248) has drawn a map sketching the geography of the developing regions, which he contrasts with 'stagnating areas' in Mexico. Not all the north is developing, and development is obviously strongly oriented to the transport lines along the north-west coast (Yaquí, Mayo, Fuerte and related irrigation areas), through the centre, where there are mines and irrigated land, and in a broader quadrangular region through the north-east, from the rail line joining San Luis Potosí to the North American border, out to the east coast. Friedmann's own 'resource frontier' example, in the Guyana region of Venezuela, draws a less rigid distinction between national and international production. Iron ore is still mostly for export from this region, though an increasing volume is for local steel mills; electricity is certainly generated for the internal market, at Caracas and locally in aluminium refineries and electric steel furnaces. To the north of the river the heavy petroleum belt is an area which must look, as does all present-day petroleum production, to overseas markets.

True, 'resource regions' may indeed be identified as those regions which are not yet incorporated into national economic life. They are *potential* resource regions, occupied in Latin America by primitive peoples who are presently isolated from modern civilization. They differ from the export base regions in that no pattern has yet been set for their exploitation.

This does not exhaust the possibilities for types of economic regions; endogenous development regions, a type not considered by Friedmann, must be included. It is true that there are no clear-cut examples in present-day Latin America (São Paulo is a metropolitan region rather than a separate endogenous one, and the Monterrey and Cauca valley areas have substantial links with the national capitals and markets), but this does not destroy the validity of the type. It will, however, be necessary to enter more important caveats on the adoption of a Friedmann-type scheme, and these may now be discussed.

Social structure

The Friedmann model modified and augmented in the last section is a fairly directly economic one, to which not even Friedmann himself would today subscribe (Friedmann and Wulff 1976; Friedmann and Weaver 1979), although it is accepted by a wide spectrum of economic, geographic and planning workers. It is based on flows obtaining between a central region and peripheral regions – flows of money, information, capital, entrepreneurship – either in response to, or as a result of, differences in levels of living or rates of growth; and it hypothesizes, with the diffusionist spread-effect theorists, that the improvement of mechanisms of modernization diffusion (transport, communications, the urban hierarchy) will bring about development. On the other hand, those who, like the dependency school, see an unbalancing mechanism in development but one which is essentially political-economic, argue for a change in the structure of power relationships via either peaceful means such as agrarian reform or revolutionary takeovers. It is, however, a logical deduction from the historical basis outlined above that another dimension should be added to development and differentiation: that of social structure. This century has seen the rapid expansion of modern market- and money-oriented societies and their economies, absorbing and apparently eliminating large remnants of non-market socio-economic structure. But it may be questioned whether traditional society has been eliminated, or indeed whether it is a much less important factor than it has been historically. It is easy to confuse the issues here because most of the regions with a more traditional, less market-oriented society and economy are also those which are economically isolated, which suffer selective out-migration of their work-force and their physical resources and which have some restrictive elements in their physical environment which make modernization difficult. The claim here is that though these are related factors, they should be distinguished and treated separately.

Primitive peoples living in societies of tribal structure and with an economic system based on reciprocity remain in isolated interior regions and even in remote coastal districts such as southern Panama. For these folk it would be idealistic to expect any long-term outcome other than replacement by modern society and economy. Total isolation, as in game parks, seems an improbable strategy; on the other hand, the social organization of these peoples cannot compete with modern structured societies and yet preserve its integrity. However, since some kind of policy must be adopted towards them, it is as well to note the distribution of such peoples. Their principal domain is within the Amazon Basin, but there are also some isolated Andean locations, such as the mountains of Perijá on the fringes of Colombia and Venezuela and the delta lands of the Orinoco, where the Guarauno Indians have long been isolated by an impassable swamp environment. The expansion of modern economic ventures and land uses to the edges of the remaining primitive territories, mostly by farmers in official or spontaneous colonization of new lands, has meant a direct cultural and economic shock for the natives as the land itself is expropriated. Usually there is a total replacement of former cultures by modern, with little in the way of adaptation or amalgamation. Indeed, in Paraguay and Brazil it is known that large numbers of natives have been killed by ranchers seeking to expand their cattle lands. As native numbers are only slight, there can be no effective opposition, and these societies are being effectively exterminated as the last step in a long history of similar actions against American Indian populations.

On a different level are what are here termed the traditional cultures of Latin America, located in the highlands of the Pacific backbone. In some areas the older forms of social organization and economy are seen only in vestigial form and do not provide a total structure for social and economic life. But in others communal organizations are still of some importance, whether formalized or of a totally informal character. Census data are not gathered on such matters and only isolated studies of individual areas are made by social scientists, so that no more than an impressionistic idea of their distribution may be gained, though in general these societies may be found to coincide with the areas of high culture in pre-Hispanic time.

In Mexico and Peru there is some formal recognition of traditional social organization through the creation of the *ejido* and the *comunidad indígena*. In both cases the focus is on rural land tenure. In the Peruvian case communal land was abolished in 1825, in accordance with Bolivar's hopes of creating nations of small independent farmers to replace the great *hacienda*. But communities whose history was already long were not thus easily destroyed, and in the 1920s they were formally recognized again, though by that time most of their lands had been taken by the large land-owners of each district. In most cases they had to fight legal battles for the communal pasture and arable lands they had once owned (Doughty 1968), and many were given only a very limited status and did not prosper or gain many members.

After the 1969 agrarian reforms, the *comunidades* were given a more formal status as the key units for land ownership and were newly endowed with lands expropriated from large land-owners.

None of the *comunidades* has been totally isolated from modern life, and a variety of modifications and adaptations is possible, some of them more successful than others. Matos Mar (1963) presents some interesting examples of the twentieth-century status of traditional communities at three separate locations in Peru. At the first, Taquile, on Lake Titicaca, a Quechua-speaking group of 650 persons occupied an island on which land was partly held privately and worked by tenant labour under servile conditions, partly operated collectively by the community. Here, in a limiting environment with no extra land available, a near-subsistence economy with minor trade in potatoes and craft items was found. Tupe, in the mountains above Lima, was another community, speaking a language (Kauke) similar to Aymara. Its former collective land ownership became private in the 1870s, apart from the *puna* land (the high pastures of the plateau). A money economy prevailed, but with only limited amounts of trade in various animal products and, again, a fixed, insufficient land resource. A third community studied by Matos was that of Muquiyauyo, a relatively progressive village of 2000 near Jauja, with 2072 hectares of good land in the Mantaro valley. In this village, as at Tupe, arable was private and pasture land held, and partially also worked, in common. In this case the stimulus from the regional centres Huancayo and Jauja – but, more particularly, the willingness to use community funds for productive investment, as in an electric power station, a textile mill and a grain mill – afforded a basis for the successful growth of the village economy, despite excessive population growth, out-migration to Lima and inefficient administration.

A general conclusion of Matos Mar's about the role of the Peruvian Indian communities was that 'they constitute ideal basic units for the development of a large region of Peru – the mountain districts where more than half of the population of the country lives' (1963, p. 138).

We need not accept that they are 'ideal basic units' in order to agree that this structure should be recognized in the context of developmental planning, and perhaps particularly in those countries that have problems of heavy out-migration from rural areas, lack of capital for rural development and lack of physical resources. The often cited conservatism, primitivism, unwillingness to change of the traditional peoples must be put also in the context of the physical environments, such as those of Taquile and Tupe cited above, isolated locations with an insufficient land resource (a frequent occurrence because of the historical process of arrogation of the best lands by powerful landlords and the preservation of old ways in remote regions).

Other countries besides Peru have attempted to incorporate the co-operative idea in their agrarian reform programmes, though for different reasons, not always associated with ancient community practices. In Chile, for example, the Frei government of 1964–70, the first government to focus directly on an agrarian-reform type of solution to the agricultural problem, instituted a collective unit, the *asentamiento*, as a transitional post-reform organization. This was basically a collective tenure form carrying on the unitary *hacienda* structure of management that had been characteristic of most of the expropriated farms. Collective ownership was maintained in the permanent forms established by the same government in its last year, the *cooperativas de reforma agraria*, though only 109 such units had been established by late 1970, the 657 others still being in the transitional form of *asentamientos*. Communal organization was continued and intensified by the Allende government of 1970–3, the membership of the *asentamientos* being made more egalitarian by the formation of new collective decision-making units, the *comites de campesinos*, and by the institution of state farms (CEP-ROs) and true collectives (CERAs), which brought in those landless labourers and *minifundistas* who had been left out by the previous reform structures (which usually only included the former labourers on the expropriated estates).

These co-operative forms, however, derive from the great private estate, the *hacienda*, not from the Indian community or any folk memory of it. The communal structure was maintained in them partly because it obviated the need for expensive surveys of individual new lots, new roads and other infrastructure, rather than out of conviction of the need for communal operation or ownership. Indeed, the communal spirit was poorly represented among the Chilean peasants affected by reform, and they created problems because of their interest in private rather than collective holdings (Broughton in Smith 1975, p. 72). Chile does have some areas, notably the Norte Chico, the irrigated valleys north of Santiago, where Indian communities are important (Weischet 1970). But in this northern region little was done to incorporate the existing *comunidades* into the new reform movement.

In like vein, we may regard the very thorough agrarian reform undertaken in Cuba after the 1959 revolution as essentially a modification of capitalist, market-oriented forms. Co-operation was a component of the Cuban formula, but it was treated largely as a means of maintaining economic scale while eliminating the North American capitalist ownership. Like Chile, in the 1950s Cuba was already a relatively wealthy country, with high levels of literacy and agricultural modernization and with no communal traditions to fall back on. The most important farm units to be expropriated were, of course, sugar plantations, which were run initially as state farms or collectives, but in 1962 state farms became the norm, very large units with paid wage labour and a considerable division of labour. Communal action is not possible under such conditions.

In Mexico tenure of communal land of two kinds was recognized by the Agrarian Reform Law of 1917: collective *ejidos*, land units held and worked communally by the village or community, and individually worked but communally owned *ejidos*. In either case the *ejidatario* is forbidden to sell or mortgage his land, and if he does not use it, it reverts to the community. This institution does build on traditional community organization, the *altepetlacalli*, a pre-Columbian (probably pre-Aztec) land-tenure organization, which had survived the land seizures of the colonial period and the abolition of communal ownership in the 1850s.

Bolivia's land reform dates from 1953. For the most part it concentrated, as in Chile, on the great *latifundios*, which were expropriated or taken over by their workers in advance of the laws of 1953 and did little to help the *comunidades*. Later, after 1969, the communities benefited from new or better surveys of their land and from titles to it, but the reform has not created new communities or helped to rebuild old ones; perhaps in Bolivia the takeover of communes by the great estates had gone so far that it was irreversible. But it remains true that community organization of work, for example at harvest time or in house construction, has survived to the present and offers an opportunity for modern economic organization.

The development model and the social factor

A development structure modified from the standard centre–periphery model was outlined above. It included, in addition to central regions and others focused on the centre, for which the relationship may or may not be beneficial, regions with an exterior, primary-export orientation and, at least in theory, regions of endogenous development. If to this largely economic model we add the social dimension, there is a further kind of modification to make. Rather than a solely economic structure based on relations with the internal or external centres, a socio-economic structure with a basic division between modern societies and those with some degree of traditional organization is appropriate. Such a model may be exemplified by reference to Venezuela, which Friedmann used as his own test-bed. Here a basic social division may be made between the core southern Andean regions, in Mérida, Táchira and Trujillo, identified by a traditional society and a residual reciprocity structure in its rural communities; regions of primitive society in the remote mountains of Perijá, the delta country of the Orinoco and the vast Guayana territory in Bolivar and Amazonas states; and the market regions which comprise the remainder of the country.

Alongside the social axis, a separate economic axis then differentiates between core, developed and underdeveloped regions, and export base regions. Individual regions may then be classified as shown in Table 20.

Obviously, the social and economic regions are for the most part

Table 20 *Venezuela: regional classification*

Economic dimension	Social dimension		
	Market regions	Traditional	Primitive
Core regions	Caracas and vicinity		
Developed regions	Caracas–Valencia axis Puerto Cabello		
Underdeveloped regions	Northern Andes Lara–Falcon Northern Llanos Oriente–Sucre and Monagas	Southern Andes Mérida–Trujillo Táchira	
Export base regions	Southern Llanos Oil regions of Zulia and Anzoategui Margarita Island		
Resource regions			Guayana Perijá Mts Orinoco Delta

parallel – modern societies occupy the core and developed regions; traditional ones may share with them the underdeveloped and the export base regions, and primitive social groups occupy remote resource regions. What it is sought to emphasize here is that the social dimension is important and should be considered prior to economic dimensions. Both social and economic divisions are likely to correspond with physical patterns. For Peru the socio-economic structure parallels the division between Costa, Sierra and Selva. On the Costa lies the modern society metropolitan region of Lima–El Callao, and the many river valleys to north and south are the modernized export base regions producing sugar cane and cotton. To the east the Sierra highlands are a traditional culture area with subsistence economy. Further east still the Selvas has primitive societies and economies and represents a resource region (oil, gas, timber, hydroelectric power) for the market-oriented regions to the west of it.

Which way to a policy?

Studies of migration and of capital movement suggest that powerful forces of centralization continue to dominate in Latin America and are evidenced too in a centralized spatial pattern and dynamic. Thus a first conclusion, in policy terms, is that a free-market approach, awaiting factor movements to reduce inter-regional differences, cannot be relied on. On the other hand, the 'developmentalist' approach as it is sometimes called, or 'diffusionist' approach, as I would prefer to call it (we are all interested in development, but diffusion specifies a mechanism) is placed in some doubt. It seems ill-advised to promote more ease in transport and urban infrastructure when one aim is to reverse or check the rural–urban flow of human and physical resources. Perhaps instead a separation between regions and their greater autonomy should be the aim?

So far this line of thought might be acceptable to the dependency school of thought (though this school has produced few practical suggestions for a balancing mechanism among regions). But doubt is cast too on the dependency interpretation. Some regions are capable of at least a semi-autonomous kind of economic growth. Others may suffer from some kind of involution, a dualism evolving to separate modern and traditional urban and rural economies; and both this kind of separation and that due to social isolation between modern, traditional and primitive peoples run counter to the dependency school's idea that there is already 'integration' in a capitalist economy.

Evidently, neither a simple diffusion–integration policy nor one of total regional autonomy is entirely acceptable as a remedy for Latin American regional imbalances. The regions are too varied in their character to allow for planning dogma, and plans must be modified to suit conditions in each country. Some suggestions for a regional policy, following a review of its current status, are made in the following pages.

6 Regional policies and recommendations

Most regional planning theory has been evolved in Western industrialized countries. It has been developed as a by-product of economics, emerging at a late stage; standing at a much lower level of generalization, it has produced much more diversified ideas and analyses (according to what kind of evidence is used and which parts of the world are the test-beds). For some economists, and certainly for a large number of policy-makers, it has been easiest to follow neoclassical thinking in regional planning, with measures that change the relative costs to regions of the two mobile factors of production labour and capital. Capital as a completely mobile factor will move from developed, industrialized regions to less developed areas where returns are higher, while labour migration will be from low- to high-wage areas. These two movements jointly will smooth the differences between rich and poor regions by progressively establishing capital/labour ratio which is near to constant over space.

Those following this line of thought have extended it by allowing some imperfections in mobility, such as incomplete knowledge on the part of entrepreneurs and potential migrants, but still see the most useful policies as those directed towards movement of labour or capital, either restricting or encouraging it. In Europe the measures commonly used, such as regional employment premiums, inducements to capital such as grants to incoming firms, tax remissions, factory buildings at low cost, credit provision and management advice, are an acknowledgement of the very real frictions that exist for capital and labour when considering movement. But this is not a renunciation of neoclassical theory, merely an adjustment to cater for imperfections in factor mobility without admissions that these might not be the main tools of regional change or that they might operate under different stimuli to the economic ones which are the common object of policy. Labour migration is the other major element in factor mobility, but since migration is usually renounced as an element of policy because it can be socially damaging, most effort is devoted to convincing firms to establish new plant in, thus moving capital to, selected regions.

In opposition to the neoclassical school, other writers have evolved theories of regional development emphasizing development as a result of technical advance at spatially defined points, principally the main cities, and spreading to other places through some kind of diffusion movement. Technical knowledge and its use are not taken as constants but as the principal dynamic forces for development. The diffusion of technology outwards is largely through the urban hierarchy, from large city to small, but large cities maintain a lead through continual innovation and the various economies of urban agglomeration. These kinds of factors are put forward by writers on spatial growth who would advise integration as the main aid to forward development for regions (Friedmann 1966, 1971a, 1971b; Melchior 1972; Pedersen 1975; Pred 1966, 1977; Richardson 1973a; Robson 1973). These writers have links with a large literature on economic development in general which emphasizes unbalanced growth, spatial or sectoral concentration, growth poles and growth centres in the promotion of economic development.

For the writers named above, the 'diffusionist' school, if we wish to give them a tag, the best regional policy must be not the modification of cost surfaces, as under neoclassical theory, but the building of an infrastructure which would optimize diffusion of development, would allow it to spread with greatest facility. Emphasis would be less on purely economic measures, such as taxes, relief from tax, credits and loans, and more on physical planning, particularly those kinds of plan devoted to the urban network and the linkages within it. There are, of course, academic debates about precisely how diffusion takes place, and particularly about the balance between local spread and hierarchical movement from larger to smaller settlements, but there is broad agreement that movement is composed of both these elements in some kind of mix. In fact, Pedersen and Robson both adopt a gravity-model formulation to simulate the diffusion processes they wish to examine (respectively, innovations in nineteenth-century Britain and economic development in South America). Such a model, of the general form $\dfrac{P_A \, P_B}{d_{AB}}$, implies both a hierarchical effect in relating diffusion between points A and B to population size, and a contagious effect in the denominator d_{AB} which is some index of distance between the points.

In this chapter we shall endorse a policy closer to that which may be derived from the 'diffusionist' school of thought than to neoclassical ideas. Urban agglomeration attractions of the metropolis must be balanced by others in secondary towns, and a stress on physical infrastructure building must be continued. Some caveats must, however, be entered with respect to the sequence of different kinds of infrastructural measures (do inter-regional roads and major regional growth poles come before smaller scale developments?) and also with respect to regions of distinctive social structure. Growth-pole-type policies may indeed be seen to be a poor tool, as applied hitherto in Latin American contexts, and it may be argued that they are wholly inappropriate because of the structure of industry (Conroy 1973). A primary emphasis, it is maintained, should be laid on intra-regional development, by which term we imply a growth process which is largely endogenous, dependent only minimally on outside stimuli. This does not obviate the need for national spatial policies; such policies are, in fact, urgently required to counteract the tendencies of national *growth* policies such as import substitution and to encourage further centralization of economic activity. Appropriate spatial policies will be found to include both directly regional measures and national policies, such as tax or land reforms designed to reduce disparities in wealth, because these latter will be most effective in helping poorer regions.

In Latin America itself the history of regional development is quite distinct from that of Europe, as shown by Gilbert (1974b) and Stöhr (1975); as a result, measures radically different from the neoclassical have been employed. Some development agencies grew out of natural disasters and the social pressure these placed on national governments. In north-east Brazil, as Kleinpenning (1971) explains, recurrent droughts from the 1870s onwards led to drought control and relief measures in the 1900s, to partial attempts at positive incentives for development, then towards integrated effort under SUDENE, created in 1959 as a regional agency with broad powers. In Chile the 1960 earthquake on the Concepción–Valdivia coastline led partially to the regionalization of the national development agency, CORFO. In Mexico frequent flooding of vast areas in the south and problems of irrigation management in the north led to the river basin commissions from 1947. Bromley

(1977) traces the origins of regional planning in Ecuador, with the CREA commission dating from 1958, to the combination of production crises in agriculture and a growing population and declining panama hat industry in the region of the southern Sierra, around Cuenca.

In other cases political expediency has predominated. In Venezuela the origins of the CVG, the agency for the Guayana territory, are in the political need to nationalize or bring under national control the mineral ore resources of Guayana, and regional programmes were attached to this need. Often political need has been allied to aims of military control and the ensuring of national security or of firming insecure national claims to border territories. This has been behind regional planning in Argentina (Morris 1972) and the Programme for National Integration (PIN) of Brazil in the 1970s, which has concentrated on road building and agricultural colonization (Cardoso and Müller 1977); similar factors underlie Amazon settlement plans of the other countries of this little-settled basin (Goulder 1979).

In all these cases the measures likely to be adopted are not those designed to alter in some way the surfaces of cost and revenue for entrepreneurs, but directly physical measures attacking problems such as transport improvement, the provision of rural settlements with basic infrastructure, power generation projects, irrigation or flood control. For the most part they do not claim to, or even seek to, change the imbalances of welfare between or within regions; they are agnostic on these issues, providing only specific physical reactions to physical situations.

For the most part, the regional policies do not amount to a national scheme, nor do they have any comprehensive viewpoint or philosophy of regional development. They are, rather, single-region schemes and may focus on an infrastructural measure which has little at all directly to do with innovation and diffusion, spread or 'backwash' effects. The positive point to be made, however, is that Latin America has established a tradition of sorts in physical planning, which is a useful background to any comprehensive regional planning effort which seeks to emphasize the physical structure of a nation. The mechanisms which have been used are those which are suited to the modification and improvement of physical structure.

Current policies

A complete state-of-the-art account of Latin American regional planning is not attempted here. There are already two excellent works on this subject written during the 1970s (Stöhr 1975; Gilbert 1974a), and the descriptions and analyses made in them are not materially out of date. It is appropriate, however, to refer briefly now to current planning to show the degree of success enjoyed by different kinds of plans and the lessons which may be learnt from them. A complete system of regions with co-ordinated plans has not been devised by any Latin American nation, though Chile had advanced quite far towards one by 1970 (Stöhr 1975, p. 32); Argentina had developed a sophisticated regional planning structure under its development agency, CONADE, before Perón's second advent in 1973; and Mexico has a national scheme for rural areas, though not for cities. Most of the effective planning has been for individual regions, which is natural enough considering the origin of most plans in a need to combat a particular local crisis or longer-term problem. Some national plans, it is true, have had considerable significance for the regions, but they have not typically been designed with regional concerns to the forefront; such are the agrarian reform programmes which, as Smith (1975) has pointed out, could be made key elements in regional policy, though they have never been so treated.

Four major types of policy seem worthy of some description. They are:

1 river basin programmes;
2 individual problem-region plans;
3 colonization and settlement plans;
4 growth-pole policies.

River basin programmes

These have often arisen in response to major floods and the need for their control. Mexico provides some of the best examples, with its modern programmes beginning under the presidency of Miguel Alemán (1946–52). Because of his personal force of character and interest as a native and former governor of the state of Veracruz, this low-lying, often flooded valley was endowed with an agency in 1947 for the multi-purpose development of the river and valley, focusing on the expansion of agricultural and power production which would add to the nation's resources rather than help local government. In the long term, because of the lack of community development or of social measures such as the provision of schools and hospitals, the stated aims of colonization on the lowlands are largely still to be fulfilled (Barkin 1972, pp. 151–85). A similar lack of a regional effect (as opposed to increased production for national markets, which has certainly been achieved) may be found in the other river basin projects of Mexico, those for the Grijalva–Usumacinta valleys in the tropical south, the Fuerte in the north-west, the Lerma–Chapala–Santiago in the centre, and the Balsas scheme, which grew out of the Tepalcatepec programme in the south-west. These schemes have the administrative advantage that their boundaries are those of the respective river basins and not state boundaries, so that rivalries between the various Mexican states do not affect regional policy; but their action is limited to irrigation, power production, soil conservation and related activities and falls short of comprehensive planning. Even if we overlook its bias towards national development rather than regional, this approach has the limitations of restriction to river basins and their physical problems, and omits the urban network altogether. At the present time Mexican politicians seem to have lost interest in river basin planning, and there are no new schemes of this kind.

In Colombia perhaps the best example of a river basin authority is the Cauca Valley Corporation (CVC), set up in 1954 with the purpose, again, of flood control on the flat Middle Cauca valley, hydroelectric power provision, and land reform and colonization on the flooded meadows of the river, fertile enough for intensive arable use but used then only for extensive cattle grazing by the owners of the great *latifundia* which occupied the valley. In this case much of the infrastructural work has been successfully completed (Morris 1979, p. 227), but the role of the agency has been gradually diminished; it was finally restricted to power provision after it lost its autonomy to the Ministry of Agriculture in 1968. (Even in power production it has had limited success and the advantages of agricultural development have largely benefited existing large land-owners.) Corporations of a similar nature (Stöhr 1975, pp. 18–19, Table 1) were set up for the Sabana of Bogotá, and for Magdalena Valley, the Guindio and the department of Chocó on the Pacific coast. Regional development in each case has been limited by the national government, which had always been envious of the initial autonomy and success of the CVC and of what Gilbert terms its 'image' (Gilbert 1974b, p. 266). While every river basin project is termed multi-purpose, the scope of them in Colombia, as much as elsewhere, is too narrow and its focus often too much on the provision of goods for other regions.

The sectoral concentration on power, irrigation or flood control is hard to reconcile with the purpose of general regional improvement, even if we admit that a lead sector is desirable in economic development, for the 'leads' given have too frequently no regional multiplier effect, the benefits being drained outwards. Even for large-scale river basin planning, such as that proposed under the River Plate Basin Treaty between Argentina, Bolivia, Brazil, Paraguay and Uruguay, the emphasis is on a few water-use-related developments such as the great hydroelectric power plants on the Paraná (this has not eliminated quarrels between Brazil and Argentina over the location of dams) and improvements in transport in border regions between adjacent countries. As to the Amazon Basin, the Treaty of Amazonian Co-operation, signed in 1978 by Bolivia, Colombia, Ecuador, Guyana, Surinam and Venezuela, is very weak (Goulder 1979). It provides only for research co-operation and data collection but has no instruments for economic or physical integration as with the River Plate Basin.

Problem-region programmes

A second general category is that of the problem regions. We need not consider here the urban plans which have been prepared for many large cities – a special sub-category of problem regions with their large slum and shanty population and congestion problems – and restrict our remarks to broader, mostly rural regions suffering from agricultural poverty, large and often dense populations in relation to resources, the lack of industry or of any dynamics in the economy, and various structural problems in agriculture such as antiquated tenure systems, the polarization of society into rich land-owners and poor peasants. The best-known programme under the heading is that of SUDENE in Brazil, though other schemes – for Ecuadorean regions for Oaxaca and the southern Mexican Balsas scheme, in Venezuela the plans for the centre-west under FUDECO and for the north-east – are all more or less aimed at improving life for a large segment of the population, often with a history of some previous development but suffering from present-day stagnation and a lack of economic prospects.

From the history of the north-east's droughts, it could be

expected that the approach to problem-solving would be initially through a relief operation. In this region attempts to solve the drought problem were begun after the great 1877–9 drought, including a long-distance interbasin river water transfer, but no effective action was taken (Kleinpenning 1971). Throughout the first half of the present century efforts were centred on a *política hidráulica*, a policy directed (through a national agency, DNOCS) at improving water supplies. A river basin authority was set up for the São Francisco valley section of the north-east in 1948. The Commissão do Vale do São Francisco (CVSF) achieved little, however, apart from its main aim of harnessing the power of the river São Francisco, from 1955 onwards, at the Paulo Afonso dam. Local regional development was encouraged by a regional bank and state organizations in the 1950s, then followed by a comprehensive regional agency, the Superintendency for the North-east (SU-DENE), in 1958. This body had relative freedom of action between that time and 1970, when it lost some of its autonomy under the military government. Emphasis in SUDENE plans was initially on infrastructural work, and two-thirds of its first budget was allocated to roads and power (Henshall and Momsen 1974); it then moved towards the encouragement of industries, with the effect of generating a few important industrial nodes at the great cities, Salvador, Recife and Fortaleza, and finally to a more rounded structure involving industry of both large-scale and cottage type, agricultural assistance and the promotion of subsistence as well as commercial crops to avoid some of the worst effects of drought. This programme has been coarse-grained, obviously missing many holes of poverty in isolated rural environments, and as in other problem regions, the impact of modern technology on rural communities has sometimes been one of confrontation and competition rather than assistance and integration. The emphasis placed on long-distance road networks rather than local roads and communications; the industrial concentration on a few major urban centres; the influence of large outside firms on industrial development because of the nature of the fiscal and capital attractions given to such firms under the well publicized '34/18' tax incentive scheme, which allowed corporations to invest taxes owed to central government in SUDENE – approved schemes – all these elements have meant a polarization of economic development within the region and have perhaps exacerbated the problem of out-migration of the best human resources to other regions, notably to the south-east.

An intermediate approach between the strictly technical river basin authority and the problem region agency is illustrated from Mexico, where the river basin agencies have had relatively wide powers. The Balsas basin, occupying 112,000 square kilometres of south-central Mexico, is an important example of the river basin approach adapted to the exigencies of rural poverty. Much of it lies in the *tierra caliente*, and much of the farmed land is steep-sloping, eroded hillsides. It has subsistence farming with some commercial ranching and sugar cane production and a dense population scattered through many small settlements. In 1947 the Tepalcatepec Commission was formed by the government to develop water use on this tributary of the Balsas. In addition to irrigation it planned hydroelectric power installations, copper, silver and iron-ore mining, a seaport on the Pacific at Las Truchas associated with a steel mill, pulp and paper manufacture (Cardenas 1972).

From 1960 the Rio Balsas Commission took over the Tepalcatepec's functions for the whole basin, with powers also involving the planning and stimulation of settlement, road, rail and communications systems, education and culture. The main thrust of planning has been directed, however, at rural areas, with emphasis on irrigation in small-scale systems on the tributary rivers. Planning even in this sector is incomplete because agrarian reform projects come under the Agriculture Ministry and because the irrigation projects effect only limited areas, primarily in the *tierra caliente*. Even this kind of river basin planning, though less restricted in character than that adopted in Colombia or the international plans for the River Plate Basin, falls far short of comprehensive planning for the region.

Although not recognized as such, agrarian reform programmes carry a sizeable regional planning element because agriculture is highly dispersed over the national territory if for no other reason. Inevitably, then, a thoroughgoing agrarian reform such as that being undertaken by Peru may be expected to have important effects on regional development. Later in this chapter some suggestions will be made for the structuring of post-reform units in different regions, but some comment on present practice, as illustrated by Peru, may help our understanding. This discussion is included here because agrarian reform is an attack on one of the principal problems of most problem regions.

Following a long history of hesitant political movement towards land reform of one kind or another, the military government which assumed power in Peru in October 1968 introduced agrarian reform in June 1969. It may be claimed that the main impact of this reform is in the problem region of the Sierra because in the coast region the expropriated sugar estates, the first to feel the effect of reform, were maintained as large-scale, modernized concerns, though under new ownership as Agricultural Production Co-operatives (CAPs). The profits are to be shared among the permanent workers, leaving temporary harvest workers without these benefits (Harding in Lowenthal 1975, p. 242). In the Sierra different kinds of community farm units had to be made, and here the formation of co-operatives led to division through the separate interests of wage-earners and communities, as in the Agricultural Societies of Social Interest (SAIS). These were composed of estates plus neighbouring communities of Indians which help to manage the reformed estate but do not directly work it. As the co-operative formed out of the estate generates income both for its workers' wages and for the Indian communities, there is always the possibility of conflict between the two interests, especially when the human groups involved are quite distinct. An attempt to overcome such difficulties, and those resulting from the exclusion of many marginal groups from the benefits of reform, is the creation of the SINAMOS, larger scale regional institutions which have so far proved difficult to organize. Apart from the divisiveness of some reform measures, the fact that the redistributive effect of agrarian reform is limited to within the agrarian sector itself may also be criticized. One calculation is that, the re-allocation of as much as 50 per cent of total farm land would transfer only 1 per cent of national income to the rural poor (Thorp and Bertram 1978, p. 308). There is no mechanism for moving investment from industry into agriculture, and indeed industry may be viewed as bleeding agriculture because the lands expropriated have been paid for in government bonds which are to be invested in industry.

Alongside agrarian reform, Peru had a defined regional policy, as stated in its Development Plan for 1975–8 (Peru 1975). Four kinds of region are singled out for special action – zones of comparative advantage where commercial production is concentrated, depressed Andean lands, economic frontiers where colonization is taking place and political frontier zones. This is not a complete regional division, as many areas are not included in any of the four; more seriously, the regional planning proposed is not integrated in any definite sense with the agrarian reform. The principal aim in the *areas deprimidas*, the problem areas of the Andes, is apparently to integrate them via farm-product exports to the nation and the exterior, using the regional town centres for the purpose of linking region and nation. Thus the plans do not capitalize on the essential differences in social structure between the poor Andean regions and the remainder of the country, seeking only to integrate them as rapidly as possible and, presumably, thus also to homogenize the whole of society, making the communal, co-operative kinds of structure endorsed by the agrarian reform movement still more difficult to put into practice.

Colonization and settlement

As shown in Chapter 5, a major feature of Latin American growth in agriculture has been a real expansion, and this fits in with the policies of many governments that have concentrated on regional development of this nature. The movement has a long history but is particularly associated with the growth of population in this century and the extension of road systems into the interior of the countries which have large undeveloped forest areas.

In Brazil the Amazon fringe has been subject to official colonization schemes from 1910 in Acre Territory, 1927 in Para state on the Tapajós river, 1930 in Amapá, 1946 in Maranhão in the Barra do Corda colony. Tavares *et al*. (1972) list projects affecting 1.4 million hectares in the Amazonian area *prior* to the organized settlement schemes from 1953 on. Because of their age, it is of interest to note the results of such programmes of colonization. Cardoso and Müller (1978) are critical of the prevalence of subsistence-level agriculture (30–50 per cent of production is for subsistence) and of the inexorable growth of a structure of large land-owners and small farmers mirroring conditions in the long-settled parts of the country and breeding, in the long term, the same tensions between social classes as are found in these older regions. Their conclusion regarding colonization is straightforward and could be applied to the other countries which have fostered settlement schemes on the rural fringe. For them, colonization has been:

a conscious effort not simply to occupy the Amazon wastes and settle the land, but to find a solution to the problem of demographic pressure in certain areas of the country; a kind of safety valve to avoid major problems without the need to take drastic measures to restructure property laws (Cardoso and Müller 1978, p. 141).

In 1953 Getulio Vargas sanctioned Law 1806, which set up the Superintendency of the Plan for Amazon development (SPVEA), an autonomous agency of central government with the function of comprehensive regional planning, including land settlement, and a separate endowment of tax revenues. Its aims could not be achieved, and more limited proposals were made by SPVEA's successor agency, SUDAM, created in 1966. This agency had officially created colonies on over 1 million hectares by 1973, together with the agrarian reform agency, INCRA, formed in 1970 out of previous agencies. But the number of families settled, some 7600 by 1973, was much less remarkable than the 1 million hectares especially in view of the aim of resettling north-easterners from overpopulated small farms in the drought region, where there were, and are still, 300,000 every year in need of relocation, on the most optimistic assumptions.

The parallel private action of land occupation in the Amazon region has little relevance to the employment problem or to regional development. On the one hand, there is continuous encroachment on the forest by private ranchers acting on their own. On the other hand, and better known, is the policy of SUDAM to support large-scale schemes for various kinds of development through fiscal remissions. Most of the projects, 335 out of 528 in June 1976 (Kleinpenning 1977), have been for agriculture, very largely livestock production on enormous ranches, many of them over 100,000 hectares with tiny work-forces and minimal infrastructure. As an example, one of them, Suia-Missu, has 678,000 hectares but will employ permanently only 250 men. The total impact of existing projects is likely to be about 15,000 jobs, while infrastructure and industrial linkages for later users of the region are almost entirely absent. SUDAM's primary incentive for these developments has been the fiscal device of allowing firms and individuals to place 50 per cent of taxes owed to government into the Banco da Amazonia, which can then be used on authorized projects. This policy is obviously biased towards the large firm, whose tax bill is correspondingly large and which has the entrepreneurial and management skills to handle large Amazonian ranches. It does not help small firms or individuals within the region. Most money, over 90 per cent, comes from the centre-south region – that is, from the metropolitan centres of São Paulo and Rio.

Colonization has, of course, been only one arm of a dual policy since 1970 under the Programme of National Integration (PIN).

The other arm is road construction, and most notable in the context of linking agricultural settlement with transport means has been the Transamazon road, at least in its intended effects. This road, running from Porto Franco on the Belém–Brasília highway, where it reaches the Tocantins river, to Humaita on the Madeira (reached in 1974) and to Porto Velho, from which access to Peru will be possible, seems to respond to two real problems, a strategic-integrative one – that of achieving access to and control over distant and isolated frontier zones – and a demographic one, in acting as a direct safety valve for movement out of the north-east's lands in drought periods and as a regular, long-term siphon of excess population. In this respect it differs somewhat from the older Belém–Brasília road, built between 1958 and 1973, when it was finally paved, or from the Northern Perimeter Highway, built north of the Amazon from 1973 on, or the Cuiabá–Santarém road; these all act more directly as inter-regional links, without focusing on the development of the land they traverse.

But even the Transamazónica, despite policy, scarcely meets the requirements of agricultural settlement; the through road is not accompanied by a network of smaller access roads to nearby settlements, let alone roads to individual farmsteads, such as would be needed for marketing bulky products. Agriculture in the colonization areas is forced into semi-subsistence operations for this if no other reason. Nor does it connect adequately the relatively fertile lands, the *terra roxa* soil areas along the fringe of the Brazilian shield, but concentrates most effectively on linking the heads of river navigation on the Amazon tributaries so as to provide a through transport network with the rivers. Like the other great roads, the Transamazon provides an inter-regional net, not a regional transport system.

The progress of colonization organized along the Transamazónica in association with road building typifies some of the main problems attaching to any intensive agricultural land use of the area. In the period 1970–3 the plans were for blocks of land to be opened by side roads and settlements of between forty-eight and sixty-four colonist families, the *agrovilas*, to be established, with basic services. Higher-order centres with administrative services, schools and industries were to be located among these and would constitute the *agropolis* with populations of 1500–3000. In the event, the 100-hectare lots of land were not totally cleared by colonists, for want of machinery or labour, and they have generally taken up farming by shifting cultivation methods, using under 10 hectares, so that the total cultivated is under 10 per cent of the planned area. Fertilizers are not used; animals are not incorporated into the farm system; major crops are rice, beans and maize for subsistence. Co-operatives have not flourished, nor have the peasants made use of the agricultural advice services available to them (Kleinpenning 1977). The *agrovilas* have placed farmers at some distance from their farms, a disadvantage when transport means are still primitive, and farmers have abandoned some of the houses they own in the *agrovilas*.

Apart from assisting with agricultural colonization, Brazilian planners also thought of the through roads as having a secondary economic function – that of helping with the exploitation of minerals. But this seems a thin line of reasoning, especially in view of the limited use of the roads to date for mineral extraction and the lack of firm knowledge about the mineral wealth of the region before the start of the PIN programme. The critique of the road projects must therefore rest with their function as colonizer agents and national integration highways. This latter function they can no doubt fulfil, though the type of threat likely from neighbouring territories would scarcely warrant the enormous road investments being made. But for the purposes of colonization and rural regional development the roads policy leaves much to be desired. Kleinpenning (1978) has noted a recent trend in Brazilian Amazon policy away from small-farmer colonization altogether, concentrating on the combination of mineral exploitation and large-scale ranching, as mentioned earlier, at agricultural–mineral 'poles' such as Carajas (iron ore), Trombetas (bauxite) and Amapá (manganese).

Rather than regional development, the colonization schemes have been a panacea for national problems (resource supply, population pressure) which have involved, in an incidental manner, some specific regions. These schemes, in following an already existent tendency towards expansion of the settled areas in tropical lowlands, fail to face up to the many structural problems of developed agricultural regions. As with the river basin planning and that for problem regions, the major emphasis is on physical planning, with little effective concern for social or economic measures. And within the physical planning of infrastructural works the spatial aspects would seem to have had insufficient consideration. It may be, as Wilson (1973) claims, that transport investments have wide indirect effects in underdeveloped countries as compared with investments in more directly productive activities, and that the emergence of entrepreneurial skills, the changing of communal attitudes and the spread of new ideas and technology are all fostered by road networks and the transport system they engender; the scale and pattern of such investments must be considered as a first priority, however, not as an afterthought.

In terms of the growth processes of Chapter 1, colonization is spatial expansion superficially like that described for Figure 1 (page 32). Any development of peripheral regions relies on that of the centre and is not autonomous; but, in fact, development is scarcely an appropriate term at all, for what occurs over wide areas (the expansion of near-subsistence agriculture with no net measurable increase in welfare for the colonists) is simply spatial growth without forward development.

Growth-pole and other urban network policies

Following the relatively successful application of a growth-pole policy in France during the 1950s and 1960s, several Latin American countries attempted to adopt such policies. Chile was one such enthusiast for these new policies, which emphasized the spread effects attributable to the urban network and the linkages of selected growth industries. After a phase of designating isolated regions as free ports (Arica near the Peruvian border in 1953, then the southern provinces of Magallanes, Aysen and Chile from 1956), Chile moved towards a national set of planning regions and plans through the creation of the National Planning Office, ODEPLAN (Larrain 1972). Each of the twelve regions was endowed with a pole of development by ODEPLAN, supported by one or more *focos*, local poles. The poles were ranked thus by ODEPLAN: (1) Santiago, as national pole; (2) Antofagasta, Valparaiso and Concepción, as interregional poles and counter-magnets to Santiago (3) regional development poles, which included most of the provincial capitals.

According to Bedrack (1974), these poles did not have the outwards radiating effect that they are supposed to have in theory, and instead of promoting growth and modernization over their whole hinterland, served instead to concentrate it in upon themselves, attracting migrants from the countryside and the greater measure of all capital investment. Bedrack cites Region 1, coincident with the province of Tarapacá, where the designed pole of

Arica certainly grew through its status as free port and through the automobile assembly industry which was directed from Santiago to this site, a highly artificial location because neither markets nor suppliers or linked industries were to be found in the northern desert region (Gwynne 1978). The *foco* of Iquique also grew, but other areas, such as the nitrate-mining regions, suffered total eclipse; the last of the nitrate mines of this province closed finally between 1965 and 1970. Some small irrigated valleys improved their infrastructure but suffered other faults in agricultural development. In Region II, Antofagasta, development was confined to Antofagasta City and Calama, and all real investment was confined to these two cities.

Such examples are, of course, not really tests of the growth-pole thesis, which is that the establishment of a modern dynamic sector or industry, with extensive linkages throughout the regional economy, will generate regional growth and spread prosperity widely in the area to which it is assigned and (notably when it is also a spatial pole) an urban centre capable of spreading modern technology around it. Antofagasta's industrial growth was copper-related, linked only with mines in the mountains (particularly Chuquicamata) and with outside markets, with the addition of a cement manufacture; Arica's was dependent on car assembly, using imported kits which were then sent on to Santiago to be sold. What multiplier effects existed were external. This experience was matched by and large in other provinces, suggesting, as Conroy (1973) argues, that growth poles are inappropriate for underdeveloped countries on economic as well as other grounds. Boisier (in ILPES 1974) comments that while the industries chosen may have been appropriate, the spatial structure of the province, and especially the lack of an urban network, hindered spread effects from the growth pole.

Chilean policy under Allende from 1970–3, despite its revolutionary aims, did not, in fact, make a major break from the diffusionist view of regional development implied in the 1960s growth poles. In place of the poles, a regional system of *centros poblados*, or settlements, was proposed as the structural element for development (Bedrack 1974, p. 74). Acknowledging the failure of growth poles to help development outside the pole itself, the tendency for them to become growth *points* within a desert of underdevelopment, ODEPLAN now sought 'concentrated deconcentration' by moving activities out from the major cities to smaller ones and by gathering together the dispersed rural population. But the system of settlements to be established, building up from the smallest (the 'basic territorial units') to microregional, then to regional and national centres, was in effect only the designation of an urban hierarchy, to which activities were to be allocated in a form not very distinct from the classical principles used by Christaller (1966) in his structuring of urban service centres. Development hopes were still pinned to the urban network as transmitter of growth.

In effect, as Hojman admits (1974, p. 103), the major changes that could be achieved through an industrial relocation policy that assigned industries to each level of the urban hierarchy were slight, as most of Chilean major industry was resource-based and its location accordingly fixed. In the copper and iron mines of the north and the oil- and gas-related industries of the far south there was little that could be done. In place of growth poles as the central concept for development, a 'corridor of development' (Hojman 1974, p. 43) was to be established between the Rio Elqui in Atacama province and the Reloncavi Basin in Llanquihue province in the south, a great north-south line of over 600 kilometres. Within it economic activity of all kinds was to be integrated by improved transport lines. This loosely defined concept did not negate the role of the major cities as nodes along the line, but hoped that the economies of north and south would become integrated with one another and that the spread effects of development would reach all urban centres along the axis, even extending out, via cross links, towards the coast and mountains in east-west directions. Such a policy was, indeed, scarcely more than the confirmation of an existing economic structure, which is based on predominantly north–south ties. Industrial growth poles were also not abandoned. La Serena–Coquimbo, Concepción and Valdivia–Puerto Montt were to serve as 'deconcentration' centres attracting industry and services away from Santiago. Talca and Temuco were envisaged as secondary centres of a similar character, and Rancagua as a centre for the direct displacement of metropolitan functions.

In Argentina the growth-pole idea was also put unsuccessfully into practice in the 1971 Plan, through an erroneous designation of both the industries and the cities which were to be poles (Morris 1972, 1975). A group of towns was named as pole for the north-west – Salta, Jujuy, Guemes and San Pedro; in the north-east, Corrientes City and Resistencia, on either side of the Paraná river, and

Posadas, Oberá and Santo Tome in the Misiones panhandle area of the far north-east. In Patagonia Zapala, Neuquén and the Upper Negro valley were seen collectively as a pole; Puerto Madryn, Trelew and Rawson, together with the iron-ore deposits at Sierra Grande, constituted another; and in the far south, Rio Gallegos and Rio Turbio. The placing of three of the six poles in Patagonia, where the total population was below 500,000, responded more to considerations of national security and control, including the affirmation of Argentina's claim to this desert territory with a substantial Chilean population, than to any regional aims.

Apart from Corrientes–Resistencia, which, when linked by a new bridge over the river, formed an agglomeration of over 500,000, the 'poles' were all loose arrangements of resource sites and small towns, which would have required substantial infrastructural improvements before any self-sustaining growth could be expected; there was in no case any adequate network of smaller towns to transmit growth outwards. Nor were the major industries chosen suitable for the growth-pole function. Electric power production (at Neuquén, Posadas and Salta), coal and oil (Rio Turbio, Guemes and San Pedro), metal-ore mining and manufacture (Puerto Madryn, Sierra Grande) were poor bases for regional multiplier effects, whether we consider their direct employment possibilities or their linkages to other industries.

In sum, the Argentine policy failed on both the spatial and the functional sides of the growth-pole idea. On the one hand, it did not identify industries with the joint characteristics of rapid growth and innovativeness, together with broad linkages, that Perroux had conceived as the essential elements of non-spatial growth poles; on the other, spatial growth-pole functions could not be fulfilled because the towns chosen were too small or, in the case of town groups, did not act as an integrated economic unit and so exercised little diffusion or spread effect.

Similar comments could be made about the equivalent policies in other countries. In Venezuela the massive efforts made in Ciudad Guayana on the lower Orinoco, with investment in steel manufacture, aluminium works and electric power production, have produced very limited linkages to the rest of the regional economy. As a sectoral choice for the growth-pole function, they thus have little to recommend them. In spatial terms, little can be expected because the Guayana region has virtually no urban network at all. What success has accrued to the Guayana project has been in terms of national production of electricity, steel and aluminium under the efficient administration of the Guayana Corporation (CVG). The relative autonomy of the CVG and the lack of competition from other regional organizations has allowed this economic success but not ensured a regional effect.

Growth poles and related policies may be seen as having functioned generally in Latin America to promote *national* growth and thus form part of a development process which approaches that modelled by Figure 1 (page 32). The centre Y achieves growth and X (representing the other regions), also grows, but only through spread effects and at a distance behind the centre, becoming more specialized in its function and thus more subject to the vagaries of the national or international markets.

Alternative policies

In Chapter 5 a set of possible regional types was outlined that included, in a social dimension, the market, traditional and primitive societies; on the economic plane, central, developing, under-developed, export base and resource regions. For each of these different policies would be appropriate to deal with their distinctive types of problem. Some general recommendations may be made at once, however, on the general nature of policy. The first is that comprehensive multi-regional planning, involving national planning agencies in place of the predominantly single-purpose, single-region bodies described above, should be introduced. This is, of course, an administrative convenience which allows co-ordination among sectoral and regional plans; but it also recognizes the interrelatedness of all the social, economic and physical characteristics of the region. Measures designed simply to attract capital, to house migrants, to build roads or factories are in themselves insufficient to solve regional problems and ineffective when not combined with other measures.

This suggestion is perhaps the greatest stumbling block in the way of regional development within many of the republics. The *ad hoc* nature of regional planning to date has been noted; given this background, it is easy to see why there are no good examples of comprehensive planning for all the regions of any nation.

Another general point is that policies for weaker regions should support truly regional (that is, intra-regional) development rather than the development of regions to fulfil national aims. As they enter the economy, export base regions and, over time, resource regions suffer exploitation to provide materials for either national or international markets. A style of development based on the building of penetration roads into such regions in order to siphon off resources is all too common, while policies for local infrastructure are infrequent and subsidiary. The principle of internationalizing development is extensible to most kinds of region and activity. Among infrastructural measures, besides road, rail and river lines of transport, the intra-regional development of communications lines, whether newspapers, radio, telephone or other services, may be encouraged. If financial stimuli to industrial or other activities are part of the regional policy, they should be stimuli which will encourage local establishments already in business or new enterprises from inside the region. They may have costs to face in the forgoing of the economic efficiency and advanced technology of large firms, but against these may be placed the creation of an optimistic environment for local enterprise. Obviously, the creation of any comprehensive policy for regions, as opposed to national policy affecting regions, must depend on a weighing of national shorter-term advantage against the longer-term regional effects of investment.

If such local regional industries are successful, they will, of course, eventually seek broader markets throughout the nation or perhaps abroad. This is all to the good, since such expansion will build on comparative advantages existing in the region, and in a way it is the opposite of import substitution, which has been widely criticized as producing an imbalanced and inefficient manufacturing sector. The concept of export promotion as a strategy for development in poor countries has itself been criticized (Jenkins 1978), both on theoretical grounds and on the evidence of progress made in this direction in one country, Mexico. But it would seem too early to make substantive criticisms of a policy that has never really been tested. In the case of Mexico, the exports are of capital-intensive, high-technology products which are produced largely by transnational companies for world markets, and they do not emanate from domestic enterprise or have much multiplier effect upon it. As to the theoretical considerations, Jenkins states that the policy is unsound because the comparative advantage idea forms part of neoclassical theory which is demonstrably unworkable in Latin America. The critique made in this book and elsewhere of neoclassical theory is, however, not of comparative advantage but of factor movements. Countries and regions may still have a relative advantage in the production of this or that good, regardless of the mobility of factors. A third and final general point before looking at types of region. In the developed countries policy has, since the experiments of the 1930s, largely eschewed the restraint or encouragement of labour movement, of migration. It has concentrated rather on capital movement, whether in the form of new plant, new firms or transferred functions from other areas. But in Latin America, as elsewhere in the poor regions of the world, migration is already taking place on a massive scale. It is therefore appropriate to incorporate some ideas on migration into policy, whether restraining or redirecting the flows.

Measures for the regions

Following the discussion of regional types in Chapter 5, a first division is made between the market-economy areas and others. The first of these includes metropolitan developing and export base regions. In all of these society is organized on economic principles and responds directly to economic stimuli, so that a set of regional economic measures is appropriate and social measures may be regarded as secondary. All these regions are displayed in Figure 20.

Metropolitan areas

Most planners would agree that Latin American great cities are too large and growing too rapidly, though optimum size or growth rate are slippery concepts that have not allowed any objective definition (Richardson 1973b). Size and growth rate are separate items that have been somewhat confused with one another in writings on the subject, and perhaps most references to size problems are, in fact, concerned with growth characteristics, such as the lack of housing infrastructure for the new immigrants to the cities and deficiencies in public transportation means. Most of the great cities have grown too quickly to allow for the provision of basic infrastructure such as roads, water pipes or electricity, especially in shanty areas, which often occupy sites – notably in the Andean countries – that have inherent difficulties for development (because of slope or drainage) and a liability to flooding, as in parts of Asunción or Buenos Aires.
    Some economists have argued that pure size, and specifically that of the primate city, is not necessarily a bad feature of urbanization in

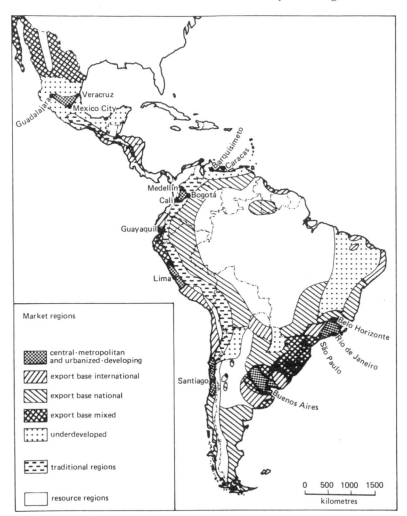

Figure 20 *Types of region for planning development. The central–metropolitan regions occupy very little space and are mapped together with the urbanized–developing regions as one type.*

less developed countries. Conroy (1976) cites other authors to show there is no constant relation between development and primacy, and that the concentration of entrepreneurial, administrative and economic activity at one point has advantages in agglomeration economies.

He also shows that over-urbanization, measured as excessive growth of service activities or underemployment of the urban labour force, is hard to prove, because the varying technologies of Latin America have different labour requirements from country to country as well as from sector to sector. Mera (1973) argues for the advantages of national growth being stimulated by concentration in one city, this growth outweighing benefits to the regions of alternative strategies. But such economistic views are too narrow; they do not recognize the social costs of agglomeration because these are not expressed in financial terms, nor do they explore the possible costs for non-metropolitan regions, and thus for the nation as a whole, of the growth of the metropolis itself.

In view of the undesirable features which obviously relate to agglomeration, excessive growth rates are arguably a basis for regional policy in metropolitan regions. Even if migration is reduced to zero, the great cities will continue to grow rapidly, an assumption based on their natural growth, which contributes heavily to the total (in the 1960s 67 per cent of Bototá's growth, 46 per cent of Caracas's, 32 per cent of São Paulo's). It is also contended, perhaps more controversially, though justified by the history of urbanization in Latin America, that metropolitan size relative to other cities (the primate city) is also a problem in Latin America because of a long history of colonial administrative convenience and trade centralization, continued in neo-colonial times through similar mechanisms. It is the weight of this tradition that forms the basis of positive policies to change urban structure.

Decentralization is thus an appropriate general policy and may be brought about by a combination of economic and physical measures. This may seem a mild recommendation, but it would constitute a major reversal of policy for at least some countries. Mexico, for example, had until fairly recently explicit subsidies for municipal services such as buses and taxis, even a subsidy on cheap foods, for the benefit of residents in Mexico City (Barkin and King 1970, p. 69). In Colombia the explicit policy of government in the period 1971–4 was development through urbanization (Ridler 1979). The advantages sought were those of agglomeration, rapid technological innovation and mechanization on new, larger farms which would be the result of a rural exodus. Congestion costs were supposed to be countered by creating semi-autonomous satellite cities just outside the metropolis.

Only two general points will be made here concerning the nature of desired metropolitan policy, first on the need for active measures, and second on the scale of region. A no-policy alternative might be proposed (as it could for the nation too), in the hope that regional problems will disappear of their own accord; this kind of interpretation does not accord with the view of factor movements and historical trends given in this book. On the other hand, it may be preferable to place the emphasis on positive attractions in other regions rather than on controls and restrictions in the metropolis. Absolute prohibition may be intolerable for some firms relying on the linkages they can obtain at the centre, and other kinds of firm may respond better to attractions from other regions than to restrictions in the centre. Active measures could be concentrated on physical controls such as land-use zoning to curb the distortions inherent in the social structure of great Latin American cities, notably the sectoral bias and irregular growth according to upper-class demand for urban space (Amato 1970; Morris 1978a).

The metropolitan region should be defined as a relatively large area, of perhaps 50 kilometres' radius, so that some part of decentralization policy can be accomplished within the metropolitan region itself. If neither labour nor capital is willing to move out to other regions, a limited deconcentration movement with satellites will allow reduction of the congestion costs of the metropolis, plus maintenance of the agglomeration advantages of the centre. This builds on the ideas of Geisse and Coraggio (1972) though without proposing, as seems to be the case in their paper, that this dispersed city, or 'great city', idea should be the sole or even principal arm of regional policy. If several large residential or industrial satellite cities can be promoted within the radius, metropolitan dwellers may maintain their access to cultural, educational and employment prospects and other metropolitan advantages, while the technical congestion and ecological problems of the large city may be shared between several centres. This kind of policy builds on and enlarges in scale one element of the policy proposed in Colombia in 1971–4 for 'cities within cities', self-contained units on the edge of the great cities, which would be built with government money and would be publicly owned (Ridler 1979). The present recommendation is not for public ownership, but to make use of existing settlements near the capitals, though more separated from it than is suggested by the suburban sites proposed in Colombia. Obviously, some countries (Chile, with Rancagua, San Antonio, Valparaiso as alternatives to Santiago; or Brazil, with São Paulo and its many satellite industrial cities) have a better chance of bringing in this 'dispersed metropolis' kind of plan than others such as Argentina, Paraguay, Venezuela or Mexico, where traditionally great *haciendas* have occupied land up to the city limits and have exercised a negative effect on the development of satellite towns.

It is not my intention to go into detail on intra-urban aspects of metropolitan regional planning. Urban land use has already been mentioned. One relatively detailed aspect of urban growth merits attention – the urban involution process mentioned in Chapter 5 and its areal connotations. The incorporation of slum and shanty town dwellers into urban life requires positive measures, beyond the passive tolerance of large areas of *barrios* in large cities. Informational services to help the migrants find jobs and homes, public transportation services, education services such as industrial training centres, post offices and telephone services are all necessary in the peripheral *barrios* or *tugurios* which spring up without any planning of infrastructure through the illegal occupation of public or privately owned sites. These measures, directed specifically at the *barrios* and not to be thought of as metropolitan-wide, are necessary if the metropolis is not to form the nation's most important area of contrasts in welfare, with all that that implies in terms of social tensions through the juxtaposition of great wealth and poverty. Friedmann (1971b) refers to these shanty town infrastructural provisions in a listing of planning priorities, but he omits reference to another group which is perhaps still more crucial, the central slum dwellers. These people are often, as in Bogotá, fresh migrants from the countryside (Flinn 1971) and therefore in greater need of help than the shanty town dwellers who are already endowed with experience of urban life. Informational and retraining schemes must be central to any aid programme for these people. Beyond all regional policies, national policy to limit inequalities between rich and poor seems also to be called for in metropolitan areas; this would reduce the need for microregional programmes which would need to be re-specified for each city every few years. National policies will be referred to again below, but the metropolitan poor would appear to be one of their targets in coalition with regional policies.

Urbanized developing regions

These are characterized by their high percentage of urban population, by the central importance of manufacturing industry and
services and by a generally good communications and transport
network among the urban centres. Their agricultural sector is
modernized and may be intensive in land use.

These regions are commonly overlooked altogether by current
policies in Latin America because of the tendency to regard them as
non-problem cities and to focus only on crisis regions. But it is
important that they be incorporated into a regional policy because
of their potential for dealing with problems both at the centre and
the periphery, to both of which they are transitional. On the one
hand, they may be used to forestall the migration movements into
the capital from peripheral regions by the attraction of housing and
job provision; on the other, they may pull capital investment out
from the centre by attractions to it. These functions might seem the
same as those for centres in the immediate metropolitan vicinity,
which were seen in the last section as having a counter-attraction
effect. But whereas such nearby centres would cater, perhaps only
with jobs or with housing, for people already installed in the
metropolitan areas and unlikely to be attracted out, the broader
regions considered now would cater to many migrants from rural
environments and small towns, and the location decisions to be
made would involve a definite choice between access to the metropolis and non-access (at least as commuters) in the developing
regions.

One leg of policy for such regions may be a growth-pole type.
Although these policies have failed in Latin America, their failure
has been in considerable measure a product of faulty application
rather than fundamental weakness. They have not been applied to
large cities in the developing regions because these have not been
sufficiently povery-stricken or lacking in industrial infrastructure.
But it is in such cities that they could best be applied, where the
transport, power and other infrastructure is sufficient and some kind
of industrial tradition is already in being. To illustrate, such policies
in Argentina would be best applied to the intermediate-sized cities
of the Pampas – Córdoba, Rosario, Santa Fé, Bahia Blanca – cities
with a substantial industrial base and a population of over
300,000 in each case, so that urban agglomeration economies are
strong; this would contract with a growth policy for remote small

towns in the distant interior. In Mexico such policies would be appropriate for what Odell and Preston (1973) term Mexico's 'core region', the axis between Guadalajara and Veracruz and would involve those two cities as well as Puebla, Queretaro and Leon, cities at some distance from, but well connected with the centre. In Peru existing strengths could be built on at those regional centres with some industrial growth and with an existing hinterland from which migrants are attracted and over which influence is spread. Cole and Mather (1978, ch. 5) show that the Costa has important regional migration foci at Piura, Chiclayo and Trujillo in the north and Arequipa in the south. These centres within the relatively modernized Costa could be counter-magnets to Lima.

The appropriate kinds of measure for such growth poles should, however, be carefully chosen. Financial aids such as credits, tax concessions, rapid depreciation of investments for tax purposes, subsidized or free factory buildings often serve to attract foreign firms which can most readily take advantage of the concessions, and such firms have known disadvantages from the point of view of regional development. They come with no existing links with local industry and may wish to operate a self-contained kind of industry in the region to avoid the complications of working with local firms. Assembly-line operations, whether of electronic calculators and other equipment or of large but still standardized objects such as motor cars, are typical of this problem. Their lack of attachment to other firms in the area makes these foreign firms footloose, able to leave at short notice when markets for their products decline. A further disadvantage is their tendency to use large capital inputs and relatively small amounts of labour. Such a tendency is inherent in modern high-technology firms, but it also relates to the fact that the attractions, if financial, as suggested above, are attractions to capital and not to labour.

If financial inducements must be adopted, they should be oriented to the local firms, defining these in terms of their place of origin and head offices, in the effort to stimulate an autochthonous development process. This kind of local bias may always be accused of being a regional version of the 'protection of infant industries', which has been often criticized by economists as a promoter of inefficiency in industry, but it is a more desirable measure at the regional than at the national level, since nations already have substantial protection through distance, customs, language and other barriers. Protection for regions has scarcely been attempted in the modern period.

If inducements to capital are to be handled with care and in a selective manner, direct implantation of industries seems still less desirable. In view of the general lack of vertical linkages among industries in Latin America, for the largely historical reasons examined in Chapter 5, little by way of a multiplier or growth-pole effect can be expected from the establishment of a steel mill, for example, or an aluminium refinery. Perhaps the best approach is infrastructural, encouraging regional development through the provision of an appropriate environment, especially at selected sites which may be termed growth poles. But this may be seen as only a part of a broader policy emphasizing road, power and water provision, the availability of industrial land, business services for industry and, on the human resource side, education at all levels, in recognition of the fact that these regions are recipients of large contingents of migrants with little preparation for modern urban living, let alone technical education. The provision of technical education should be a priority among educational goals. This kind of policy may intensify its effort at the growth poles but would be best applied over whole regions, or at least those parts which form the areas of influence of the proposed poles, if any spread effects are intended.

Alongside measures aimed chiefly at the manufacturing industries, other measures concerning the tertiary sector seem worth mentioning. Input–output studies often indicate the service industries to be linked most closely with other economic activities in the region (Schaffer 1976), so that any growth they achieve, other things being equal, will have maximum multiplier effects within the region. In Latin American countries the tertiary sector is already large and important; it has a relatively low capital–labour ratio and, as a substantial part of it is government employment, it is in the power of governments to redirect this industry to non-metropolitan locations. As yet another advantage, many of the office functions that are associated with central government could be easily decentralized because they have no geographic need to be located in the centre. Given the importance attached by industrialists to personal access to important ministries in the capital cities, a deconcentration of some government departments, or of segments of them, might be a first priority in regional policy.

International export base regions

Internationally oriented export base regions, such as the coffee lands of Central America, the cocoa and oil palm lowlands of Pacific Coast Ecuador and the sugar plantations of Guyana and Cuba, apparently have a difficult choice of target. If they choose to develop their specialized export products, they achieve efficient production levels and high returns but at the expense of over-specialization in the long term, with the consequent difficulty of conversion to other activities if markets decline. A constant danger is leaving redirection until a crisis has already emerged. In the long term the history of Peruvian guano, of Chilean nitrates, of Brazilian sugar or of Venezuelan oil suggests strongly the dangers of monocultural agriculture, of single-export economies in general and the lack of any real attack on the problems of market change. The choice of target (productive efficiency or regional welfare) is not, of course, left to the region, and because of the importance of these regions and their products (they may be the main earners of foreign currency for the nation), policy depends heavily on political will to help the region at national level, much more than in other regions, where large electorates may support measures for the region and where national efficiency aims are not greatly disturbed by, for example, a reshuffle of industry between major cities.

To some extent, a solution for the internationally oriented export base regions may be apparent in their redirection towards internal markets, especially in those larger countries whose national markets can absorb many of the raw materials from such regions. But this kind of reorientation must be viewed carefully by the region, because the national capital may replace overseas centres as dominant partners in a system which favours, in the long term, only the centre. The improvement of infrastructure connecting the region to the metropolis should be held, chronologically and in importance, behind the build-up of the local economy.

To illustrate, plans for the Argentine Pampas region should include investment in agricultural processing industries in market towns. Dairying, already important in parts of Santa Fé and Buenos Aires province (Morris 1972), could be linked more closely with the processing of dried milk, casein and cheese and butter production, as already has taken place successfully in part of central Santa Fé. For the beef-producing *estancias*, processing could be brought in through the establishment of regional slaughterhouses and meatpacking centres, to cater for internal markets if not the overseas markets. Fruit and vegetable crops could be introduced elsewhere in conjunction with processing plants. Outside agriculture, timber industries may utilize poorly drained lands, and tourism represents a major potential for the Buenos Aires coast. Such plans must be accompanied by infrastructural improvements. Cross-links among the various internal urban centres need improvements to counterbalance the already strong links with Buenos Aires and to establish an intra-regional network of towns and functions.

In other regions a more drastic spatial policy is desirable because the export base has led to an infrastructure entirely geared to the export markets. This is the case with the copper- and iron-mining regions of northern Chile, for example. Here the infrastructural elements of policy would be more prominent than in the Pampas, in order to improve roads and rail networks within the irrigated valleys and between them, to create a regional electric power grid, to build up regional fishing ports and facilities for freezing and processing, and especially to improve both domestic and agricultural water supplies throughout the region so as to allow for wider settlement and a broader economy. In this region such policies are eminently preferable to the artificial cultivation of manufacturing industries looking outwards for both supplies and markets because of special economic inducements, as was the case with the motor industry at Arica in the period 1967–74 (Johnson 1967; Gwynne 1978).

National export base regions

Argentina, Mexico and Brazil offer the best examples of export base regions oriented to domestic markets. In most of the cases (in Patagonia, the Chaco; Brazil's provinces of Goiás and Mato Grosso; the Mexican Mesa del Norte) physical limitations are dominant. Patagonia, the Argentine, Paraguayan and Bolivian Chaco and the Mesa del Norte are all desert lands. Brazil's centre-west suffers from poor soils. In human terms, though, these are not important poverty regions because they have few inhabitants, and the per capita income levels are frequently quite high. Policies for such regions thus may have a distinctive complexion.

For Patagonia, to promote an internal development presents substantial difficulties because of the physical restrictions. Hydroelectric power is abundantly available from the El Chocón–Cerros Colorados scheme, and other sites have great potential, but the power is transmitted to Buenos Aires. HIDRONOR, the company managing El Chocón, can control floods over the whole Negro valley and cultivate 1 million hectares, but there is no demand for land here, nor have industries been attracted by the cheap power. On the northern fringe of Patagonia inter-provincial disputes over the Rio Colorado were solved in 1978 (Morris 1978b) but this has not led to any massive settlement or development programme. Rather than use the water *in situ*, indeed, Mendoza province plans eventually to divert it northwards into existing irrigated lands of that province. But an apparently permanent export-base-type economy does not pose welfare problems for Patagonia. Its harsh environment deters large-scale settlement so that a good man/resource ratio is maintained. Poverty from unemployment is not a problem. In Argentina and Mexico (and possibly in other emerging national export base regions such as Venezuelan Guayana) policy is thus best directed towards the improvement of infrastructure rather than the attraction of industries or agricultural development aimed at increasing employment in what must remain thinly peopled regions. And the improvements may be inter-regional to allow exploitation of the region by the nation.

Other export base regions may be transitional towards the traditional region type, with relatively dense populations of impoverished rural folk. In Tucumán, the northern Argentine province producing sugar for the national market, the situation is complex because the environment offers more alternatives than does that of Patagonia, and the population is much denser. The 1966 crisis in the domestic sugar market and the withdrawal of subsidies to producers led to a government emergency plan for this province designed to attract new industries using credits and tax reliefs. Such policies, adopted in imitation of those of Western industrial countries, had very limited success, restricted to inducing Buenos Aires and foreign companies to produce footwear, electrical goods and sugar-related products such as alcoholic drinks and confectionery. But these industries were footloose; they established only branch factories for the most part and had few local linkages (Rofman 1974, pp. 254–5). Many of them have since left, and unemployment remains high. In such regions there is an urgent need to formulate comprehensive regional plans, based on more than temporary incentives, in order to use local enterprise for economic growth. Given the existing dominance of links with Buenos Aires, it is of importance to establish local infrastructure of road, communications and power and fuel supplies and, where incentives must be used, to use them for the encouragement of a diversification of local agriculture away from the plantation. Beef cattle, managed timber production, cotton and citrus crops are all possibilities for the region. Craft industries could be important to absorb some of the large body of unemployed.

But for this and some other export base regions which attract migrants, infrastructure and the direct encouragement of production is only one side of the coin. The other is a population policy; large numbers of migrants come from the whole north-west, and even from Paraguay and Bolivia, to work in the sugar industry in Tucumán and elsewhere in western Argentina during the harvest seasons. This seems illogical in view of the high rates of unemployment in Tucumán and generally in the north-west. It also forms part of a migration chain in which migrants from the rural areas to Argentine cities are replaced by Bolivians and migrants from the most distant rural areas to the commercial harvest lands of Mendoza, Tucumán or Salta. In this way it is an unsettling factor which does not make for a stable rural population, and therefore migration controls, at least for the incoming foreigners but also possibly for migrants from outside provinces, should be used. In other regions of export-base character, such as the humid Pampas or the Pacific coastlands of Ecuador, a modestly positive immigration policy is in order, to divert flows from metropolitan areas during difficult periods. The central point to be made here is that a migration policy should not be disdained in Latin America. In Europe or North America it may be looked upon as socially disruptive, but in Latin America migration is already a powerful process; a migration policy would merely serve to steer the migrants towards the most suitable areas for their settlement. It would not be intended actively to promote immigration, as this cannot be a solution for the densely peopled regions of emigration. But tolerance of it and some aid to settlers would provide a temporary solution during the demographic transition.

Resource regions

Those regions in which there has been, up to the present, very little development of a modern economy have developmental problems of a different order. First, there is no regional pressure for development, and where development plans have been made for such regions, they have been devised by central governments and in the interest of national development only. The natural tendency is for policy to centre on the use of these regions to promote national aims and to overlook negative effects on the region itself. Second, such areas often have a local population, but one which is very sparse, with a non-market socio-economic structure. The question thus arises of whether any special measures should be taken to care for these populations. The size of the native population in the Amazon Basin countries, where this problem is most obvious, is small compared with the large groups endowed with more advanced socio-economic structure. Goulder (1979) estimates the Colombian Amazon territory to have only 70,000 inhabitants and the total population density to be only 1.2 per square kilometre; in Ecuador the Oriente has only 1.0 persons per square kilometre. In Peru native population is estimated at 200,000 in the Selvas, again with a density of about 1 per square kilometre.

If we consider first the possible long-term outcome for the primitive peoples, there would appear to be little doubt that their societies and economies will be changed, and that a policy of 'native reservations' cannot be successful because of the inexorable spread of modern civilization. But if total isolation is not possible, their gradual incorporation into more advanced society may be attained and would be compatible with the utilization of the regions within a modern society over the long term. We may compare the current course of events, for example, Brazil with an alternative and more desirable scenario that could be achieved. In the Amazon region agricultural colonies have been set up on the Transamazónica, bringing in some *Nordestinos* to farm on a near subsistence basis. Along the Belém–Brasília and Rondon highways settlement has been unplanned; the process has preceded any legislation but still brings in outsiders, squatters occupying sites along the roadsides and linked with civilization only tenuously via the road. This rural–rural migration is only a panacea for the problems of overpopulated regions such as the north-east but could be used to spur local development in resource regions through a dual policy of social adjustment among the Indian groups and the spatially restricted settlement of outsiders within the region. Rather than sudden, often hostile confrontation with new settlers, a policy for the Indian groups should move ahead of modern settlers and be educational in content, teaching co-operative and individual craft industries, production for markets, adjustment of shifting farming systems to allow for commercial production, the creation of larger communities and the enlargement of communal interests. Agricultural investigations may be conducted at the same time so as to find some compromise between shifting cultivation, ecologically sound but space-consuming, and modern agriculture, which depletes tropical soils though it economizes on land.

Some areas may be chosen for settlement by migrants from other regions, but a careful selection of these areas is required. Linear settlement along penetration roads, as at present, cutting across ecological and tribal boundaries, is undesirable and totally lacks selectivity except with respect to transport. Selection principles might include planned settlement near mineral bodies which are due to be exploited in any case and where outside effects are bound to be felt or in limited areas near hydroelectric or other power projects. Joint development of minerals and farming is, in fact, part of the most recent Amazon policy (Kleinpenning 1978) in Brazil, but Brazil's kind of development is too dependent on outside capital to be commendable. Resource regions present one of the types of area where an alternative technology may be employed, simply because there is no pre-existing competition from conventional technology.

Traditional regions

Social and cultural dimensions enter still more interestingly into the equation when regions preserving something of the more sophisticated non-market societies are concerned. In Chapter 5 traditional regions were found to include, for the most part, those lands regarded as 'underdeveloped' – areas of dense population, agricultural vocation and structural problems in the division of ownership and control of production and marketing. Some of them (north-east Brazil, central Chile outside the metropolitan vicinity, north-east Venezuela, eastern Paraguay) have little traditional culture to build on, either because the original social structure was destroyed by colonial plantation organizations or because of serfdom in Indian areas where slavery was not practised. On the other hand, as they commonly lack organization under capitalist economic principles too, much of the following prescription must hold.

For regions combining traditional culture with economic problems, the argument is that cultural and social measures must precede and predominate over economic, in accordance with the existing precedences in such cultures, as posited by Polanyi (1977).

One set of measures for development which already recognizes traditional structure in some countries is agrarian reform, and in countries or regions of largely agricultural economy this might well be used as the machine of regional development. It is in this kind of region that the differentiation process termed 'agricultural involution' (Geertz 1963) may be observed, if not in complete Asiatic form, at least producing a kind of agricultural dualism between rich and poor farmers: the former arrogate to themselves increasing amounts of land and labour; the latter respond by pooling communal resources and creating work through the intensification of land use on diminishing farm plots. To break the circle of poverty capital accumulation is necessary, impossible for the individual but achievable, as in the case of the Peruvian communities cited in Chapter 5, by group organization.

However, to achieve the level of community organization needed for such schemes as local power generation, grain milling or an irrigation system in regions where the communal spirit has been eroded by centuries of challenge from alternative organizations requires some kind of move from central or regional government beyond the recognition of communities. Ideally, both levels of government are involved, central government to pass agrarian reform laws, to enforce them and to recognize community forms of organization and landholding, and regional governments to promote regional institutions such as the councils of village elders, and specific kinds of regional post-reform agrarian structure suited to a new market orientation for production. As Smith (1975) has pointed out, reform makes a considerable difference to the potential intensity of agricultural production. Whereas pre-reform intensity, because it was mostly for subsistence, may have been fairly even across space, post-reform agriculture, if it moves towards commercial production, will adjust type of land use to distance from markets and other mobile factors, so that intensive production will emerge near to markets where transport costs are low, and less intensive land uses will occupy more distant areas. Thus the coming of commercial, market-oriented agriculture to a densely peopled region of subsistence farming means a complex set of adjustments in different directions. Areas near to markets may need no adjustment beyond the adoption of modern technology, but areas at some distance may find themselves with excessive population on the farms and too intensive a form of land use. Migration out of such regions, the creation of relatively large farms and radical changes from, say, intensive grain-crop production to beef-cattle farming may be required.

For example, in the reform of agriculture in the Sierra of Peru it may be appropriate to develop intensive post-reform agriculture in the Huancayo region, close to both a regional market centre, the city of Huancayo, and to the capital, Lima. But a similar intensity is, at least initially, not suitable for the area around Cuzco in the southern Sierra, with its small regional market for commercial goods and greater distance barrier from the Lima market. In Mexico development of the Balsas valley within 160 kilometres of the capital may be relatively intensive; for Oaxaca state, densely peopled and equally or more capable of intensive production, the distance from the capital places is at some disadvantage and, again, temporary out-migration to local urban centres or to other regions may be encouraged.

The organization of community structures to assist in regional development need not be restricted to those places where a formal community exists. In Venezuela and Colombia a fairly informal, vestigial community structure is evident in simple work-sharing at the time of major tasks, such as house building and harvesting. Such institutions can be built upon by their endowment with formal status and prestige, meeting places and central warehouses to enable them to manage bulk purchases of inputs and the storage of harvested goods.

The above comments may suggest that the recommendation is basically just a 'grass-roots' policy, tempered by regional considerations. But 'grass-roots' or community action is only one side of the policy. Given that these regions are economically at a subsistence or near-subsistence level, any development they achieve must produce a need for transport systems, towns and marketing organizations to move and exchange the goods now produced. Infrastructural works are therefore an appropriate tool to prepare for and help in the transition to a market economy.

As with market economy regions, care must be taken to select those elements of infrastructure which are geared to the intra-regional economy and society. Rather than an opening up of the region to the influence of the national metropolis, regional networks focusing on new or resuscitated market and craft industries (that is, using the existing talents of the human resource base) are desirable. It is possible that some centres, in distant isolated regions, though with a comparatively dense rural population (places such as Cuzco in the southern Peruvian Sierra or Oaxaca in southern Mexico), may be encouraged to emerge as local growth poles in the long term and thus to limit the permanent out-migration from the region and the need for a reduction in land-use intensity, with all that that implies for the rural communities. Not that such a growth-pole policy would have much in common with growth-pole measures currently and recently employed in Latin America. Continuing the theme of social change preceding economic, the emphasis in such centres would be to promote them first as centres for education, welfare and information, second as economic centres through the development of their infrastructure (and only to a minor degree through the attraction, by fiscal or other devices, of new or transferred firms to the centre).

One way of ensuring a more intra-regional, endogenous development of industry at such growth poles is by a selective procedure in granting aid or providing infrastructure, favouring physical structure which is inherently regional in its effects and aiding firms with a specifically local origin and with strong local multiplier effects through the use of local labour, materials and other inputs and through supplying local markets. Such recommendations are, of course, Utopian if we wish to carry them out with precision – to decide on the degree of local linkage of an industry it is necessary to compile a complete regional input-output table, and it is precisely in the backward regions under consideration here that such tables are likely to be unavailable. Obviously, some kind of estimating procedure and the judgement of regional authorities has to be used in the absence of precise measures, but this does not make selection less desirable. What can never be accurately estimated is the degree to which the encouragement of local firms will produce a tradition or habit of local entrepreneurship which might help regional development in general. It is, however, important to bear this kind of effect in mind; some kinds of industry form a particularly suitable outlet for budding local entrepreneurship and could be encouraged for that reason alone. One such is the passenger road transport industry, involving buses, trucks and converted vehicles of various kinds, owned in ones or twos by individuals who at most employ one or two other individuals and who often expand into various non-transport activities such as agriculture and merchant functions at either the rural or the urban terminals of their routes, as well as acting as general conveyors of information. Such a role for road transport firms has long been recognized but scarcely incorporated into any kind of planning (see, for example, Hay 1973).

A matter which is related to those of firm origins and relationships just discussed is the kind of inputs which may be used. Much has been written about alternative technologies in relation to development problems, and it is not proposed here to make any specific analysis. But it is self-evident that many of the concepts of alternative technology apply with particular vigour to the kind of small-scale industry advocated for Latin American poverty regions. The difference of the present approach is that rather than the straightforward advocacy of small, capital-saving industries on purely technological grounds, the emphasis here is on industries suited to poor regions because of their structure and the strength of their intra-regional ties. The link between small-scale industry and a distinctively regional structure is appreciated by Schumacher, father of the alternative technology school, who argues for small-region coherence as both cause and effect of the adoption of intermediate technology (Schumacher 1973, pp. 159–77). Technological arguments come in second place, to back up those already given which broadly favour the alternative-technology type of industry. Many of the features of alternative technology – such as the use of local solar or wind power, bio-gas generation from animal waste in place of imported oil, coal or electricity, the use of local materials and home-made machines in place of imported tractors and other items – fit in well with the concept of endogenous regional development. Street (1977) sees the use of alternative technology as linked with the exploration of internal frontiers, and resource areas have already been mentioned as foci for use of these techniques. But they seem to be equally relevant to the traditional regions where mechanization and modern technology have not made much impact. What is seen as most important is the fact that local enterprise is encouraged and may eventually provide the basis for a self-perpetuating growth process which goes further than the respectable idea of independence with respect to material inputs. Alternative technology is unlikely to be able to compete with modern large-scale industry where the latter already exists, but it may be able to flourish where industry has *not* been developed – that is, in traditional regions and also in resource regions.

Inter-regional processes and policies

Most of the foregoing suggestions relate to single regions or types of region. They by-pass to some extent the question of inter-regional flows, such as the 'backwash' effects described by Friedmann (1966) and Myrdal (1957) and the spread effects envisaged by other economists. These problems could be skirted because the intra-regional measures would, if successful, obviate the need for broader-scale measures by eliminating inter-regional differences or at least reducing the socio-economic slopes to manageable proportions.

Yet there are cases where densely peopled regions border on very sparsely inhabited lands, and massive migrations of labour seem likely, or where inter-regional capital flows seem likely temporarily to disadvantage peripheral regions. In the long term intra-regional measures would take care of these movements, but by that time the inter-regional balance of advantage may have swung too far to be capable of recovery.

The most obvious cases of this gross disparity are where the inter-regional boundaries are also international ones, and one of the nations involved is unable to control the attractions to migrants of conditions in the other country; such situations produce not only inter-regional imbalances but also international political problems (the more important labour migration flows are shown in Figure 15 (page 128). For example, in north-western Argentina Bolivians are attracted in to work seasonally in commercial agriculture, as already noted for the case of Tucumán, a major employer because of the seasonal demand for cane cutters and mill workers. This immigration creates social tensions because of the minority status of the Bolivians, their distinctive culture, their poverty and lack of education and their mobility, with its resultant lack of integration into any community. Still more acute is the Central American boundary problem between El Salvador and Honduras, where the 'football war' declared in July 1969 and continued in some form ever since, despite efforts at a settlement from 1973 onwards, has been the consequence of the fact that as many as 300,000 Salvadoreans live in rural Honduras as a result of a migration process over fifty years old, as well as the Hondurans' resentment of the relative economic success of the Salvadoreans, who appear to enjoy a better preparation and penchant for business (Miller 1971a). El Salvador's dense population of over 160 per square kilometre, and in particular the rural population on excessively small farms, has seen an outlet in the settlement of sparsely peopled western Honduras. To solve this problem, a policy attracting the migrants back both to the rural areas and to towns is necessary. Agrarian reform allied to urban industrialization in Salvador might achieve this. The urgency of the political question means that some measures designed directly to control migration are in order, though only on a temporary basis. Longer-term policy should be devoted to the alleviation of the causes of migration. Honduras's own claim is for less developed status within the Central American Common Market, which would certainly help its position *vis-à-vis* its more advanced neighbours. Regional policies can be replaced here by national policy.

In other cases of an apparent juxtaposition of overpopulated Andean uplands with underpeopled Amazonian plains, the contrast does not lead to massive migration because the rural lowland frontiers are not very attractive to the highlanders, whether in Bolivia, Peru, Ecuador, Colombia or Mexico. Physical contrasts present a sufficient barrier to movement and are likely to continue to do so. Brazil's Amazonian frontier is a different case and requires much more positive controls, since the tropical environment changes only gradually from the core area of the densely peopled Nordeste in, say, Pernambuco, through the transitional areas of Maranhão, to the true *selvas* environment of the state of Pará. Indeed, the whole western Brazilian frontier of settlement, in view of this gradualness of environmental change, seems to require some form of control beyond the simple geographic discipline of distance, which still isolates some parts and delays settlement. This frontier is possibly the most important area for the testing of regional planning methods on the fringe of settlement.

The 'meso-economic' sector

Another area of policy which lies outside the control of individual regions and which has been deliberately avoided hitherto is that of the multinational firm. This is a matter for resolution more at national than at regional level, though it presents its problems at regional level. Multinational firms express preferences for central locations within peripheral countries, locating plant in the capital or at least in one of the largest cities. In the long term regional policy might make non-central regions equally attractive to such firms, but in the short or medium term they represent an unbalancing force.

Holland (1976) has recognized these firms as constituting a separate and identifiable 'meso-economic' sector, lying between the macro-economic (government) and micro-economic (individual firms of relatively small size). They are separate because they do not operate as government does, with its social responsibility influencing many of its actions, nor do they operate as private firms in classical manner by competing for markets, labour or materials. These negative features make the 'meso-economic' firm an unbalancing force in development which can only be resolved by national or even, as suggested by Holland (1976, p. 123), by international controls.

The argument in this work has been that regional development should not rely on outside firms and entrepreneurship beyond the essential, that it should be endogenous wherever possible, though this has been advanced primarily as an expedient to contain the 'backwash' effects of flows from the region to the national capital. Here the motivation is different – to restrict the spread effects of great enterprises of this world's major industrial centres *to* the national capitals, where they concentrate their effort at the expense of the other regions. As the multinational companies of the meso-sector usually make use of advanced technology and represent growth industries, their presence cannot be entirely rejected; but simply to redirect them from the capital city to peripheral regions is likely to mean that they will not establish plant at all but will choose to move to other countries instead. In any case, their effect, if allowed into the region in undiluted form, is likely to be a mixed blessing because of their capital intensity, their polarization of the regional economy into modern and traditional and various 'back-wash' effects in their labour hinterland.

Perhaps the best compromise is to accept these firms but only where they have established, or can establish, important links with local industry, thus acting in the Perrouxian growth-pole fashion as *industries motrices*. This kind of policy is recommended also by Holland, but his argument seems faulty in recommending assembly-line-type operations for peripheral regions because of their lower technical input requirements. Such operations have few contacts with local industry or spin-off effects in promoting the development of new local industries to supply specific commodities or products for the factory. Assembly-line operations are relatively self-contained and help the region very little, as was shown above (page 198) in the extreme example of the Arica motor industry in northern Chile. Rather than such industries, industries much less self-contained and with a much lower level of standardization are desirable – the manufacture of toys and agricultural equipment, the construction industry and the making of building materials such as ceramics, wood-using industries in general – seem more promising, though every case would need judging on its regional merits.

Only if there is some choice and selection among trans-national companies can there be any reconciliation with the ideas mentioned earlier of low-capital, alternative-technology industry in the regions. Allowing undiluted trans-national enterprise to compete directly with alternative-technology industry will produce only a new dualism in which the low technology makes use of the unemployed, the underemployed, the more isolated, less well educated segments of society.

National spatial policies

A no-policy alternative, allowing regional problems to solve themselves through market forces, has been rejected here. Some kind of intervention is desirable, and some overtly regional policies have been outlined. Two further questions may be examined briefly. One concerns the utility of regional versus sectoral policies, which latter might have spatial implications; the other concerns the timing of intervention by national government.

To this second question the final answer can only be put in terms of national aims, which may be very varied, including, for example, maximum economic growth, economic efficiency, the stability of socio-economic structure, equity, participation, the long-term husbanding of resources and ecological balance. If we suppose that regional policy must be considered as an instrument for fulfilling one or more of these aims, then the timing of intervention must be considered. Richardson (1977, pp. 21–2) lists ten possible keys for the timing of first government intervention to aid the regions towards what he calls 'polarization reversal', the replacement of 'backwash' by spread effects. They are as follows:

1 Evolution of industrial structure to point where branch plants become feasible.
2 Emergence of scale diseconomies in the primate city.
3 Relaxing of capital constraints to policy through a period of national economic health.
4 Construction of a skeletal national transport network.

5 When political or social pressures for measures to help the regions have emerged.

6 After the introduction of sound rural development and small-scale industry programmes in the periphery.

7 When per capita incomes in the periphery have risen to levels justifying industries for local demand.

8 When stable (*sic*) exports have been subject to chronic instability.

9 When the national supply of administrators, planners, managers and so on permits decentralization of control functions.

10 When some non-core cities begin to grow faster than the primate city.

In fact, most of these seem inappropriate as signs of the correct moment for intervention, or else they apparently leave intervention too late, so that forces for imbalance may take an irreversible hold. Key 1 requires a modern industrial structure to have emerged in order to allow branch plants to be the agent of decentralization. But branch plants of large firms, it has already been argued, are undesirable agents of industrialization for various reasons. Key 4 is inappropriate for similar reasons, as it constrains development to a type which is dependent on the centre and not autonomous. Key 3, waiting for a period of prosperity before attempting regional policy, seems dangerous in that such periods can scarcely be predicted and are unlikely to coincide with other important factors.

Waiting for social and political pressures to emerge seems a dangerous policy, which could lead to a distorted, biased programme designed simply to meet the specific demands of one region which was more vociferous than others. In addition, such a policy would be politically unwise; once disaffection has given rise to local movements, the leaders of such movements are unlikely to give up on achieving their first goals. Similarly, waiting for peripheral regions to pass market size thresholds (Key 7), for scale economies to disappear (Key 2), for staple exports to become unsteady (Key 8), for administrators to emerge who are prepared to move out and manage the periphery (Key 9), or for non-core cities to grow more rapidly than those of the core (Key 10) all seem to be leaving action too late or assuming changes that may not occur at all. Market-size thresholds for modern industry are themselves constantly rising and may do so at a faster rate than regional purchasing power. Staple exports may become uncertain at any moment and are outside national control of markets; administrators are unlikely even to wish to move out of the centre, and their supply will itself adjust to the centre's demand, not to that of the nation.

This leaves the suggestion of rural development programmes, including agriculture and small-scale industry, as the most satisfactory priority and that which fits in best with our scheme. Yet there is a central difference between Richardson's proposals and those of this chapter, since Richardson makes rural development a matter *separate* from regional development (which presumably, for him), refers to urban industrial development. Here it is proposed, rather, that rural development and small-scale industries should be an integral and foremost part of regional policy.

Sectoral versus regional policies

The discussion so far has been restricted to the kinds of policy which might be elaborated specifically for regions and has purposely avoided some aspects of national policy which have a major bearing on the fate of regions. But it must be acknowledged at once that national sectoral policies may have as much importance for the region as some directly regional policies, and that national government often carries out its sectoral policies with no stated regional bias more fully and with more significant consequences for the region. National governments are often chary of organizing truly regional policies, through a combination of unwillingness to compromise national growth, the lack of any tradition or experience in this field, the fear of favouring one region at the expense of disaffection of the rest of the electorate and the real difficulties of enacting such policy. On the other hand, they are not afraid to enact national sectoral policies with profound regional effects.

In a review of Argentine policy under the second Perón regime, this author concluded (Morris 1975) that regional effects and perhaps policy were alive but acting against the peripheral regions to help the centre. The giant steel industry on the River Plate and petrochemicals at various sites around Buenos Aires were massive investments aiding the central development of Buenos Aires and the humid Pampas region but not the various interior regions. In Colombia Gilbert (1978) noted an intentional concentration of hospital beds in the cities because of the greater cost-effectiveness this provision could have. The whole broad area of import-substitution policy for manufacturing development, it was argued in Chapter 5, was itself a centralizing, polarizing process under

governmental guidance. Effective protection for consumer industries meant a largely centralized, metropolitan agglomeration of
manufacturing industry. Indeed, the large and growing role of the
state in the economy seems itself to be a major centralizing factor of
this 'unconscious' variety because the proliferation of state agencies
and functions usually means more offices and employment in the
capital city, and the important linkages between private industry
and government ministries which supply them with credits and
licences promote still more centralization.

In other countries some ostensibly regional programmes are, in
fact, national plans which incidentally, almost accidentally, have a
strong regional effect. To some extent the Mexican river basin
programmes are of this nature, their greatest achievement being
power and raw-material production for national markets. More so
were the Argentine growth-poles programme, the Brazilian PIN
programme for the Amazonia region and the Guayana programme
in Venezuela. Often quite effective in the provision of resources to
spur national growth, they have few identifiably positive results for
the region itself. Where regional and national plans have worked in
opposite directions, as in Colombia during 1971–4, the national plan
designating the construction industry as the lead sector and concentrating heavily in Bogotá has been more effective than policies
designed to favour smaller cities and improve infrastructure in all
the regions (Gilbert 1975).

There are, of course, ways in which the state may act, through
national policy, so as to aid the regions positively outside the
framework of strictly regional policy. Some of the measures are
negative – the de-emphasis of resource-exploitation schemes for
export to the metropolis or abroad when these are seen to be
damaging to long term development for the region, the dropping of
import substitution policies and the tariff barriers they imply so as to
reduce the tendency to concentrate unsuitable and inefficient industries in the central region. Other possible schemes are positive. For
example, if we admit as evident the greater poverty of peripheral
regions, then any scheme to exclude from income taxation the
poorest sections of national population or to make the tax structure
more progressive, placing the major burden on the richest elements
of society, will be of value in promoting development in these
peripheral regions.

Similar measures are the provision of free public schools, which
are currently under-provided in the peripheral regions where

private schools are scarce and where the population cannot in any case afford the cost of private education, and the provision of medical treatment facilities and doctors, public transport facilities and low-interest mortgages for housing. One important kind of measure we have already covered in some degree is land or agrarian reform, the modification of tenure arrangements and the redressing of gross inequalities in farm size. Where agrarian reform has been attempted measures have been adopted as a national policy, without particular regard for regional considerations, but again the effects of such policies must be greatest in the peripheral regions, where agriculture is still an important sector of the economy and essential to the employment of the regional population.

Again, the question of national political will is uppermost, and although there may occasionally be governments which look favourably on redistributive welfare measures, few have any experience of handling them. This is a paradoxical situation, in that the state has a relatively large hand in many economic enterprises, including most of the capital industries and the public services, but neither tradition nor experience, with the possible exception of Uruguay, exists to promote or support welfare measures, which have not been envisaged as part of the state's functions until recently, although with the large disparities in income and welfare between regions as well as between distinct socio-economic groups within each region, welfare measures are more appropriate to Latin America today than to Europe or North America.

This chapter's recommendations are summarized in Table 21, which sets out relevant regional and national policies for each major type of region.

There is no absolute superiority of national sectoral measures over regional or spatial measures for the region, but one of the merits of national measures over a spatial approach is that they avoid the promotion of a meaningless 'place prosperity' over 'people prosperity'. Subsidies or other aid directly to the region may, if not carefully administered, help rich people in the region, the larger farmers and firms, at the expense of the nation as a whole. One guide-line (though very approximate) to the appropriateness of 'regional' versus 'national' policies for the region is the degree of poverty of peripheral regions. National policies of land reform or tax reform to help the poor are of most value to the regions of massive poverty such as north-east Brazil, eastern Paraguay and southern Mexico. Regional policies, emphasizing infrastructure or

Table 21   *Regional and national policies*

Region type	Regional policy	National policy
Metropolitan	Decentralization or dispersed-city policy; urban land-use controls	Tax structure reforms; urban speculation controls
Urban developing regions	Growth poles at large cities; social and economic infrastructure; selective industrial incentives; tertiary-sector development	
Export base regions	Infrastructure, local or inter-regional; migration policy	Foreign trade measures for diversification; migration policy
Resource regions	Policy *re* indigenous population; settlement restrictions; alternative technology	Settlement restrictions
Traditional regions	Social measures; community development; alternative technology; infrastructure	Tax reforms; public service provision; agrarian reform

the movement of capital or labour, are more appropriate to countries whose peripheries are not peculiarly poor but where a direct push is required to induce development. Countries such as Mexico, with a relatively wealthy northern periphery and a poor southern periphery, must use a combination of both kinds of measure in order to achieve regional development in a balanced fashion.

The suggestions made in this chapter have not been in a systems framework and, indeed, have not been precisely enough defined to allow systems analysis. But one general conclusion may be drawn from earlier chapters showing the historical continuity of physical, social and economic structures, including spatial and non-spatial aspects on the one hand and, on the other, the generally unsuccessful outcome of regional policies applied over the last few years: it is that regional response to any kind of measure is likely to be slow because of the long-term stability of the inter-regional socio-economic system – indeed, only a major effort will have any long-lasting effect on this system. We may take the side of Forrester (1969), who considers the more restricted field of urban systems and claims that modern urban economic theory has suffered from an excessively narrow view of the urban economic system, in particular from a view of it as a simple system in which direct cause-and-effect association may be identified both in space and in time. In fact, Forrester says that urban systems have deep historical roots (they have existed for centuries rather than for years or decades), and the feedbacks may themselves be long-term, acting over several decades, so that they fall outside all the frameworks commonly employed by urban analysts. In addition, many of the feedback mechanisms are non-linear relations, and they are intricately interwoven with one another. These kinds of characteristics are all the more likely to be present in national systems of economy, larger and inherently more complex.

For these reasons it is unreasonable to expect short-term or direct results from a crude regional policy such as credits to manufacturing industry. The appropriate tools for moving such a system may not be at all easily identified because of their complexity and the frequent non-association in time or place of cause and effect. Their long-term stability is itself evidence of a resistance to change which will be hard to eradicate by the alteration of one or two major parameters. And perhaps most important, in complex systems short-term and long-term changes may move in opposite directions; temporary up-turns in the economy may not last longer than the special measures introduced to help it, and in no case can we rely on measures brought in for a few years only and then allowed to lapse.

This may seem a counsel of pessimism. Forrester's view is that the urban system can only be modelled by simulation techniques and not by extracting significant variables and relating them; but simulation cannot be expected to yield good results for national–regional systems where there is so much that is specific to the individual country, nor will it satisfactorily identify the key variables which one must suppose exist and whose identification will allow us to take measures with some chance of success. What one may hope for is that Latin American countries will at least try regional policies, and national policies with regional effects, over substantial periods and with a degree of flexibility and willingness to adapt and improve policy with experience, so that the regional experience of one generation becomes the laboratory experiment from which the next generation of policies may be derived.

References

Amato, P. (1970), 'Elitism and settlement patterns in the Latin American city', *Journal American Institute of Planners*, vol. 36, pp. 96–105

Arriaga, E. E. (1968), 'Components of city growth in selected Latin American countries', *Milbank Memorial Fund Quarterly*, vol. 46, pp. 237–52

Baer, Werner (1965), *Industrialization and Economic Development in Brazil*, Homewood, Illinois: Irwin

Bagu, Sergio (1950), *Estructura Social de la Colonia*, Buenos Aires: El Ateneo

Bailey, Helen M., and Nasatir, A. P. (1960), *Latin America: The Development of Its Civilization*, Englewood Cliffs, New Jersey: Prentice-Hall

Balan, Jorge (1976), 'Regional urbanization under primary-sector expansion in neo-colonial societies', in A. Portes and H. L. Browning, *Current Perspectives in Latin American Urban Research*, ch. 7, pp. 151–79, Austin, Texas: University of Texas

Barkin, David, and King, Timothy (1970), *Regional Economic Development: The River Basin Approach in Mexico*, Cambridge University Press

Barkin, David (ed.) (1972), *Los Beneficiarios del Desarrollo Regional*, Mexico City: Secretaría de Educación Pública

Bazant, Jan (1950), 'Feudalismo y capitalismo en la historia económica de Mexico', *El Trimestre Económico*, vol. 17, no. 1, pp. 1–30

Bedrack, Moises (1974), *La Estrategia de Desarrollo Espacial en Chile 1970–73*, Buenos Aires: Ediciónes SIAP

Berry, Albert, and Urrutia, Miguel (1976), *Income Distribution in Colombia*, New Haven, Conn.: Yale University Press

Berry, B. J. L. (1961), 'City size distributions and economic development' *Economic Development and Cultural Change*, vol. 9, no. 4, pp. 573–87

Berry, B. J. L. (1972), 'Hierarchical diffusion: the basis of development filtering and spread in a system of cities', in N. M. Hansen (ed.), *Growth Centres in Regional Economic Development*, New York: Free Press

Boisier, S., Smolka, M., and de Barros, A. A. (1973), *Desenvolvimento Regional e Urbano: Diferenciais de Produtividade e Salarios Industriais*, Relatorio de Pesquisa, no. 15, Rio de Janeiro: IPEA/INPES

Borah, Woodrow (1954), *Early Colonial Trade and Navigation between*

Mexico and Peru, Ibero-Americana Series, Los Angeles: University of California Press

Borts, G. H., and Stein, J. L. (1962), *Economic Growth in a Free Economy*, New York: Columbia University Press

Boserup, Ester (1965), *The Conditions of Agricultural Growth*, Allen & Unwin

Boudeville, J. R. (1966), *Problems of Regional Economic Planning*, Edinburgh University Press

Bourde, Guy (1974), *Urbanization et Immigration en Amérique Latine: Buenos Aires*, Paris: Aubier-Montaigne

Breton, F. (1976), 'Working and living conditions of migrant workers in South America', *International Labour Review*, vol. 114, no. 3, pp. 339–54

Brito Figueroa, Frederico (1975), *Historia Económica y Social de Venezuela*, Caracas: Universidad Central de Venezuela

Bromley, R. J. (1977), *Development and Planning in Ecuador*, Latin American Publications Fund

Brookfield, Harold C. (1975), *Interdependent Development*, Methuen

Brown, Jonathan C. (1979), *A Socio-Economic History of Argentina 1776–1860*, Latin American Studies Series No. 35, Cambridge University Press

Brown, Larry A., and Lentnek, Barry (1972), 'Innovation diffusion in a developing economy; a mesoscale view', *Economic Development and Cultural Change*, vol. 21, no. 2, pp. 274–92

Browning, H. L. (1975), 'Variación de la primacia en América Latina durante el siglo XX', in L. Unikel and A. Necochea, *Desarrollo Urbano y Regional en América Latina*, ch. 6, pp. 147–72

Browning, H. L., and Feindt, W. (1971), 'The social and economic context of migration to Monterrey, Mexico', in F. F. Rabinovitz and F. M. Trueblood (eds.), *Latin American Urban Research*, vol. 1, ch. 3, pp. 45–70

Cardenas, Cuauhtemoc (1972), 'Regional rural development: the Mexican Rio Balsas Commission', in F. F. Rabinovitz and F. M. Trueblood (eds.), *Latin American Urban Research*, vol. 2, pp. 143–50

Cardona, R., and Simmons, Alan (1975), 'Toward a model of migration in Latin America', in Brian Du Toit and Helen I. Safa, *Migration and Urbanization; Models and Adaptive Strategies*, pp. 19–48

Cardoso, Fernando, and Müller G. (1978), *Amazonia: Expansão do Capitalismo*, São Paulo; Editora Brasiliense

Cardoso, Fernando H., and Faletto, Enso (1979), *Dependency and Development in Latin America*, Berkeley: University of California Press

Carmagnani, Marcello (1973), *Le Chili 1680–1830; Formation d'un Marché Colonial*, Paris: SENPET

Carol, Hans (1964), 'Stages of technology and their impact upon the physical environment; a basic problem in cultural geography', *Canadian Geographer*, no. 1, vol. 8, pp. 1–9

Castells, M. (1973), *Imperialismo y Urbanización en América Latina*, Barcelona: Gustavo Gili

Chapman, Anne (1957), 'Trade enclaves in Aztec and Maya civilization', in Polanyi *et al.*, *Trade and Markets in the Early Empires*, pp. 114–53

Chaunu, P. (1964), *Historia de América Latina*, transl. F. Monjardin, Buenos Aires: EUDEBA

Chevalier, François (1963), *Land and Society in Colonial Mexico: The Great Hacienda*, ed. L. B. Simpson, Berkeley: University of California Press

Christaller, W. (1966), *Central Places in Southern Germany*, transl. C. W. Baskin, Englewood Cliffs, NJ: Prentice-Hall

Clark, C. (1957), *The Conditions of Economic Progress*, Macmillan

Clark, C. (1967), *Population Growth and Land Use*, Macmillan

Cobb, Gwendolin (1949), 'Supply and transportation for the Potosi mines, 1545–1640', *Hispanic American Historical Review*, vol. 29, pp. 25–45

Cochran, Thomas C., and Reina, Ruben E. (1962), *Entrepreneurship in Argentine Culture*, Philadelphia: University of Pennsylvania Press

Cole, J. P. (1973), *Economic and Social Geography of Latin America*, Butterworth

Cole, J. P., and Mather, P. M. (1972), 'Peru province level factor analysis', *Revista Geográfica*, vol. 77, pp. 7–37

Cole, J. P., and Mather, P. M. (1978), *Peru 1940–2000; Performance and Prospects*, vol. 1, chs. 1–7, Department of Geography, Nottingham University

Connell, John, Dasgupta, B., Laishley, R., Lipton, M. (1976), *Migration from Rural Areas*, IDS Village Studies Programme, Delhi: Oxford University Press

Conroy, Michael E. (1973), 'Rejection of growth center strategy in Latin American regional development planning', *Land Economics*, vol. 49, pp. 371–80

Conroy, Michael E. (1976), 'Towards a policy-oriented theory of the economy of cities in Latin America', in A. Portes and H. L. Browning, *Current Perspectives in Latin American Urban Research*, ch. 4, pp. 71–98

Cordova, Armando (1973), *Inversiones Extranjeras y Subdesarrollo*, Caracas: Universidad Central de Venezuela

Cortes Conde, Roberto (1968), 'Algunos Rasgos de la expansión territorial en Argentina en la segunda mitad del siglo 19', *Desarrollo Económico*, vol. 8, no. 9, pp. 3–29

Cortes Conde, Roberto (1974), *The First Stages of Modernization in Spanish America*, transl. Tony Talbot, Harper and Row

Crow, John A. (1946), *The Epic of Latin America*, New York: Doubleday

Cunningham, Susan (1979), 'Brazil: recent trends in industrial development', *Bank of London and South America Review*, vol. 13, no. 4, pp. 212–20

Datoo, B. A. (1978), 'Towards a reformulation of Boserup's theory of agricultural change', *Economic Geography*, vol. 54, pp. 135–44

Denevan, W. M. (1966), *The Aboriginal Cultural Geography of the Llanos de Mojos of Bolivia*, Berkeley: University of California Press

Denevan, W. M. (1970), 'Aboriginal drained-field cultivation in the Americas', *Science*, vol. 169, pp. 647–54

Denevan, W. M. (1976), *The Native Population of the Americas in 1492*, Madison, Wisconsin: University of Wisconsin

Dickenson, John P. (1978), *Brazil: Studies in Industrial Geography*, Dawson

Diffie, B. W. (1947), *Latin American Civilization: Colonial Period*, Harrisburg, Pennsylvania: Stackpole

Di Tella, Guido, and Zymelman, Manuel (1967), *Las Etapas del desarrollo económico argentino*, Buenos Aires: EUDEBA

Dolfuss, O. (1973), *Le Pérou: Introduction Géographique*, Paris: Institut des Hautes Etudes de l'Amérique Latine

Domike, Arthur L., and Barraclough, Solon (1965), *Evolución y Reforma de la Estructura Agraria América Latina*, Santiago de Chile: FAO

Doughty, Paul L. (1968), *Huaylas: An Andean District in Search of Progress*, Ithaca, NY: Cornell University Press

Dozer, D. M. (1962), *Latin America: An Interpretative History*, New York: McGraw-Hill

Dozier, Craig L. (1963), 'Mexico's transformed Northwest: the Yaqui, Mayo and Fuerte examples', *Geographical Review*, vol. 53, pp. 548–71

Du Toit, Brian, and Safa, Helen I. (eds.) (1965), *Migration and Urbanization: Models and Adaptive Strategies*, The Hague: Mouton

Eidt, R. C. (1959), 'Aboriginal Chibcha settlement in Colombia', *Annals, Association of American Geographers*, vol. 49, pp. 374–92

El-Shakhs, S. (1972), 'Development, primacy, and systems of cities', *Journal of Developing Areas*, vol. 7, pp. 11–36

Erasmus, Charles J. (1965), 'The occurrence and disappearance of reciprocal farm labour in Latin America', in D. B. Heath and R. N. Adams, *Contemporary Cultures and Societies of Latin America*, pp. 173–99

Fagg, John E. (1969), *Latin America*, 2nd edn., Macmillan

Flinn, William L. (1971), 'Rural and intra-urban migration in Colombia; two case studies in Bogotá', in F. F. Rabinovitz and F. M. Trueblood (eds.), *Latin American Urban Research*, vol. 1, ch. 5, pp. 83–93

236   *References*

Forrester, J. W. (1969), *Urban Dynamics*, Cambridge, Mass.: MIT Press
Frank, A. G. (1967), *Capitalism and Underdevelopment in Latin America: Historical Studies of Chile and Brazil*, New York: Monthly Review Press
Fried, M. (1967), *The Evolution of Political Society*, New York: Random House
Friedmann, John (1966), *Regional Development Policy: A Case Study of Venezuela*, Cambridge, Mass.: MIT Press
Friedmann, John (1971a), 'The role of cities in national development', in J. Miller and R. A. Gakenheimer (eds.), *Latin American Urban Policies and the Social Sciences*, ch. 5, pp. 167–88
Friedmann, John (1971b), 'Urban-regional policies for national development in Chile', in F. F. Rabinovitz and F. M. Trueblood (eds.), *Latin American Urban Research*, vol. 1, pp. 217–46
Friedmann, John, and Weaver, Clyde (1979), *Territory and Function; The Evolution of Regional Planning*, Edward Arnold
Friedmann, John, and Wulff, Robert, (1976), *The Urban Transition*, Edward Arnold
Furtado, Celso (1970), *The Economic Development of Latin America*, Cambridge University Press

Garfield, Viola, (ed.) (1961), *Symposium: Patterns of Land Utilization and Other Papers*, Proceedings of the 1961 Spring Meeting of the American Ethnological Society, Seattle: University of Washington Press
Gauthier, Howard L. (1975), 'Migration theory and the Brazilian experience', *Revista Geográfica*, vol. 82, pp. 51–62
Geertz, Clifford (1963), *Agricultural Involution: The Process of Ecological Change in Indonesia*, Berkeley: University of California Press
Geisse, G., and Coraggio, J. L. (1972), 'Metropolitan areas and national development', in F. F. Rabinovitz and F. M. Trueblood (eds.)., *Latin American Urban Research*, vol. 2, pp. 45–60
Giberti, Horacio (1961), *Historia Económica de la Ganadería Argentina*, Buenos Aires: Solar/Hachette
Gibson, Charles (1969), 'Spanish-Indian institutions and colonial urbanism in New Spain', in J. E. Hardoy and R. Schaedel, *The Urbanization Process in America*, pp. 225–39
Gilbert, Alan (1974a), *Industrial Concentration, Urban Growth and Regional Development in Colombia since 1951*, Occasional Papers No. 24, Department of Geography, University College, London
Gilbert, Alan (1974b), *Latin American Development*, Penguin
Gilbert, Alan (1975), 'Urban and regional development programmes in Colombia since 1951', in Cornelius and F. M. Trueblood (eds.), *Latin American Urban Research*, vol. 5, pp. 241–74
Gilbert, Alan (ed.) (1976), *Development Planning and Spatial Structure*, Wiley

Gilbert, Alan (1978), 'The state and regional income disparity in Latin America', *Bulletin of the Society for Latin American Studies*, vol. 29, pp. 5–30

Gilbert, Alan G., and Sollis, Peter J. (1979), 'Migration to small Latin American cities: a critique of the concept of "fill-in" migration', *Tijdschrift voor Economische en Sociale Geografie*, vol. 70, no. 2, pp. 110–13

Gould, Peter R. (1969), *Spatial Diffusion*, Association of American Geographers Commission on College Geography Resource Paper No. 4, Washington DC

Goulder, Paul (1979), 'The Amazon Basin: utilization or conservation', *BOLSA Review*, vol. 13, no. 9, pp. 522–8

Gwynne, Robert (1978), 'Government planning and the location of the motor vehicle industry in Chile', *Tijdschrift voor Economische en Sociale Geografie*, vol. 69, pp. 130–40

Hanke, Lewis (1956), *The Imperial City of Potosí, an Unwritten Chapter in the History of Spanish America*, The Hague: Martinus Nijhoff

Hardoy, J. E. (1975), *Urbanization in Latin America: Approaches and Issues*, New York: Anchor Books

Hardoy, J. E., and Aranovich, Carmen (1969), 'Urbanización en América Hispánica entre 1580 y 1630', *Boletín del Centro de Investigaciónes Históricas y Estéticas*, Universidad Central de Venezuela, Caracas, vol. 11, pp. 9–89

Hardoy, J. E., and Schaedel, Richard (1969), *The Urbanization Process in America from its Origins to the Present Day*, Buenos Aires: Di Tella Institute

Haring, C. H. (1947), *The Spanish Empire in America*, Oxford University Press

Harvey, David (1973), *Social Justice and the City*, Edward Arnold

Hay, Alan (1973), 'The importance of passenger transport in Nigeria', in B. S. Hoyle (ed.), *Transport and Development*, pp. 125–38

Heath, D. B., and Adams, R. N. (1965), *Contemporary Culture and Society in Latin America*, New York: Random House

Hennessy, Alistair (1978), *The Frontier in Latin American History*, Edward Arnold

Henshall, Janet D., and Momsen, R. P. (1974), *A Geography of Brazilian Development*, Bell

Herrick, Bruce (1972), 'Urbanisation and Urban Migration in Latin America: an economist's view', in F. F. Rabinovitz and F. M. Trueblood (eds.), *Latin American Urban Research*, vol. 2, ch. 4, pp. 71–81

Herring, Hubert (1968), *A History of Latin America*, 3rd edn., Cape

Hill, A. David (1971), *Latin American Development Issues*, Proceedings of Latin American Geographers' Conference No. 3, Muncie, Indiana

Hirschman, Albert O. (1958), *The Strategy of Economic Development*, New Haven, Conn.: Yale University Press

Hodder, B. W. (1968), *Economic Development in the Tropics*, Methuen

Hojman, David A. (1974), *Desarrollo Regional y Planificación Regional; Efectos del Modelo Económico de la Unidad Popular sobre el Desarrollo Espacial Geográfico; El Caso Chileno*, Caracas: Universidad Central de Venezuela

Holland, Stuart (1976), *The Regional Problem*, Macmillan

Hoyle, B. S. (ed.) (1973), *Transport and Development*, Macmillan

Hudson, John C. (1976), 'Theory and methodology in comparative frontier studies', in D. H. Miller and J. O. Steffen (eds.), *The Frontier: Comparative Studies*, pp. 11–52

ILPES, Instituto Latinoaméricano de planificación económica y social (1974), *Planificación Regional y Urbana en América Latina*, Mexico City: Siglo XXI

Isaac, Erich (1970), *Geography of Domestication*, Englewood Cliffs, NJ: Prentice Hall

Jameson, Kenneth P. (1976), *Industrialización regional el Perú*, Serie de Documentos de Trabajo No. 30, Universidad Católica del Perú, Lima

Jenkins, Rhys O. (1978), 'Manufactured exports – development strategy or internationalization of capital', *Bulletin, Society for Latin American Studies*, no. 28, pp. 64–82

Johnson, E. A. J. (1970), *The Organization of Space in Developing Countries*, Cambridge, Mass: Harvard University Press

Johnson, L. J. (1967), 'Problems of import substitution: the Chilean auto industry', *Economic Development and Cultural Change*, vol. 15, pp. 202–16

Jones, D. M. (1977), 'The Green Revolution in Latin America; success or failure', *Proceedings, Conference of Latin Americanist Geographers*, vol. 6, pp. 55–64, Muncie, Indiana: Department of Geography, Ball State University

Kay, George (1975), 'Stages of technology and economic development: an approach to the study of human geography', *Geography*, vol. 60, pp. 89–98

Kirsch, Henry W. (1973), *The Industrialization of Chile 1880–1930* (PhD dissertation reproduction), University of Florida, Miami

Kleinpenning, J. M. G. (1971), 'Objectives and results of the development policy in Northeast Brazil', *Tijdschrift voor Economische en Sociale Geografie*, vol. 62, no. 5, pp. 271–89

Kleinpenning, J. M. G. (1977), 'A critical evaluation of the policy of the

Brazilian government for the integration of the Amazon region', paper to annual meeting of Society for Latin American Studies, York

Kleinpenning, J. M. G. (1978), 'A further evaluation of the policy for the integration of the Amazon region 1974–76', *Tijdschrift voor Economische en Sociale Geografie*, vol. 69, no. 1/2, pp. 78–85

Kukliński, A. (ed.) (1972), *Growth Poles and Growth Centres in Regional Planning*, The Hague: Mouton

Kuznets, S. (1959), *Six Lectures on Economic Growth*, New York: Free Press of Glencoe

Lall, Sanjaya (1975), 'Is dependence a useful concept in analyzing underdevelopment?', *World Development*, vol. 3, pp. 799–810

Lapa, José do Amaral (1968), *A Bahia e a Carreira da India*, São Paulo: Universidad de São Paulo

Larrain, Manuel A. (1972), 'Chilean regional development policy', in F. F. Rabinovitz and F. M. Trueblood, *Latin American Urban Research*, vol. 2, ch. 6, pp. 133–41

Lederman, Esteban (1969), *Los Recursos Humanos en el Desarrollo de América Latina*, Serie II, No. 9, Santiago: ILPES

Leeds, Anthony (1961), 'The port-of-trade in pre-European India as an ecological and evolutionary type', in Viola Garfield (ed.), *Symposium: Patterns of Land Utilisation and Other Papers*

Lösch, A. (1954), *The Economics of Location*, New Haven, Conn.: Yale University Press

Lowenthal, Abraham F. (1975), *The Peruvian Experiment*, Princeton, NJ: Princeton University Press

Mabogunje, Akin L. (ed.) (1973), *Planificación Regional y Desarrollo Nacional en Africa*, Buenos Aires: SIAP

McGee, Terence G. (1971), *The Urbanization Process in the Third World: Explorations in Search of a Theory*, Bell

McGreevey, William P. (1971), 'A statistical analysis of primacy and lognormality in the size distribution of Latin American cities 1750–1960', in R. M. Morse (ed.), *The Urban Development of Latin America 1750–1920*, ch. 10

Mason, J. Alden (1957), *The Ancient Civilizations of Peru*, Penguin

Matos Mar, J. (1963), 'Three Indian communities in Peru', in J. Meynaud (ed.), *Social Change and Economic Development*, pp. 130–8

Melchior, E. R. (1972), 'The integration of space in Latin America', in F. F. Rabinovitz and F. M. Trueblood (eds.), *Latin American Urban Research*, vol. 2, ch. 4, pp. 85–100

Mera, K. (1973), 'On the urban agglomeration and economic efficiency', *Economic Development and Cultural Change*, vol. 21, no. 2, pp. 309–24

Meynaud, Jean (ed.) (1963), *Social Change and Economic Development*, Paris: UNESCO

Miller, David H., and Jerome O. Steffen (eds.), (1976), *The Frontier: Comparative Studies*, Norman, Okla.: University of Oklahoma Press

Miller, John (1971a), 'The rapprochement of nations with contiguous regions', in J. Miller and R. A. Gakenheimer (eds.), *Latin American Urban Policies and the Social Sciences*, ch. 2, pp. 43–72

Miller, John (1971b), 'Channelling national urban growth in Latin America', in J. Miller and R. A. Gakenheimer (eds.), *Latin American Urban Policies and the Social Sciences*, ch. 4, pp. 107–66

Miller, John, and Ralph A. Gakenheimer (1971), *Latin American Urban Policies and the Social Sciences*, Sage

Miller, R., Smith, C. T., and Fisher, J. (eds.), *Social and Economic Change in Modern Peru*, Monograph No. 6, Centre for Latin American Studies, Liverpool University

Moreno Toscano, Alejandra (1968), *Geografía Económica de México siglo XVI*, Mexico City: El Colegio de Mexico

Morris, A. S. (1972), 'The regional problem in Argentine economic development', *Geography*, vol. 57, no. 4, pp. 289–306

Morris, A. S. (1975), *Regional Disparities and Policy in Modern Argentina*, Institute of Latin American Studies Occasional Papers No. 16, University of Glasgow

Morris, A. S. (1977), 'The failure of small farmer settlement in Buenos Aires province', *Revista Geográfica*, vol. 85, pp. 63–77

Morris, A. S. (1978a), 'Urban growth patterns in Latin America with illustrations from Caracas', *Urban Studies*, vol. 15, pp. 299–312

Morris, A. S. (1978b), 'The Argentine Colorado – interprovincial rivalries over water resources', *Scottish Geographical Magazine*, vol. 94, pp. 169–80

Morris, A. S. (1978c), *Sociedad, Economía y Estructura Geográfica en Iberoamérica*, Geocrítica, vol. 16, Barcelona: Universidad de Barcelona

Morris, A. S. (1979), *South America*, Hodder & Stoughton

Morse, Richard M. (1951), 'São Paulo's economy in the nineteenth century: economic roots of the metropolis', *Inter-American Economic Affairs*, vol. 5, no. 3, pp. 19–27

Morse, Richard M. (1971a), *The Urban Development of Latin America 1750–1920*, Stanford, California: Centre for Latin American Studies

Morse, Richard M. (1971b), 'São Paulo: case study of a Latin American metropolis', in F. F. Rabinovitz and F. M. Trueblood (eds.), *Latin American Urban Research*, vol. 1, ch. 7

Morse, Richard M. (1974), *From Community to Metropolis: A Biography of São Paulo*, New York: Octagon Books

Myrdal, Gunnar M. (1957), *Economic Theory and Underdeveloped Regions*, Duckworth

North, Douglass C. (1955), 'Location theory and regional economic growth', *Journal of Political Economy*, vol. 63, pp. 243–58
North, Douglass C. and R. P. Thomas (1973), *The Rise of the Western World*, Cambridge University Press

O'Brien, Philip (1974), *A Critique of Latin American Theories of Dependency*, Institute of Latin American Studies Occasional Papers No. 12, University of Glasgow
Odell, P. R., and Preston, D. A. (1973), *Economies and Societies in Latin America*, Butterworth

Parsons, J. J. (1968), *Antioqueño colonization in Western Colombia*, Ibero-Americana Series No. 32, Berkeley: University of California
Pedersen, P. O. (1975), *Urban-Regional Development in South America; A Process of Diffusion and Integration*, The Hague: Mouton
Peru (1975), *Plan Nacional de Desarrollo 1975–78*, Lima: Instituto Nacional de Planificación
Polanyi, Karl (1977), *The Livelihood of Man* (ed. H. W. Pearson), New York: Academic Press
Polanyi, Karl, Arensberg, A., and Pearson, Harry W. (1957), *Trade and Markets in the Early Empires*, Glencoe, Ill.: Free Press
Portes, Alejandro, and Browning, Harley L. (1976), *Current Perspectives in Latin American Urban Research*, Austin, Texas: University of Texas Press
Pottier, A. (1963), 'Axes de communication et développement économique', *Revue Economique*, vol. 14, pp. 58–132
Pounds, N. J. G. (1969), 'The urbanization of the classical world', *Annals, Association of American Geographers*, vol. 59, pp. 135–50
Prado Junior, Caio (1967), *The Colonial Background of Modern Brazil*, transl. Suzette Macedo, Berkeley: University of California Press
Prebisch, Raúl (1971), *Change and Development; Latin America's Great Task*, New York: Praeger
Pred, Allan (1966), *The Spatial Dynamics of U.S. Urban-Industrial Growth, 1800–1914: interpretative and theoretical essays*, Cambridge, Mass.: MIT Press
Pred, Allan (1975), 'Diffusion, organizational spatial structure and city-system development', *Economic Geography*, vol. 51, pp. 252–68
Pred, Allan (1977), *City-Systems in Advanced Economies*, Hutchinson

Rabinovitz, F. F., and Trueblood, F. M. (1971), *Latin American Urban Research*, vol. 1, Berkeley: Sage
Rabinovitz, F. F., and Trueblood, F. M. (1972), *Latin American Urban Research*, vol. 2, *Regional Development*, Berkeley: Sage

Ramos, Demetrio (1970), *Minería y Comercio Interprovincial en Hispanoamérica Siglos 16, 17 y 18*, Valladolid: Universidad de Valladolid

Reis Filho, N. G. (1968), *Evolucão Urbana do Brasil*, São Paulo: Universidad de São Paulo

Richardson, Harry W. (1973a), *Regional Growth Theory*, Macmillan

Richardson, Harry W. (1973b), *The Economics of Urban Size*, Farnborough: Saxon House

Richardson, Harry W. (1977), *City Size and National Spatial Strategies in Developing Countries*, World Bank Staff Working Papers No. 252, Washington DC: World Bank

Riddell, J. Barry (1970), *The Spatial Dynamics of Modernization in Sierra Leone: Structure, Diffusion and Response*, Evanston, Ill.: Northwestern University Press

Ridler, Neil B. (1979), 'Development through urbanization: a partial evaluation of the Colombian experiment', *International Journal of Urban and Regional Research*, vol. 3, no. 1, pp. 49–59

Robson, Brian (1973), *Urban Growth: An Approach*, Methuen

Rofman, Alejandro Boris (1974), *Dependencia, Estructura de Poder, y Formación regional en América Latina*, Buenos Aires: Siglo XXI

Rofman, Alejandro B. (1975), 'Influencia del proceso histórico en la dependencia externa y en la estructuración de las redes regionales y urbanas actuales', in L. Unikel and A. Necochea, *Desarrollo urbane y regional en América Latina*, pp. 61–82

Rostow, W. W. (1960), *The Stages of Economic Growth: A Non-Communist Manifesto*, Cambridge University Press

Rowe, John H. (1947), 'The distribution of Indians and Indian languages in Peru', *Geographical Review*, vol. 37, pp. 202–15

Sanchez-Albornoz, Nicolás (1974), *The Population of Latin America; A History*, Berkeley: University of California Press

Sanders, W. T., and Marino, J. (1970), *New World Prehistory*, Englewood Cliffs, NJ: Prentice-Hall

Santos, Milton (1971), *Les Villes du Tiers Monde*, Paris: Gemin

Santos, Milton (1973), 'La Urbanización Dependiente en Venezuela', in M. Castells, *Imperialismo y Urbanización en América Latina*, pp. 97–110

Scalabrini Ortiz, Raúl (1958), *Historia de los Ferrocarriles Argentinos*, Buenos Aires: Ediciónes Devenir

Schaffer, William (1976), *On the Use of Input-Output Models for Regional Planning*, Leiden: Nijhoff Social Sciences

Schumacher, E. F. (1973), *Small is Beautiful: A Study of Economics as if People Mattered*, Blond & Briggs

Scobie, James (1972), 'Buenos Aires as a commercial-bureaucratic city 1880–1910; characteristics of a city's orientation', *American Historical Review*, vol. 77, pp. 1035–73

Selwyn, Percy (ed.) (1975), *Development Policy in Small Countries*, Croom Helm

Service, Elman R. (1951), 'The *encomienda* in Paraguay', *Hispanic American Historical Review*, vol. 31, pp. 230–52

Slater, David (1975), 'Underdevelopment and spatial inequality; approaches to the problems of regional planning in the Third World', *Progress in Planning*, vol. 4, no. 2, pp. 97–167

Smith, C. T. (1970), 'Depopulation of the Central Andes in the sixteenth century', *Current Anthropology*, vol. 11, pp. 453–64

Smith, C. T. (1975), 'Agrarian reform and regional development', in C. T. Smith (ed.), *Studies in Latin American Agrarian Reform*, Monograph No. 5, Centre for Latin American Studies, Liverpool University

Stann, E. Jeffrey (1975), *Caracas, Venezuela, 1891–1936: A Study of Urban Growth* (PhD dissertation), Nashville, Tennessee: University of Tennessee

Stearman, Allyn Maclean (1978), 'The highland migrant in lowland Bolivia: multiple resource migration and the horizontal archipelago', *Human Organization*, vol. 37, pp. 180–5

Sternberg, Rolf (1972), 'Occupance of the Humid Pampas: 1856–1914', *Revista Geográfica*, vol. 76, pp. 61–102

Steward, J. H., and Faron, L. C. (1959), *Native Peoples of South America*, McGraw-Hill

Stöhr, Walter, (1975), *Regional Development Experiences and Prospects in Latin America*, The Hague: Mouton

Stöhr, Walter, and Tödtling, Franz (1977), 'Spatial Equity – some antitheses to current regional development strategy', *Papers of the Regional Science Association*, vol. 38, pp. 33–54

Street, James H. (1977), 'The internal frontier and technological progress in Latin America', *Latin American Research Review*, vol. 12, pp. 25–56

Taaffe, E. J., Morrill, R. L., and Gould, P. R. (1963), 'Transport expansion in underdeveloped countries; a comparative analysis', *Geographical Review*, vol. 53, pp. 503–29

Tavares, Vania P., Considera, Claudio M., and de Castro e Silva, Maria T. I. (1972), *Colonizacão Dirigida no Brasil*, Rio de Janeiro: IPEA/INPES

Thorp, Rosemary, and Bertram, Geoffrey (1975), 'Industrialization in an open economy: a case-study of Peru 1890–1940', in R. Miller, C. T. Smith and J. Fisher (eds.), *Social and Economic Change in Modern Peru*, ch. 3, pp. 53–86

Thorp, Rosemary, and Bertram, Geoffrey (1978), *Peru 1890–1977: Growth and Policy in an Open Economy*, Macmillan

Turner, Frederick Jackson (1893), 'The significance of the frontier in American History', *Annual Report of the American Historical Association*

Unikel, L., and Necochea, A. (eds.) (1975), *Desarrollo Urbano y Regional en América Latina*, Mexico City: Fondo de Cultura Económica

Utria, Ruben (1972), 'The social variables of regional development in Latin America', in F. F. Rabinovitz and F. M. Trueblood (eds.), *Latin American Urban Research*, ch. 3, pp. 61–84

Vance, James (1970), *The Merchant's World: The Geography of Wholesaling*, Englewood Cliffs, NJ: Prentice-Hall

Vapñarsky, César A. (1969), 'On rank-size distribution of cities; an ecological approach', *Economic Development and Cultural Change*, vol. 17, no. 4, pp. 584–95

Villalobos, Sergio (1968), *El Comercio y la Crisis Colonial*, Santiago: Universidad de Chile

Weischet, Wolfgang (1970), *Chile: seine länderkindliche Individualität und Struktur*, Darmstadt; Wissenschaftliche Buchgesellschaft

Weller, Robert H., Macisco, John J., and Martine, George R. (1971), 'The relative importance of the components of urban growth in Latin America', *Demography*, vol. 8, no. 2, pp. 225–32

West, Robert, and Augelli, John P. (1966), *Middle America*, Englewood Cliffs, NJ: Prentice-Hall

Wilkinson, Richard G. (1973), *Poverty and Progress: An Ecological Model of Economic Development*, Methuen

Williamson, J. G. (1965), 'Regional inequality and the process of national development: a description of the patterns', *Economic Development and Cultural Change*, vol. 13, no. 4 (pt 2), pp. 3–45

Wilson, George (1973), 'Towards a theory of transport and development', in B. S. Hoyle (ed.), *Transport and Development*, ch. 12, pp. 208–230

Worcester, D. E., and Schaeffer, W. G. (1956), *The Growth and Culture of Latin America*, New York: Oxford University Press

Zalduendo, Eduardo A. (1975), *Libras y Rieles*, Buenos Aires: El Coloquio

Zipf, G. K. (1949), *Human Behaviour and the Principle of Least Effort*, Reading, Mass.: Addison-Wesley

Index

Acapulco, 65, 76–9
access and isolation, 50–2
administration changes, 83–8
agglomeration, urban, 20–1, 137–9
agrarian reform, *see* agriculture
agriculture: change in, 139–44;
co-operative, 178–80, 193, 197,
218–19; development of, 24;
dualism in, 72–5; European, 68,
71–5; and migration, 130–1; and
population density, 67; productivity of, 152–4; reform of, 179–80,
192–7, 218–19, 223, 227; shifting, 98; state, 179–80; subsistence, 53–5, 71–5; and trade, 77,
81–2, 95–9; wages in, 125; *see
also* sugar
airlines, 163; *see also* transport
Alemán, Miguel, 188
Allende, Salvador, 135
altepetlacalli, 180
altiplano, 46, 62
aluminium, 201–2; *see also* bauxite
Amato, P., 207
Amazon Basin: missions in, 61,
68–70; population in, 176, 187,
195–6, 216, 223; regional policies
in, 150, 190, 217; rubber in, 98,
102; transport in, 102, 160
Andes, 48–53, 193
Antofagasta, 163, 198–9
applied models of economic
development, 25–6
Aranovich, Carmen, 65–6

Arequipa, 80, 86, 111, 159, 164,
169, 210
Argentina: agriculture in, 75, 95–7,
100. 118, 140, 148, 152, 173,
212–15, 222; frontiers, 68, 92,
96; growth poles in, 26; incomes
in, 125, 167; industry in, 115–16,
131, 134–7, 172; physical environment of, 47–8; population of,
52, 123–9, 152, 160; regional
policies in, 187–8, 190, 200–1,
205, 209, 212–14, 222, 227–8;
trade in, 76, 78, 83, 93, 95–7,
100, 114, 132, 145, 213; transport in, 103–7, 115, 161–3;
urbanization in, 86–7, 110, 114,
156, 158, 171, 208–9
Arica, 76, 80, 198–9
Arriaga, E. E., 129
asentamiento, 179
Asunción, 51, 128, 204
audiencia, 63–6
Ayacucho, 86, 111
ayllu system, 89
Azara, Felix de, 96
Aztecs, 39, 44, 53–6, 59, 75, 89; *see
also* indigenous settlement

'backwash' effect, 31, 222
Baer, Werner, 164
Bagu, Sergio, 72
Bahia, *see* Salvador
Bahia Blanca, 115, 209
Bailey, Helen, 70

Index compiled by Ann Hall